LANDSCAPE PLANTS OF THE SOUTHEAST

ABOUT THE AUTHORS

R. Gordon Halfacre, Alumni Distinguished Professor at Clemson University, received a Master of Landscape Architecture from North Carolina State University, a Master of Science in Horticulture from Clemson University, and a Ph.D. in Horticulture from Virginia Polytechnic Institute. He received V.P.I.'s Sigma Xi Research Award and was named Outstanding Teacher at North Carolina State University. The National Council of State Garden Clubs presented to him the Silver Seal Award and the Helen S. Hull Award for Literary Horticulture. The American Society for Horticultural Science in the Southern Region chose him for the L. M. Ware Outstanding Teacher Award. He is the author of *Fundamentals of Horticulture, Keep 'Em Growing, Plant Science, Horticulture,* and *Carolina Landscape Plants.* Dr. Halfacre is a registered, practicing landscape architect and full member of the American Society of Landscape Architects.

Anne Rogers Shawcroft, a landscape writer who lives in Raleigh, North Carolina, studied botany and landscape design at North Carolina State University and received a Bachelor of Arts in Art Education from the University of North Carolina at Greensboro. She has worked professionally with plants and landscape design for over 30 years. She coauthored *Carolina Landscape Plants* and previous editions of *Landscape Plants of the Southeast.*

LANDSCAPE PLANTS OF THE SOUTHEAST

R. GORDON HALFACRE

ANNE ROGERS SHAWCROFT

Publisher
SPARKS PRESS, INC.
P.O. Box 26747
Raleigh, NC 27611

Landscape Plants of the Southeast

First Edition, 1971   Second Edition, 1975
Third Edition, 1979   Fourth Edition, 1986
Fifth Edition, 1989

Fifth Edition — Second Printing, 1992
Fifth Edition — Third Printing, 1994

ISBN 0-916822-14-1
Library of Congress Catalog Card Number 88-092591

*To Angela and Robert Halfacre
and Cathy Rogers*

CONTENTS

ACKNOWLEDGMENTS

Many people have contributed to the material in *Landscape Plants of the Southeast* and we gratefully acknowledge their support. Special thanks are extended to Edgar H. Sparks, publisher and to Dr. Clive W. Donoho, Jr., for their inspiration and encouragement. For assistance in the organization and preparation of the manuscript, appreciation is expressed to Robert E. Marvin, Landscape Architect, Walterboro, South Carolina; Richard C. Bell, Landscape Architect, Raleigh, North Carolina; Howard M. Singletary, Dr. J. C. Raulston, and Dr. Roy A. Larson, Horticultural Science, North Carolina State University; Dr. J. C. Wells, Plant Pathology, North Carolina State University; Dr. Robert L. Robertson, Entomology, North Carolina State University; Richard R. Wilkinson, Landscape Architecture, North Carolina State University; Charles O. Bell, Grounds Superintendent, University of North Carolina at Greensboro; Ellis Jourdain Moore, and John P. Fulmer, Horticulture Department, Clemson University; Ronald Copeland, Apex Nursery, Apex, North Carolina; Martha Finkel, Oxford, North Carolina; Ruth Sparks Knight, Raleigh, North Carolina; Dr. Henry Orr, Horticulture Department, Auburn University; Dr. Alfred E. Einert, Landscape Architect, Horticulture Department, University of Arkansas.

Illustrations are by Jim Kellison, John Norton, Angela Halfacre, and Helen Weaver. Photographs were contributed by David Mikulcik, Dr. R. Daniel Lineberger, Adrienne Halfacre, Robert Halfacre, Angela Halfacre, and Dr. David Bradshaw.

R. G. H.
A. R. S.

INTRODUCTION

Landscape Plants of the Southeast presents information on 1500 plants most useful for landscaping purposes in the Southeast. It brings together all facts on plant materials needed to create interesting and successful landscape designs.

In this book plants are grouped by type and height for landscape use. Usually shrubs and trees are arranged according to plant families. Since this is of little value to landscape gardeners, another method has been employed. All plants are grouped into 7 easily distinguished main categories — ground covers, vines, shrubs 1-4 feet high, shrubs 4-6 feet high, shrubs 6-12 feet high, small trees, and large trees.

The Latin and common names of plants conform to the International Code for the Nomenclature of Cultivated Plants which went into effect in January 1959. Clonal or English varietal names are given in single quotation marks; horticultural varieties are in italics.

The scientific name of a plant is made up of 2 words, for example, *Ajuga reptans*. The first word represents the genus or group to which the plant belongs and is always written with a capital letter. The second word indicates the species or kind and is rarely capitalized. The meanings of the genus and species are given to aid in understanding the scientific terms.

The following illustration will relate the association of species, genus, and family. In this book there are 5 kinds or species of roses, Memorial Rose, Rugose Rose, Japanese Rose, Climbing Rose, and Banks Rose. They all belong to the group or genus *Rosa* and are known respectively as *Rosa wichuraiana*, *Rosa rugosa*, *Rosa multiflora*, *Rosa hybrida*, and *Rosa banksiae*. Somewhat closely related to roses are strawberry, spirea, pyracantha, photinia, hawthorn, cotoneaster, and quince. These different genera (plural of genus) together with several others form a larger relationship that is known as the rose family, or Rosaceae. The ending — aceae, which is generally used to denote a family, is the feminine plural of the Latin suffix—aceus, meaning like or related to.

Information on the individual species is presented uniformly for ease in comparison of characteristics. Following is an explanation of this descriptive information.

Zones. The zone numbers listed for each plant refer to the map of average minimum temperatures for zones 6,7,8, and 9 on page xvi. These zones indicate areas of the Southeast where the plant grows well without protection.

Size. Size indicates the height and spread of mature plants. The extremes are given, as 4-6 feet, which means that somewhere between these figures is the average height of growth attained within a reasonable time under average cultural conditions. Immature plants will be below that average, but many plants under optimum conditions will exceed heights shown in this book. The spread indicated is the average width of the plant when it is not affected by crowding.

Size in planting design is essential. Plants should be in proportion with the background; a small garden may be overpowered by a large tree. With a limited garden area and a small house, emphasis should be on low and medium sized shrubs and trees. However, small shrubs against a massive building will usually seem lost and completely out of scale.

Form. There is great variation of form or shape in plants. Form may be called the architecture of plants. Line patterns of branches vary from upright to spreading, arching, or horizontal.

Select plants that will achieve the desired visual effect. Vertical branching leads the line of view upward; horizontal branching ties the view to ground forms. Weeping forms in plants complement rolling terrain and steep banks. Tall and upright plant forms are useful emphasis points in the repetition and regularity of formal gardens. Tight, neatly rounded plants such as boxwood are used in formal design. Informal design usually calls for loose-growing plants, such as azalea and waxmyrtle.

Density of habit of growth must be considered in achieving balance in design. Plants such as boxwood and yew are heavy and compact in form, while waxmyrtle and azalea are light and open. Compact hollies balance the loose form of taller dogwoods; light white pines balance heavy pyracanthas. Many deciduous trees and shrubs have interesting line patterns when they are dormant. Crape-myrtle and dogwood branches are especially attractive in winter.

Texture. Texture is the relationship of size, surface, appearance, and general distribution of branches, twigs, and foliage to the complete plant. Plants are classified as either fine, medium, or coarse in texture. Examples are fine — weeping willow, cotoneaster, and spirea; medium — azalea, sasanqua, and cleyera; and coarse — Southern magnolia, loquat, and aucuba.

As a general rule, fine-textured plants enrich architecture having smooth surfaces and fine lines; coarse textured plants complement large spaces and coarse building materials.

Variety should be introduced but handled carefully to avoid confusion. Change in size, texture, form, or color may be used to bring emphasis to a certain area. Maintain unity in at least two of the basic qualities, such as size and foliage color, and vary the third. For example, to emphasize a particular feature, use varying leaf textures while maintaining similar color and form throughout the planting.

Color. Far too much dependence upon flower color for interest in garden design is evident. Color is seasonal but good foliage and lines are relatively permanent. Use color with restraint and as an accent. Color is provided by leaves, berries, and bark as well as flowers. Care should be taken to maintain harmony between plant colors and background elements.

Culture. Often plants are selected for landscape design without considering the cultural aspects such as sun or shade exposure, soil, moisture, pruning, pest problems, and growth rate. When plants are placed in an unsuitable environment, constant maintenance problems will occur.

The terms sun, part shade, or shade refer to the quantity of light in which a plant grows best. Some plants cannot endure sun, while others require full sun for best display.

Soil requirements for plants vary widely. For best growth and development, plant only in the soil conditions recommended. The term"drainage" indicates the freedom of moisture movement downward through the soil and not the slope of the soil surface. The following conditions affect soil drainage. Poor drainage is found in very heavy clay; medium drainage is found in good garden soil consisting of a desirable combination of sand or gravel, clay, and organic matter; good drainage is found in gravelly soil or very sandy loam with no obstructing formations to impede water movement. Fertility of the soil is judged by the amounts of nitrogen, phosphate, and potassium present. Organic matter and trace minerals are also factors in soil fertility. With few exceptions, most landscape plants require at least medium soil fertility for best growth.

Plants are classified as either low, medium, or high in moisture requirements. For example, santolina and yucca thrive in low moisture conditions, but photinia and spirea prefer medium moisture. Weeping willow and waxmyrtle require high moisture conditions for best results.

Pruning for most plant materials involves thinning and heading back to maintain desired sizes. For plants which require special practices, specific recommendations have been made.

Most plants are susceptible to some diseases or insects. Select plants for landscape use that are relatively free of pest problems or be prepared to follow a spray schedule. Plants that are grown out of their habitat are more subject to pest problems than those growing in their native environment.

Plants have characteristic rates of growth. Although growth rate is of minor importance, it is a factor to consider in choosing a plant for a specific purpose. Sometimes rapidly growing plants are needed to fill a space quickly or to protect finer but slower-growing plants. However, many rapidly growing plants are brittle and can be used only temporarily or in protected locations.

Landscape Notes. In this section are suggestions and characteristics of plants for landscape use. Many of the comments are personal observations from experience in planting design.

Plant materials should be used to serve definite functions or solve specific problems. If a plant does not do this, it should be left out of the design. Shrubs should not be scattered over the yard to try to show off each plant. This detracts from the overall design and also creates a mowing problem. Remember, the object is to complement the house and not compete with it for interest. Some of the functions of plant materials are accent, softening, separation or screening, shade, framing, and background.

Accent shrub plantings may be used to attract or focus attention on the main entrance of the house, and both shrubs and trees may be used for this purpose in the family living area. Normally these are the only two areas where accent plantings should be used. A good design can be destroyed by using upright evergreens or other accent plants along the front of the house or on corners.

As an accent, a plant must possess one or more distinctive characteristics. It must be outstanding in form, texture, size, color, or have a combination of these qualities. Often an accent plant is most effective when used with other plants that emphasize its characteristics. For example, a plant with coarse texture used with plants having fine texture would make a good combination. The same principle works with form, color, or size.

Corners, sharp angles, exposed high foundations, and massive walls should be visually softened by plantings. Plants selected should not attract attention or dominate. Consider these questions. If a corner of a house is to be softened, how large will the plants need to grow? Will the choices blend with other nearby plants? Plants should be massed at the corners of a building; a single plant is rarely effective. Use a small group of shrubs spaced so that they will grow together upon reaching maturity. Medium and small shrubs work well for one-story houses. Two-story houses may require large or medium shrub plantings; the best are irregular and inconspicuous in form but not unusual in foliage, color, and texture.

Shrubs are often used in borders to separate areas, to screen unpleasant views, to serve as wind barriers, and to give privacy or enclosure. In a border or mass planting, use several shrubs of one type before changing to another species. For example, place 10 or 12 ligustrums in a group or row, then continue with 8 or 10 photinias. If further extension is needed, a third choice may be used, or continue with more ligustrums. This approach will result in unity, harmony, and a well-planned border.

The choice of shrubs to serve as screening material is nearly limitless. The best shrubs for screening are large in size, irregular or oval in form, and standard in color and texture; an ultimate height of 6-12 feet is often best. Dense, low-branching plants should be used.

Trees provide protection from undesirable winter and summer winds and screen unsightly views. For winter wind protection evergreen trees are best. Deciduous trees dense in twig and branch mass also afford excellent wind protection. Nearly all small trees grow larger than even the largest shrubs and are used most effectively where extra tall or massive screening is needed. Small trees may be used alone or combined with shrubs in screen or border planting. The variations in height provide an interesting and pleasant change.

Summer shade is an asset to both indoor and outdoor living areas. To shade a roof or wall of a one-story house, plant medium to large trees as close as 15-20 feet from the side or 12-15 feet from the corner of the building. The lower branches should be removed as the tree grows and the canopy allowed to reach over the roof. Trees may be planted for shade on lawns and patios, but do not shade vegetable gardens or flower beds.

Trees are usually located diagonally from the corners of the house for framing; the best for this purpose are medium to large in size and round or irregular in form.

Background trees located behind the house or view are important along with framing trees in providing a total setting. Background trees should be large enough to visually break the roofline of the house when viewed from the front.

Varieties. Often a plant variety can provide the designer with superior or different features. Those included are representative of the wide choice available for general use in the Southeast.

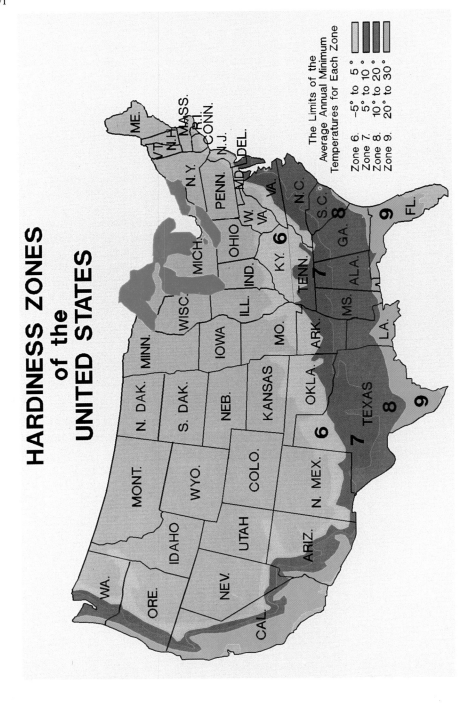

HARDINESS ZONES of the UNITED STATES

The Limits of the
Average Annual Minimum
Temperatures for Each Zone

Zone 6.   −5° to   5°
Zone 7.   5° to 10°
Zone 8.   10° to 20°
Zone 9.   20° to 30°

GROUND COVERS — EVERGREEN

Ajuga (aj-oo'ga)
   Latin for not yoked,
   alluding to calyx

reptans (rep'tanz)
   creeping

BUGLEFLOWER

Family Labiatae

Size	Height 3-5 inches; spread indeterminate. Zones 6, 7, 8, 9.
Form	Compact, dense mat, spreading by stolons similar to strawberry. Foliage — 3-4 inches long, 1 inch wide. Flower — mid-April; small, compact pyramidal spikes.
Texture	Medium to coarse.
Color	Foliage — dark green. Flower — blue.
Culture	Part shade. Soil — well-drained; medium fertility. Moisture — high. Pruning — none. Pest Problems — aphids during rapid growth in early spring and crown rot. Growth Rate — rapid.
Notes	Excellent ground cover especially for moist locations. Good used in rock gardens and in odd corners. Space plants 6 inches apart. *A. genevensis* grows more slowly.
Varieties	**alba** — white flowers. **Atropurpurea** — bronze foliage and blue flowers. **Burgundy Glow** — new leaves bright burgundy-red, mature leaves cream-white and dark pink. **Rubra** — rose flowers, more vigorous. **Variegata** — gray-green leaves with cream markings.

Aspidistra (as-pi-dis'tra)
   Greek for small, round shield
   in allusion to stigma

elatior (ee-lay'ti-or)
   taller

CAST-IRON PLANT

Family Lilaceae

Size	Height 1-2 feet; spread 2-3 feet.	Zones 7, 8, 9.

Form
Upright clumps of foliage; spreads slowly by rhizomes. Foliage — to 20 inches long, 2-3 inches wide. Flower — inconspicuous, bell-shaped at surface of ground.

Texture
Coarse.

Color
Foliage — blackish-green. Flower — purple.

Culture
Shade. Soil — very tolerant. Moisture — medium. Pruning — periodically remove damaged and dead foliage. Pest problems — scale. Growth Rate — slow.

Notes
Not strictly ground cover but used in densely shaded spots for massing or accenting. Adaptable to areas with limited soil volume. Will grow under roof overhangs and in containers. Good to contrast with other textures. Grows best in Coastal Plains.

Variety
variegata — leaves alternately striped, green and white in varied widths. Loses stripes if planted in rich soil.

Cotoneaster (ko-to'nee-as-ter)
   Greek meaning like quince

dammeri (dam'mer-eye)
   named for Udo Dammer,
   German botanist

BEARBERRY COTONEASTER

Family Rosaceae

Size	Height 6-12 inches; spread to 3 feet.	Zones 6, 7, 8.
Form	Prostrate with branches often rooting in moist soil. Foliage — alternate, entire, 1 inch long. Flower — early June; 1 inch diameter. Fruit — fall; berries ¼ inch, usually with 5 nutlets.	
Texture	Fine.	
Color	Foliage — lustrous dark green above, light green beneath. Flower — white. Fruit — bright red.	
Culture	Sun to part shade. Soil — good drainage; medium to low fertility. Moisture — medium to high. Pruning — none. Pest Problems — fire blight, lacebug, red spider, and borers. Growth Rate — slow.	
Notes	Effective in rock gardens or on low banks. Limit quantities in warmer locations to avoid pest and disease problems. Mulch to control weed growth between plants.	
Varieties	**Coral Beauty** — height 15-18 inches; spreads rapidly. **Lowfast** — good selection for warm areas; fairly resistant to fireblight. **Major** — strong grower; leaves 1-1½ inches long. **Radicans** — leaves smaller than species. **Skogholm** — height less than 1 foot, but stems may trail to 3 feet.	

Cyrtomium (sir-to'mi-um)
Greek for arching and
merging

falcatum (fal-kay'tum)
sickle-shaped

HOLLY FERN

Family Polypodiaceae

Size	Height 1-2 feet; spread 2-3 feet. Zones 8, 9.
Form	Upright stems forming compact clumps. Foliage — hollylike leather pinnae, 1-2 feet long. Sori bearing spores on underside of leaves in late summer or fall.
Texture	Coarse.
Color	Foliage — glossy dark green.
Culture	Shade or part shade. Soil — good drainage; medium fertility with high organic content. Moisture — medium. Pruning — remove dead and damaged fronds in spring. Pest Problems — none. Growth Rate — moderate.
Notes	Lends interest to small city gardens. Does not spread. Excellent as accent plant or ground cover in Coastal Plain areas.
Varieties	**Butterfieldii** — deeply serrated leaf margins. **Compactum** — leaves shorter than species. **Rochefordianum** — excellent foliage. More popular than species.

Dianthus (di-an'thus)
Greek meaning divine
and flower

plumarius (plu-ma'ri-us)
plumed (fringed petals)

COTTAGE PINK

Family Caryophyllaceae

Size	Height 10-16 inches; spread 1-2 feet.	Zones 6, 7, 8.
Form	Low tufted perennial forming mat-like growth. Foliage — narrow, thick, linear, 1-4 inches long. Flower — May-July; very fragrant; 1½ inch across, 5 petals often fringed, single to double.	
Texture	Fine.	
Color	Foliage — glaucous blue. Flower — rose, pink, white, or multicolored with darker center.	
Culture	Sun. Soil — well-drained; rich humus, slightly alkaline pH. Moisture — high. Pruning — after flowers fade, prune to promote new growth. Pest Problems — leaf spots. Growth Rate — moderate.	
Notes	Old fashioned in character. Used in edging, rock gardens and foreground in perennial border. Mass in naturalized areas. Fragrant, coloful blossoms provide excellent cut flowers. Good companion for Blue Fescue.	
Varieties	**Cyclops** — red flowers. **Dinah** — semi-double rose flowers with maroon centers. **Highland Queen** — vivid scarlet flowers borne over long period. **Moon Mist** — 8-10 inches; pure white double flowers; very fragrant. **Pink Princess** — coral rose flowers, fragrant, long blooming period; very hardy. **Spring Beauty** — 12-18 inches; double mixed flowers.	

Dichondra (di-kon'dra)
   creeping tropical vines,
   morning glory family

repens (ree'penz)
   creeping

carolinensis (ka-ro-ly-nen'sis)
   from Carolinas

DICHONDRA

Family Convolvulaceae

Size	Height 2-3 inches; spread indeterminate.	Zones 8, 9.
Form	Creeping with leaves upright forming thick cover. Foliage — ½ inch diameter, rounded.	
Texture	Medium to fine.	
Color	Foliage — medium green.	
Culture	Sun or part shade. Soil — tolerant; medium drainage; medium fertility; fertilize annually. Moisture — medium; water periodically in dry weather. Pruning — mow 3-4 times during year. Pest Problems — rust fungus, cutworms, red spider, slugs, and nematodes. Growth Rate — rapid.	
Notes	Used as substitute for grass over large areas. May be sown with seeds in March to May and is sometimes called 'Leaf Lawn.' Will not stand traffic as well as grass lawn. Not hardy in mountains. Requires practically no maintenance when established.	

Festuca (fes-tu'ka)
    fescue grasses

ovina (o-vi'na)
    pertaining to sheep

glauca (glaw'ka)
    glaucous

BLUE FESCUE

Family Poaceae

Size	Height 8-12 inches; spread 8-12 inches.	Zones 6, 7, 8, 9.
Form	Singular dense tufts or clumps of grass. Foliage — narrow, 10-12 inches long. Fruit — panicles 12-14 inches long.	
Texture	Fine.	
Color	Foliage — silvery-blue. Fruit — light brown.	
Culture	Sun to part shade. Soil — tolerant. Moisture — tolerant. Pruning — remove seed heads. Pest Problems — none. Growth Rate — medium to rapid.	
Notes	Best color in full sun. Protects soil against erosion and is drought resistant. Use gravel mulch for best appearance. Excellent edging or border material but does not form solid carpet.	
Varieties	**Blue Fox** — height 6 inches; blue foliage. **Sea Urchin** — compact growth habit with blue foliage; height 10 inches. **Silver Egret** — height 5 inches; silver blue foliage.	

Fragaria (fra-gair'i-a)
   Latin for fragrance

chiloensis (chill-o-en'sis)
   from Chile

ananassa (a-nan'as-sa)
   resembling pineapple

STRAWBERRY

Family Rosaceae

Size	Height 4-12 inches; spread indeterminate. Zones 6, 7, 8, 9.
Form	Non-climbing; medium density, propagates naturally by runners. Foliage — leaf of three dentate leaflets each 1-2 inches long. Flower — spring and summer; 1 inch in clusters. Fruit — May to June; berry ¾-1 inch diameter.
Texture	Medium.
Color	Foliage — medium green; winter, reddish-brown. Flower — snowy white. Fruit — red.
Culture	Sun or very light shade. Soil — good drainage; medium to high fertility. Moisture — medium. Pruning — periodic thinning. Pest Problems — parasitic nematodes, mites, beetles, weevils, and other insects. Growth Rate — moderate.
Notes	Use for border planting along walks, drives and flower beds and as garden plant. Wild strawberry also excellent for similiar uses.
Varieties	**Earlibelle** — early, bright red fruit. **Lester** — early, prolific fruit; disease resistant. **Sunrise** — early, orange-red fruit. **Surecrop** — midseason, red fruit; vigorous plant. **Tribute** — everbearing; July through October. **Tristar** — everbearing; July through October.

Helleborus (hell-e-bor us)
   Christmas rose

orientalis (or-i-en-ta'lis)
   oriental, eastern

LENTEN-ROSE

Family Ranunculaceae

Size	Height 12-18 inches; spread to 12 inches.	Zones 6, 7.

Form   Low, erect clumps. Foliage — palmately compound, arising directly from crown, 12 inches wide. Flower — January, often remains until April; bell-shaped, 2 inches wide, 2-6 in cluster. Fruit — late spring; capsule.

Texture   Coarse.

Color   Foliage — dark green. Flower — white, fading to green or purple. Fruit — black.

Culture   Shade. Soil — tolerant; low to medium drainage; medium fertility with humus added. Moisture — medium. Pruning — none. Pest Problems — none. Growth Rate — slow until established.

Notes   Excellent cover for shaded areas; strong texture and attractive winter flowers. Space 1½ to 2 feet apart. Maximum life 10 years.

Varieties   **atro-rubens** — flowers dark purple outside, greenish-purple inside. **White Magic** — hybrid with *H. niger*; white flowers becoming pale pink, 4 inches diameter. Blooms in late winter.

Hypericum (hy-per'i-kum)
  under or among
  heather

calycinum (kal-ee-sy'num)
  calyxlike

AARONSBEARD

Family Hypericaceae

Size	Height 12-18 inches; spread 1-2 feet. Zones 6, 7, 8, 9.
Form	Procumbent, low and spreading with tufted stoloniferous growth. Foliage - opposite, 2 inches long. Flower — May and June; 3 inches wide in terminal clusters. Fruit — fall, persisting; capsules. Stems — 4-angled.
Texture	Medium.
Color	Foliage — bluish-green; fall, purplish-green. Flower — yellow with reddish anthers. Fruit — red-brown. Bark — reddish.
Culture	Sun or part shade. Soil — tolerant. Moisture — low to medium. Pruning — may discolor during cold winters and need shearing back in early spring. Pest Problems — scale. Growth Rate — rapid.
Notes	Flowering mass which completely covers the ground; useful as under-shrub in woods and for rockeries; also useful in sandy soil. Good for covering large, rough areas and for erosion control. Shade limits flower production.

Iberis (eye-beer'is)
  candytuft

sempervirens (sem-per-vy'renz)
  evergreen

EVERGREEN CANDYTUFT

Family Cruciferae

Size	Height 6-10 inches; spread 1-2 feet. Zones 6, 7, 8.
Form	Rounded mounds. Foliage — alternate, 1 inch long, narrow. Flower — late March to early May; small umbels, 1 inch in diameter.
Texture	Fine.
Color	Foliage — dark green. Flower — white.
Culture	Sun. Soil — good drainage; medium fertility. Moisture — medium. Pruning — shear after flowering. Pest Problems — none. Growth Rate — moderate.
Notes	Excellent ground cover for edging. Effective in rockeries. Named varieties often more compact. Best in southeastern exposure for morning sun.
Varieties	**Christmas Snow** — blooms again in fall. **Purity** — very low spreading mound; neat in appearance. **Snowflake** — stems and leaves larger and thicker than species. **Snowmantle** — compact growth; deep green leaves and large flowers.

Juniperus (jew-nip'er-us)
   juniperlike

chinensis (chi-nen'sis)
   from China

sargentii (sar-jent'ee-eye)
   named for C. S. Sargent,
   first director of Arnold Arboretum

SARGENT JUNIPER

Family Cupressaceae

Size	Height 1 foot; spread 6-8 feet. Zones 6, 7, 8, 9.
Form	Low spreading, forming broad mat with procumbent stems. Foliage — needlelike, opposite on many conspicuous twigs. Fruit — fall; ¼-½ inch across, 2-5 seeded.
Texture	Fine.
Color	Foliage — steel blue. Fruit — brownish-violet.
Culture	Sun. Soil — good drainage; low fertility. Moisture — low. Pruning — none. Pest Problems — mites, bagworms, and scale. Growth Rate — moderate.
Notes	Best variety for adverse conditions. Withstands heat and salt spray. Effective in raised planters.
Varieties	**Compacta** — compact form with needle-shaped dark green leaves. **Glauca** — height 1½ feet, spread 4-6 feet; leaves blue-green when young. **J. c. Expansa Aureovariegata** — spreading form; height 2 feet; spread 7-8 feet. Uniformly variegated foliage.

Juniperus (jew-nip'er-us)
   juniperlike

conferta (kon-fer'ta)
   crowded, pressed
   together

SHORE JUNIPER

Family Cupressaceae

Size	Height 12-18 inches; spread 4-6 feet.	Zones 6, 7, 8.
Form	Spreading with medium density. More open in growth than Andorra or Sargent Juniper and more vigorous. Foliage — needles to ½ inch long, usually in 3's. Fruit — fall; berrylike, ½ inch diameter.	
Texture	Fine.	
Color	Foliage — gray-green with white line on top. Fruit — black.	
Culture	Sun but will tolerate part shade. Soil — good drainage; low fertility; prefers sandy loam. Moisture — low. Pruning — none. Pest Problems — red spiders. Growth Rate — rapid.	
Notes	Drapes well on banks or in planters. Will grow on beach dune or in clay. Spreads rapidly by underground stems. Effective in masses. Useful as foreground for taller plantings. Withstands severe exposure.	
Varieties	**Blue Pacific** — more compact; withstands heat well. Most popular selection. **Boulevard** — horizontal main branches with shiny green foliage. **Compacta** — prostrate growth when young with closely spaced needles and branches; needle color light green. **Emerald Sea** — height 1 foot with dense growth and prostrate habit. Blue-green foliage; good salt tolerance. **Silver Mist** — bright blue-gray foliage; compact growth.	

Juniperus (jew-nip'er-us)
   juniperlike

horizontalis (hor-ri-zon-tay'lis)
   horizontal

CREEPING JUNIPER

Family Cupressaceae

Size	Height 12-18 inches; spread 3-5 feet.	Zones 6, 7, 8, 9.
Form	Low and open. Foliage — needlelike. Fruit — fall; berries ⅜ inch diameter, 1-4 seeds.	
Texture	Fine.	
Color	Foliage — bluish-green; winter, rust-green. Fruit — blue.	
Culture	Sun. Soil — good drainage; low fertility; prefers slightly alkaline conditions. Moisture — low. Pruning — none. Pest Problems — bagworms and mites. Growth Rate — moderate to rapid.	
Notes	Serviceable for difficult locations. Named varieties more colorful and interesting in habit of growth than species. Withstands city conditions.	
Varieties	**Bar Harbor** — dwarf form; slow growing and very hardy. Blue-green foliage turning purple in fall. **Douglasii** — trailing form with blue-gray foliage turning pale purple in fall; rapid growth. Waukegan Juniper. Excellent in containers. **Emerald Spreader** — very low growing emerald green branches with fern-like appearance. **Green Acres** — dark green spreading form. **Plumosa** — light green, feathery foliage turning reddish-purple in fall; height 1-2 feet. Andorra Juniper. **Wiltonii** — extremely low-growing form with blue foliage. Blue Rug Juniper.	

Liriope (li-ri'o-pe)
    lily-turf

muscarii (mus-cay'ree)
    grape hyacinth; from Latin
    for musky, in allusion to
    musky scent

LILYTURF

Family Liliaceae

Size	Height 12-18 inches; spread 12-18 inches.	Zones 6, 7, 8, 9.

Form   Grasslike with leaves recurving toward ground. Forms clumps. Foliage — 1-2 feet long and 1/3-1 inch wide. Flower — July to August; small clusters on center spike above leaves. Fruit — fall; berrylike in clusters.

Texture   Medium.

Color   Foliage — dark green. Flower — lavender-pink. Fruit — shiny black.

Culture   Shade but tolerates full sun. Soil — tolerant. Moisture — medium. Pruning — each March cut tops to within 1 inch of ground with lawn mower or by hand shearing. Pest Problems — scale. Growth Rate — moderate to rapid.

Notes   Thrives in practically any situation and is often used to border walks and drives. Frequently used in beds around trunks of trees. Effective in mass. Requires little care. Withstands salt spray.

Varieties   **Big Blue** — improved strain with large leaves; large flower spikes. **Majestic** — strong grower, foliage dark green; large deep lavender flower in July and August. **Monroe White** — white flowers; shade only. **Silvery Sunproof** — white variegated form, leaves more yellow in dense shade. Lavender flowers held well above foliage. **variegata** — leaves yellow-striped.

Liriope (li-ri'o-pe)
  lily-turf

spicata (spy-ka'ta)
  spiked; or having
  flowers in spike

CREEPING LILYTURF

Family Liliaceae

Size	Height 10-15 inches; spread indeterminate. Zones 6, 7, 8, 9.
Form	Grasslike with leaves recurving toward ground. Foliage — 13-15 inches long and ¼ inch wide. Flower — July to August; small clusters on center spike above leaves. Fruit — fall; berrylike.
Texture	Fine.
Color	Foliage — dark green. Flower — pale lilac or nearly white. Fruit — black.
Culture	Shade but tolerates sun. Soil — tolerant. Moisture — medium. Pruning — cut leaves to 1 inch in March. Pest Problems — scale. Growth Rate — rapid.
Notes	Excellent for preventing soil erosion. Withstands neglect when established; maintains neat appearance all seasons. Fast suckering habit.
Variety	**Franklin Mint** — height 12-15 inches; very large flower spikes. May be hybrid with *L. muscari*.

Ophiopogon (o-fi-o-po'gon)
    Greek snake's beard

jaburan (jab'ur-ran)
    oriental vernacular name

vittata (vit-tay'ta)
    striped

SNAKEBEARD

Family Liliaceae

Size	Height 8-12 inches; spread indeterminate. Zones 7, 8, 9.
Form	Grasslike with leaves recurving toward ground. Foliage — ¼-½ inch wide, 12-18 inches long, oblong lanceolate. Flower — small clusters on center spike usually hidden by foliage. Fruit — berrylike.
Texture	Medium.
Color	Foliage — green with white stripes. Flower — white to lilac. Fruit — dark blue.
Culture	Shade or sun. Soil — tolerant; good drainage; medium fertility. Moisture — medium; withstands drought well. Pruning — cut leaves to 1 inch in March with shears or mower. Pest Problems — none. Growth Rate — rapid.
Notes	Most attractive planted in small masses. Often used as border for flower beds and walks or thick plantings on gently sloping banks. Attractive in containers. Not as hardy as Liriope. Withstands salt spray. Little care required.
Varieties	**aureus** — yellow-striped leaves. **Sunproof** — tolerates full sun.

Ophiopogon (o-fi-o-po'gon)
  Greek snake's beard

japonicus (ja-pon'i-kus)
  from Japan

MONDO GRASS

Family Liliaceae

Size	Height 6-10 inches; spread indeterminate. Zones 7, 8, 9.
Form	Stemless clumps spreading to form grasslike cover. Foliage — grassy, 9-12 inches long and ⅛ inch wide, curving toward ground. Flower — July; tiny spikes usually hidden by foliage. Fruit — berrylike.
Texture	Fine.
Color	Foliage — dark green. Flower — pale lilac to white. Fruit — blue.
Culture	Sun or shade. Soil — good drainage; medium fertility with humus added. Moisture — medium. Pruning — cut leaves to 1 inch in March. Pest Problems — none. Growth Rate — rapid.
Notes	Resistant to drought. Excellent cover for large or small areas; especially useful under trees. Set plants 4-6 inches apart or 3 inches in heavy shade. Excellent control of erosion when well established.
Varieties	**Gyokuruu** — dark green grass-like foliage; height 2 inches. **Nana** — compact slow-growing form; height 4-5 inches. **Shiroshima Ryu** — dark green and white striped leaves; height 3-4 inches. **Variegatus** — leaves with white and green striping.

Pachysandra (pack-i-san'dra)
   evergreen

terminalis (ter-mi-nall'is)
   at end

JAPANESE SPURGE

Family Buxaceae

Size	Height 5-12 inches; spread indeterminate.	Zones 6, 7.

Form   Low and stoloniferous with matted, creeping rootstalks. Fleshy, erect stems with leaves tufted at top, forming loose carpets. Foliage — alternate, wedge-shaped to 2 inches long in clusters. Flower — midspring; inconspicuous terminal spikes. Fruit — summer; 3-horned drupe, 1/3 inch diameter.

Texture   Medium.

Color   Foliage — olive green. Flower — white. Fruit — white.

Culture   Shade. Soil — tolerant. Moisture — medium. Pruning - pinching tops in spring makes plants thicker. Pest Problems — scale and stem rot. Growth Rate — slow to moderate.

Notes   Excellent ground cover for shade. Of uniform height. Most effective planted thickly. Good texture accent on level ground under trees where grass will not grow. Blends well with plants of yellow or yellow-green coloration. Spreads by underground stolons. Does not grow well in warm areas.

Varieties   **Cut Leaf** — deeper green leaves with serrated and cut edges. **Green Carpet** — grows close to ground forming compact low cover. Waxy dark green foliage. **Variegata** — leaves marked on edges with white; not as vigorous as species.

Phlox (flocks)
    showy garden plant

subulata (sub-you-lay'ta)
    awl-shaped

THRIFT

Family Polemoniaceae

Size	Height 2-4 inches; spread indeterminate. Zones 6, 7, 8, 9.
Form	Dense and creeping, forming mounds of foliage merging into solid carpet. Foliage — opposite, ½ inch long, awl-shaped, crowded. Flower — March to May; covering foliage, ¾ inch diameter.
Texture	Fine.
Color	Foliage — yellow green. Flower — white, pink, blue or purple.
Culture	Sun. Soil — good drainage; medium to low fertility. Moisture — low. Pruning — none. Pest Problems — fairly clean. Growth Rate — moderate.
Notes	Good for use in rock gardens, borders, and on small banks. Valued for ability to survive under adverse conditions. May be used as soil stabilizer. Useful in mass for ground cover. Best in small areas. Colors other than rose-crimson blend better with surroundings. Little care required after established except division every 3 or 4 years.
Varieties	**alba** — white flowers. **Alexander's Pink** — pink flowers. **Emerald Cushion** — pink flowers, habit dwarf and compact. **Eventide** — blue flowers. **Moerheimii** — deep pink flowers. **Nelsonii** — compact form with white rose-centered flowers. **Sky Blue** — blue flowers. **White Delight** — large pure white flowers.

Rosa (ro'za)
    old Latin name
    for rose

wichuraiana (wy-shur-ee-ay'na)
    in honor of Wichuray,
    Russian botanist

MEMORIAL ROSE

Family Rosaceae

Size	Height 1-2 feet; spread 20 feet or more.	Zones 6, 7, 8, 9.
Form	Dense, creeping, and prostrate sending out long trailing shoots. Foliage — alternate, 7-9 oval leaflets 2-3 inches long. Flower — May; single or semidouble in fragrant corymbs about 2 inches across. Fruit — late summer; ovoid hips.	
Texture	Medium.	
Color	Foliage — dark green. Flower — white. Fruit — red.	
Culture	Sun or part shade. Soil — fairly tolerant. Moisture — medium. Pruning — cut out dead or weak wood; fasten stolons for cover. Pest Problems — fire blight. Growth Rate — rapid.	
Notes	Beautiful cover for banks in full sun and rockeries. Roots along procumbent stems and aids in erosion control. Good barrier planting; may be trained on fence for screen.	
Varieties	**Evangeline** — large clusters of soft-pink fragrant flowers. **Phyllis Bide** — small buff-yellow flowers. **poteriifolia** — extremely dense growth; disease and pest resistant and drought resistant. White flowers in summer and clusters of red fruit in fall.	

Santolina (san-to-ly'na)
  lavender cotton, aromatic
  undershrubs

chamaecyparissus (kam-ee-sip-a-ris'sus)
  Greek for dwarf cypress

LAVENDER-COTTON

Family Compositae

Size	Height 1-2 feet; spread 3-4 feet.

Zones 6, 7, 8, 9.

Form	Very dense and compact low-spreading mounds. Foliage — alternate, ½ inch long, aromatic. Flower — June; buttonlike, ½-¾ inch diameter.
Texture	Fine.
Color	Foliage — silvery gray-green. Flower — yellow.
Culture	Sun. Soil — very good drainage; low fertility. Moisture — low. Pruning — remove top growth to crown every 2 to 3 years for renewal; remove flowers annually. Pest Problems — fungus during damp seasons. Growth Rate — moderate.
Notes	For foliage effect in rock gardens and foreground planting. Will not tolerate wet soil or high fertilization. Highly aromatic foliage. Useful on poor, sandy, or gravelly soils. Stems root where they touch ground. Somewhat salt tolerant.
Variety	**nana** — forms 1 foot compact mound.

Santolina (san-to-ly'na)
   lavender cotton, aromatic
   undershrubs

virens (vy'renz)
   green

GREEN SANTOLINA

Family Compositae

Size	Height 12-18 inches; spread 2-3 feet.	Zones 7, 8, 9.
Form	Very dense mounds. Foliage — alternate, pinnate, aromatic, 1-2 inches long and 1/16 inch wide. Flower — summer; buttonlike, ⅝ inch.	
Texture	Fine.	
Color	Foliage — emerald green. Flower — yellow.	
Culture	Sun. Soil — very good drainage; low fertility. Moisture — low. Pruning — remove top growth to crown every 2 to 3 years for renewal; remove flowers annually. Pest Problems — excess moisture may cause fungus. Growth Rate — moderate.	
Notes	Excellent for mass or border plantings. For foliage effect in rock gardens. May be clipped to form dwarf hedge. Useful in poor, sandy or gravelly soils. Foliage aromatic.	

Sarcococca (sar-ko-kok'a)
Greek for flesh and berry

hookeriana (hook-er-i-a'na)
named for J. D. Hooker

humilis (hu'mi-lis)
dwarf or low-growing

SMALL HIMALAYAN
SARCOCOCCA

Family Buxaceae

Size	Height 1-2 feet; spread 1½-2½ feet. Zones 6, 7, 8.
Form	Loose and informal. Foliage — alternate, entire, 1-2 inches. Flower — fragrant; inconspicuous. Fruit — round, 1/3 inch diameter, inconspicuous.
Texture	Medium.
Color	Foliage — lustrous dark green. Flower — white. Fruit — blue-black. Stem — green.
Culture	Part shade. Soil — medium drainage; medium fertility with humus added. Moisture — medium to low. Pruning — remove dead wood. Pest Problems — none. Growth Rate — moderate.
Notes	Useful in groups as filler and background, as informal border, or as ground cover.
Variety	**S.h. digyna Purple Stem** — height 4-6 feet; stems and midribs purple.

Teucrium (too'kri-um)
     named for King Teucer,
     first king of Troy

chamaedrys (kam-ee'dris)
     pre-Linnaean name for
     some germander

GERMANDER

Family Labiatae

Size	Height 10-12 inches; spread 8-10 inches. Zones 6, 7, 8, 9.
Form	Irregularly spreading mounds with moderate branching. Foliage — opposite, small, dense, arranged in whorls. Flower - late summer; ¾inch long on showy spikes.
Texture	Medium to fine.
Color	Foliage — very pubescent, giving grayish color to dark green leaves. Flower — rose-purple.
Culture	Sun. Soil — good drainage; medium fertility. Moisture — medium. Pruning — shear after flowering if dwarf hedge desired. Pest Problems — none. Growth Rate — moderate.
Notes	Fine border plant suitable for rock and herb gardens, formal and informal edgings. Useful for summer bloom in front of evergreens.
Variety	**prostratum** - to 8 inches. Flowers heavily.

Vinca (vin'ka)
    periwinkle, creeping myrtle

major (ma'jor)
    greater, larger

BIG PERIWINKLE

Family Apocynaceae

Size	Height 1 foot; spread indeterminate. Zones 7, 8, 9.
Form	Upright and more open and loose than *V. minor.* Foliage — opposite, 3 inches long. Flower — March and April; 1-2 inches wide.
Texture	Medium.
Color	Foliage — glossy light green. Flower — light blue.
Culture	Sun or shade; competition from weeds in sun. Soil — very tolerant. Moisture — low. Pruning — needs some clipping. Pest Problems — fungus in fertile soils. Growth Rate — rapid.
Notes	Excellent for naturalizing. Good ground cover for banks; can compete with worst root conditions under trees. Suitable for window boxes. Requires little maintenance.
Variety	**Variegata** — cream-colored markings on leaves.

Vinca (vin'ka)
   periwinkle,
   creeping myrtle

minor (my'nor)
   smaller

PERIWINKLE

Family Apocynaceae

Size	Height 5-8 inches; spread 3-4 feet. Zones 6, 7, 8.
Form	Wide-spreading with stems rooting along ground, non-climbing, medium density. Foliage — opposite, 1-2 inches long. Flower — March and April; single, ¾ inch diameter.
Texture	Medium.
Color	Foliage — lustrous dark green. Flower — blue.
Culture	Part shade or shade; competition from grass in sun. Soil — medium drainage; low fertility. Moisture — low to medium. Pruning — crowded, neglected plantings improved by severe thinning to increase vigor. Pest Problems — stem canker, fungus in fertile soils. Growth Rate — rapid.
Notes	Excellent ground cover under trees and for covering shady banks. Usually more desirable ground cover than V. *major*. Roots along stems to make new plants.
Varieties	**Alba** — white flowers. **Alpinia** — large blue flowers. **Azurea Flore Pleno** — sky-blue double flowers. **Gertrude Jekyll** — abundant white flowers, small leaves. **La Grave** — larger lavender flowers and large leaves. **Multiplex** — purple-blue double flowers. **Sterling Silver** — leaves with cream-white margins; lavender blue flowers.

GROUND COVERS — DECIDUOUS

Epimedium (ep-i-me'di-um)
  from land of Medes

x youngianum (yun-jee-ay'num)

'Niveum' (niv'ee-um)
  white flowers

BARRENWORT

Family Berberidaceae

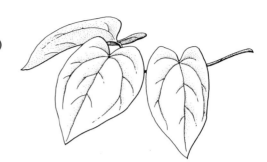

Size	Height 8-10 inches; spread indeterminate. Zones 6, 7, 8.
Form	Dense, upright and rounded mounds; spreads by underground stems (rhizomes). Foliage — thrice compound on wiry petiole, leaflet 2-2½ inches long, heart-shaped. Flower — spring; ½ inch diameter in pendulous sprays held above leaves.
Texture	Medium to coarse.
Color	Foliage — new growth pale bronze; summer, green; fall, reddish green. Flower — white.
Culture	Part shade to shade. Soil — tolerant; medium drainage; medium fertility. Moisture — high to medium. Pruning — shear in late winter. Pest Problems — none. Growth Rate — slow to moderate.
Notes	Handsome foliage and decorative flowers; tolerates full sun in moist soil. Semi-evergreen in warm areas. Plant 12 inches apart for quick ground cover.

Hemerocallis (hem-er-o-kal'is)
  from Greek meaning
  beautiful for one day

hybrida (hy'brid-a)
  hybrid

DAYLILY HYBRIDS

Family Liliaceae

Size	Height — foliage 18 inches, scape to 5 feet; spread 3-4 feet.	Zones 6, 7, 8, 9.

Size
: Height — foliage 18 inches, scape to 5 feet; spread 3-4 feet.

Zones 6, 7, 8, 9.

Form
: Herbaceous perennial spreading from crown by fleshy rhizomes. Foliage — 2 feet long, 1 1/3 inches wide. Flower — summer; 5 inches long and 3½ inches wide, 6-12 on tall scapes, not fragrant.

Texture
: Medium to coarse.

Color
: Foliage — light green. Flower - yellow, orange, dark red, pink, and combinations.

Culture
: Sun or shade. Soil — tolerant; prefers loam. Moisture — very tolerant. Pruning — remove scapes after flowering. Pest Problems — none. Growth Rate — rapid.

Notes
: Select evergreen varieties whenever possible; mulch until established. Inexpensive species useful in masses for large scale or roadside plantings and to control erosion on banks and near water. Will grow in difficult areas with minimum care. Space 1½-3 feet apart. More than 12,000 varieties now grown.

Varieties
: **Buttercurls** — 4 inch ruffled lemon yellow flowers on 26 inch plants. Mid-season bloomer. **Dragon Mouth** — 6 inch red flowers on 30 inch plants. Late season bloomer. **Happy Returns** — 3½ inch ruffled lemon yellow flowers, long blooming period. **Hyperion** — citron yellow flowers. Midseason bloomer; very hardy. **Sirocco** — salmon pink flowers on 26 inch plants. Early-midseason bloom. **Stella d' Oro** — height 12-16 inches; dark green foliage and yellow flowers, exceptionally long blooming period. Hardy and beautiful in sun or partial shade.

Hosta (hos'ta)
   plantain lily

lancifolia (lan-si-fo'li-a)
   lance-shaped leaves

NARROW-LEAVED
PLANTAIN LILY

Family Liliaceae

Size	Height 1½-2 feet; spread 4 feet. Zones 6, 7, 8, 9.
Form	Perennial herb forming clumps. Foliage — slender, lanceolate, 6 inches long, 1½-2 inches wide, tapering at both ends. Flower — August; 2 inches long, bell-shaped on scapes.
Texture	Coarse.
Color	Foliage — dark green. Flower — lilac or pale lavender.
Culture	Shade or part shade. Soil — tolerant if fertile. Moisture — high. Pruning — remove dead foliage in winter. Pest Problems — slugs. Growth Rate — rapid.
Notes	Low maintenance perennial beautiful in foliage and flower as specimen or border plant. Plant close together for immediate covering under trees. Most useful massed or in planter boxes. Many other species equally attractive.
Varieties	**Albo-marginata** — margins of leaves white. **tardiflora** — autumn flowering. **Thunbergiana** — shiny green twisted leaves.

Hosta (hos'ta)
  plantain lily

plantaginea (plan-ta-ji-nee'uh)

FRAGRANT PLANTAIN

Family Liliaceae

Size	Height 1½-2½ feet; spread 4 feet.	Zones 6, 7, 8, 9.
Form	Perennial herb forming clumps. Foliage — 4-5 inches wide, 6 inches long on stem to 2 feet long. Flower — late summer; 4 inches long, fragrant, on scapes 1½-2½ feet above foliage.	
Texture	Coarse.	
Color	Foliage — green. Flower — white.	
Culture	Part shade. Soil — medium drainage; high to medium fertility. Moisture — high. Pruning — remove dead foliage. Pest Problems — none. Growth Rate — rapid.	
Notes	Excellent for bordering walks and drives in shaded areas or as specimen. Only *Hosta* with scented flowers.	
Variety	**Grandiflora** — spectacular flowers in August and September.	

Plant textures and forms blend naturally to complement shady suburban garden.

VINES — EVERGREEN

Akebia (a-kee'bi-a)
  Asian woody vines

quinata (kwi-na'ta)
  in fives

FIVELEAF AKEBIA

Family Lardizabalaceae

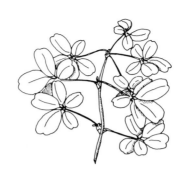

Size	Height 30-40 feet; spread indeterminate. Zones 6, 7, 8.
Form	Climbs by twining. Foliage — alternate, 5 leaflets palmately compound, each 2 inches long. Flower — April to May; ½-1 inch diameter in clusters, fragrant. Fruit — 2-3 inch pods.
Texture	Medium to fine.
Color	Foliage — pale to medium green; winter, purplish. Flower — purple. Fruit — purple.
Culture	Sun or light shade. Soil — good drainage; medium to low fertility. Moisture — low. Pruning — control growth to desired height. Pest Problems — none. Growth Rate — rapid.
Notes	Excellent foliage for fences or trellis if carefully controlled. Spreads by long underground runners. May lose some leaves in severe winters. Other species include A. *trifoliata*, 3 leaflet type.

Anisostichus (an-i-sos-tic'us)

capreolata (kap-re-a-lay'ta)
winding, turning

CROSSVINE

Family Bignoniaceae

Size	Height 50-60 feet; spread indeterminate. Zones 6, 7, 8.
Form	Climbs by tendrils. Foliage — opposite and compound, 2 leaflets to 6 inches long, terminal tendrils, entire, stiff. Flower — mid-April; trumpet-shaped, 2 inches wide. Fruit — July; pods 1 foot long.
Texture	Coarse.
Color	Foliage — dark green, glabrous; winter, purplish. Flower — orange-red. Fruit — green turning brown.
Culture	Sun for best flowering. Soil — tolerant; prefers loam. Moisture — medium. Pruning — train. Pest Problems — none. Growth Rate — rapid.
Notes	Excellent fast-growing screen for wire fences and can be trained on masonry walls. Grown for handsome foliage and flower production. Formerly named *Bignonia capreolata*.
Variety	**atro-sanguinea** — flowers dark purple. Leaves longer and narrower than species.

Clematis (klem'a-tis)
   woody flowering vines

armandii (ar-mon'de-i)

ARMAND CLEMATIS

Family Ranunculaceae

Size	Height 15-20 feet; spread indeterminate.	Zones 7, 8, 9.
Form	Climbs by twisting petioles. Foliage — 5 inches wide with 3 leaflets, linear and entire. Flower — spring; 1-2½ inches in showy panicles, fragrant, blooms on growth of previous year.	
Texture	Coarse.	
Color	Foliage — medium to glossy green. Flower — white.	
Culture	Sun for top growth, cool shade over roots. Soil — fertile; neutral to akaline. Moisture — medium to low. Pruning — mid-summer after bloom if necessary. Pest Problems — clematis borer, leaf spot, and root rot. Growth Rate — rapid.	
Notes	Prefers cool areas. Fast-growing with beautiful flowers; use as accent to cover pergolas and trellises. Does not tolerate cultivation.	
Varieties	**Apple Blossom** — white flowers flushed with pink; leaves bronze-green. **Farquhariana** — light pink flowers. **Snowdrift** — very large white flowers.	

Euonymus (you-on'i-mus)
   hardy shrubs and vines

fortunei (for-too'nee-i)
   named for Robert Fortune

WINTERCREEPER

Family Celastraceae

Size	Height 3-6 feet when clinging to wall; spread 2-4 feet. Zones 6, 7, 8, 9.
Form	Vinelike, climbing by aerial roots on solid surfaces. Foliage — opposite, ¼-2 inches long.
Texture	Medium.
Color	Foliage — dark green with whitish veins; fall, reddish. Stem — green.
Culture	Sun or shade. Soil — medium drainage; medium fertility with high organic content. Moisture — medium to high. Pruning — thin. Pest Problems — scale and aphids on new growth. Growth Rate — moderate.
Notes	Desirable as low screen against masonry or tree trunks, and may be used as low ground cover for difficult situations in shade or with poor drainage. Tolerates salt spray. Excellent as bank cover. Allows little weed competition.
Varieties	**Coloratus** — 1-2 inch leaves which turn reddish-purple in winter. **Emerald Cushion** — dwarf mounded form, dense branching habit; holds rich green foliage; 12 inches by 18 inches. **Kewensis** — ¼ inch leaves; slow growing, use in small areas. **Minimus** — ½ inch leaves. **radicans** — 1-2 inch leaves. **Silver Queen** — compact shrub, 3-4 feet height; leaves deep green with cream-white margins. Excellent container plant.

X Fatshedera (fats-hed'e-ra)
    bigeneric hybrid; English
    ivy and Fatsia japonica

lizei (li-ze'i)
    named for Messrs. Lizé
    of France

BUSHIVY

Family Araliaceae

Size	Height 8-9 feet; spread indeterminate. Zones 7, 8, 9.
Form	Vinelike, requires support. Foliage — alternate, starfish in shape reaching 10 inches in width on established plants. Palmately 5-lobed. Flower — fall; 1 inch spherical heads. Fruit — berry on old wood.
Texture	Coarse.
Color	Foliage — dark lustrous green. Flower — pale green. Fruit — blue. Stem — green.
Culture	Shade or part shade with protection in Piedmont and mountains. Soil — tolerant; good drainage; medium fertility. Moisture — medium to low. Pruning — train or confine. Pest Problems — aphids. Growth Rate — rapid.
Notes	Excellent espalier plant. Outstanding for use in exterior and interior planter boxes. Good filler in narrow strips between walk and wall. Tolerates beach conditions if protected from strong winds. Plant in protected areas west of coastal regions.
Variety	**Variegata** — leaves bordered with white.

Ficus (fy'kus)
    classical Latin
    for fig

pumila (pew'mi-la)
    dwarf, small

CLIMBING FIG

Family Moraceae

Size	Height to 30 feet; spread indeterminate.	Zones 8, 9.
Form	Climbs by aerial rootlets with leaves held flat against wall. Foliage — alternate, simple, entire; juvenile leaves about 1 inch long, mature leaves 2-4 inches long. Fruit — 2 inch figs on older plants; inedible.	
Texture	Fine to medium.	
Color	Foliage — light green. Fruit — yellowish-green.	
Culture	Part shade or shade. Soil — tolerant. Moisture — medium. Pruning — remove young, erect growth and cut back old main stems to forestall maturity. Pest Problems — harbors insects in dense mat if not thinned. Growth Rate — rapid.	
Notes	Very good for covering masonry walls. Avoid planting near wood construction. Forms lacy pattern of stems and foliage over support until completely covered. Not hardy in Piedmont or mountains.	
Varieties	**Minima** — dwarf climbing fig, juvenile form. **Variegata** — small green and white leaves, pointed.	

Gelsemium (gel-see'mi-um)
    Latin version of jessamine

sempervirens (sem-per-vy'renz)
    evergreen

CAROLINA JESSAMINE

Family Loganiaceae

Size	Height to 20 feet; spread indeterminate. Zones 6, 7, 8, 9.
Form	Twining vine with wiry thin stems; growth becoming stockier with generous exposure to sun. Delicate growth character. Foliage — opposite, narrow and pointed, small and waxy. Flower — late February to early April; fragrant, single or in small cymes. Fruit — flattened winged capsule.
Texture	Fine.
Color	Foliage — shiny dark green; winter, wine-red. Flower — yellow. Fruit — brown.
Culture	Sun or shade. Soil — tolerant. Moisture — medium. Pruning — shear after flowering. Pest Problems — none. Growth Rate — moderate; rapid when established.
Notes	Good screening material. Flower production best in sun. Grows well on fences and trellises; train first growth horizontally to cover wire. Will climb on small trees and downspouts. Native to Southeast.
Variety	**Pride of Augusta (Plena)** — double flowered.

Hedera (hed'er-a)
  classical name of ivy

canariensis (ka-nay-ri-en'sis)
  from Canary Islands

ALGERIAN IVY

Family Araliaceae

Size	Height to 30 feet; spread indeterminate. Zones 8, 9.
Form	Mass of trailing vines climbing by aerial roots. Foliage — alternate, thick and leathery, 5-7 lobed, 2-6 inches long, 3-5 inches wide. Fruit — berry.
Texture	Coarse.
Color	Foliage — glossy dark green. Fruit — blue-black. Twigs — green when young, red when older.
Culture	Shade. Soil — tolerant; good drainage; medium fertility. Moisture — medium to high. Pruning — none. Pest Problems — snails and scale insects. Growth Rate — moderate to rapid.
Notes	Must be confined if used in small garden. Easy and inexpensive to establish. May be used as ground cover. Not cold hardy in mountain areas.
Varieties	**Canary Cream** — green leaves with cream-colored margins. **Shamrock** — for small, refined areas. **Variegata** — leaves with dark green, gray, and cream markings.

Hedera (hed'er-a)
  classical name of ivy

colchica (kol'chi-ka)
  from Colchis, ancient
  name of region of N. E.
  shore of Black Sea

COLCHIS IVY

Family Araliaceae

Size	Height of 30 feet; spread indeterminate. Zones 7, 8, 9.
Form	Mass of vines clinging by aerial roots. Foliage — alternate, heart-shaped and thick, very slightly 3-lobed, 2-6 inches long, fragrant when crushed. Fruit — berrylike.
Texture	Coarse.
Color	Foliage — dark green. Fruit — black.
Culture	Shade. Soil — very tolerant. Moisture — medium. Pruning — thin. Pest Problems — aphids. Growth Rate — moderate.
Notes	Useful on fences or as accent. May be sheared to form topiary object. Can be used as ground cover. Must be confined if used in small garden.
Varieties	**Dentata-Variegata** — very large dark green leaves variegated with gray and yellow. **Sulphur Heart** — leaves marked with central splash of yellow.

Hedera (hed'er-a)
classical name of ivy

helix (he'licks)
Latin for ivy

ENGLISH IVY

Family Araliaceae

Size	Height to 50 feet; spread indeterminate. Zones 6, 7, 8, 9.
Form	Climbs on solid surfaces by aerial roots; dense. Foliage — alternate, to 4 inches long with 3-5 lobes, margins entire. Flower — inconspicuous. Fruit — berry.
Texture	Medium to coarse.
Color	Foliage — dark green with gray veins. Fruit — bluish-black.
Culture	Part shade to shade. Soil — medium drainage; medium fertility with high organic content. Moisture — medium to high. Pruning — needs control to prevent damage to wood trim or siding. Pest Problems — scale, aphids, mealybug, fungus leaf spot, and bacterial leaf spot under moist conditions. Growth Rate — rapid once established.
Notes	May be used as ground cover; should not be permitted to grow in valuable trees. Aggressive in adapted conditions. Numerous small-leaved forms available for limited ground areas. Variegated foliage types also in nursery trade. Easy and inexpensive to establish. Some low temperature injury in mountains.
Varieties	**baltica** — small-leaved form, very hardy. **Buttercup** — leaves dark green with light veins, new leaves yellow. **Gnome** — grows very close to ground; fine-textured dark-green leaves less than 1 inch long. **Gold Heart** — small dark green leaves with cream centers; very hardy and holds color all year. **Hahn's** — small green leaves, bushy growth. **Harrison** — broad dark green leaves turning reddish purple in winter. Best appearance when grown on wall; very hardy. **Marginata** — gray-green leaves with white margins. **Wilson** — very hardy form; smaller leaves than species. 6-8 inches in height.

Jasminum (jas'min-um)
   Arabic name for jasmine

officinale (of-fish-i-na'lee)
   medicinal

COMMON JASMINE

Family Oleaceae

Size	Height to 15 feet; spread indeterminate.	Zones 7, 8, 9.
Form	Semi-climbing and shrublike requiring support. Foliage — opposite, pinnate, 5-7 pairs of leaflets each ½ to 2 inches long. Flower — late spring and summer; ¾-1 inch wide in clusters, fragrant. Fruit — 2-lobed berry.	
Texture	Medium.	
Color	Foliage — green. Flower — white. Fruit — black.	
Culture	Sun or part shade. Soil — tolerant. Moisture — tolerant. Pruning — none. Pest Problems — none. Growth Rate — moderate.	
Notes	Popular for summer flowers and fragrance. Useful on arbors or trellises, having graceful, airy effect.	
Varieties	**Affine** — flowers tinged pink outside. **aureo-variegatum** — variegated leaves. **grandiflorum** — flowers larger and more showy, to 1½ inches wide.	

Kadsura (kad-soo'ra)

japonica (ja-pon'i-ka)
from Japan

SCARLET KADSURA

Family Schisandraceae

Size	Height 8-12 feet; spread indeterminate. Zones 7, 8, 9.
Form	Climbs by twining. Foliage — alternate, simple, entire or dentate, thick, 4 inches long. Flower — June-September; solitary, axillary, ¾ inch across; dioecious. Fruit — fall; 1 inch diameter, globose; pendulous clusters.
Texture	Coarse.
Color	Foliage — glossy medium green with reddish petioles. Flower — sulfur-yellow. Fruit — scarlet.
Culture	Part shade. Soil — good drainage; humus soil. Moisture — high. Pruning — shape. Pest Problems — none. Growth Rate — moderate.
Notes	Excellent foliage and striking fruit display of red berries against green foliage. Not aggressive. Useful as ground cover.

Lonicera (lon-iss'er-a)
  honeysuckles

sempervirens (sem-per-vi'renz)
  evergreen

TRUMPET HONEYSUCKLE

Family Caprifoliaceae

Size	Height 50 feet; spread indeterminate. Zones 6, 7, 8, 9.
Form	Twining vine. Foliage — opposite, thin, 1½-3 inches long, perfoliate. Flower — mid-April through summer; trumpet-shaped, 2 inches long. Fruit — fall; berries ⅛-¼ inch diameter.
Texture	Medium.
Color	Foliage — gray-green. Flower — gold to scarlet red. Fruit — translucent red.
Culture	Sun to part shade. Soil — tolerant. Moisture — tolerant. Pruning — maintain desired size. Pest Problems — aphids. Growth Rate — rapid.
Notes	Excellent for naturalizing. Begins bloom with dogwood and continues throughout summer if grown in sun. Flowers and foliage interesting at close range on trellis or fence.
Varieties	**Magnifica** — bright scarlet flowers; late flowering. **Sulphurea** — yellow flowers. **Superba** — bright scarlet flowers; leaves broadly oval.

Rosa (ro'za)
old Latin name
for rose

banksiae (banks-i'a)
named for
Lady Banks

BANKS ROSE

Family Rosaceae

Size	Height 10-20 feet; spread indeterminate. Zones 7, 8, 9.
Form	Requires support for climbing. Foliage — alternate, 3 to 5 leaflets, 1½-2½ inches long, shining, glabrous. Flower — April to May; single or double on slender smooth pedicels in many flowered umbels, about 1 inch diameter, slightly fragrant. Stem — nearly thornless.
Texture	Fine.
Color	Foliage — deep green. Flower — white or creamy yellow. Stems — new growth green.
Culture	Sun or part shade. Soil — tolerant. Moisture — medium. Pruning — train. Pest Problems — none. Growth Rate — rapid.
Notes	Forms good screen; has numerous flowers. Needs space for massive growth and must be trained to support. Requires little maintenance. Tolerates salt spray. Not reliably hardy in mountains.
Varieties	**Alba-plena** — very fragrant white double flowers. **Lutea** — double yellow flowers. **Lutescens** — single yellow flowers. **Normalis** — single white flowers.

Smilax (smi'laks)
   ancient Greek
   name of obscure
   meaning

lanceolata (lan-see-o-lay'ta)
   shaped like lance head

SMILAX

Family Liliaceae

Size	Height 20-30 feet; spread indeterminate.	Zones 6, 7, 8, 9.
Form	Climbing by extending tendrils. Foliage — alternate, simple, 2-6 inches long, ovate or rounded with broadly heart-shaped base. Fruit — berry.	
Texture	Medium.	
Color	Foliage — shining bright green. Fruit — dark red.	
Culture	Sun or shade. Soil — tolerant. Moisture — medium. Pruning — should be heavily pruned annually in December. Pest Problems — none. Growth Rate — rapid.	
Notes	Handsome foliage frequently used in bouquets and Christmas decorations. Forms dense screen on trellises and fences. Excellent vine that should be more widely used. Spreads by underground shoots.	

Trachelospermum (trak-ee-lo-sperm'um)
  star jasmine

asiaticum (a-shi-at'i-kum)
  of Asia

YELLOW STAR-JASMINE

Family Apocynaceae

Size	Height to 12 feet; spread to 15 feet.	Zones 7, 8, 9.
Form	Climbs by twining. Foliage — opposite, 2 inches. Flower — May and June; ¾ inch wide, star-shaped, very fragrant.	
Texture	Medium.	
Color	Foliage — dark glossy green; new growth reddish-brown. Flower — pale yellow.	
Culture	Part shade. Soil — medium drainage; high fertility. Moisture — high to medium. Pruning — shape. Pest Problems — scale and white fly. Growth Rate — slow to moderate.	
Notes	Somewhat more cold hardy than *T. jasminoides*. For spot interest on fences and walls where fragrance may be appreciated. Elegant and interesting foliage.	
Varieties	**Asia Minor** — very small leaves and dense, compact growth. **Nortex** — slender, spear-shaped leaves with light gray center midrib. **oblanceolatum** — smaller leaves and more cold hardy. **Variegatum** — slow-growing; variegated foliage.	

Trachelospermum (tra-ke-lo-sper'mum)
   star jasmine

jasminoides (jas-min-oy'deez)
   jasminelike

CONFEDERATE JASMINE

Family Apocynaceae

Size	Height 10-12 feet; spread indeterminate. Zones 8, 9.
Form	Twining vine or ground cover. Foliage — opposite, simple, entire, leathery; 1½-3 inches long, ½-1 inch wide. Flower — May to June; very fragrant and in small clusters; 1 inch in diameter.
Texture	Medium.
Color	Foliage — dark glossy green above; pale green beneath with veins darker green. Flower — white.
Culture	Part shade. Soil — good drainage; high fertility. Moisture — high. Pruning — shape each year. Pest Problems — scale and white fly. Growth Rate — moderate to rapid.
Notes	Fragrance of flowers outstanding. Useful for screen on pergolas and arches and as ground cover.
Varieties	**Japonicum** — leaves white-veined, turning bronze in fall. **Madison** — hardy in zone 7. **nana** — dwarf form; attractive ground cover in light shade. **Variegatum** — leaves green and white; hardier than species.

VINES — DECIDUOUS

Actinidia (ak-tin-id'ee-a)
   from Greek for ray,
   referring to radiate styles

deliciosa (de-lis-i-o'sa)
   delicious

KIWI VINE

Family Dilleniaceae

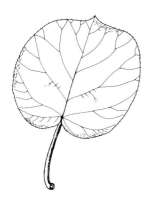

Size	Height 25 feet; spread 30 feet.	Zones 7, 8, 9.
Form	Climbs by twining. Foliage — alternate, 5-8 inches long and 4-7 inches wide. Flower — May; inconspicuous, sexes separate. Fruit — summer; globular berry 1½ inch diameter, edible.	
Texture	Coarse.	
Color	Foliage — medium to yellow-green with prominent red hairs on new shoots. Flower — white. Fruit — brownish green, hairy.	
Culture	Sun or shade. Soil — well-drained; medium to high fertility. Moisture — high. Pruning — none or as needed to maintain size. Pest Problems — none. Growth Rate — rapid.	
Notes	Grown mainly for luxuriant effect of foliage but also bears delicious fruit. Use as texture contrast in large scale areas or as accent plant for pergolas and trellises. Plant staminate and pistillate plants if fruits desired. *A. arguta* — small fruit; for northern climates.	

Clematis (klem'a-tis)
   woody flowering vines

hybrida (hy'brid-a)
   hybrid

LARGE-FLOWERED CLEMATIS

Family Ranunculaceae

Size	Height 5-30 feet; spread indeterminate. Zones 6, 7, 8, 9.
Form	Climbs by twining; woody, fragile stems. Foliage — opposite, compound, 3- 8 leaflets. Flower — late spring through early summer; large and solitary, or few flowers in clusters or small flowers in profuse clusters, 2 to 10 inches in diameter; single or double.
Texture	Medium to fine.
Color	Foliage — bright green. Flower — white, red, purple, blue, or lavender.
Culture	Sun for top growth, cool shade over roots. Soil — good drainage; medium high fertility; prefers rich loam. Moisture — high. Pruning — sometimes required to train and to increase flower production. Pest Problems — stem rot. Growth Rate — moderate.
Notes	Easily trained to wall or form. Requires care throughout year. Restrained and delicate growth habit. Weak climber. Best in Piedmont or mountain regions.
Varieties	**Belle of Woking** — double silvery gray flowers; prune after flowering. **Comptesse de Bouchard** — satiny rose flowers, 5-6 inch diameter; prune in early spring. **Duchess of Edinburgh** — double pure-white flowers, fragrant; prune after flowering. **Elsa Spaeth** — bright blue flowers in July and August on current year's wood. **Henryi** — creamy-white flowers with dark center; prune in early spring. **jackmanii** — large purple flowers. **Nelly Moser** — mauve-pink flowers with dark pink bars; prune in early spring.

Clematis (klem'a-tis)
    woody flowering vines

maximowicziana (maximo-veech-i-a'na)
    named for C.J. Maximowicz

JAPANESE CLEMATIS

Family Ranunculaceae

Size	Height to 30 feet; spread indeterminate. Zones 6, 7, 8, 9.
Form	Dense and heavy; climbing by twining stems and petioles, forming thick tangle heaviest at top. Foliage — midspring to late fall; opposite, 3-5 entire or lobed leaflets, glabrous. Flower — late August; panicles of 1 inch flowers, light, lacy, with bitter-sweet odor. Fruit — fall, persisting; 1-seeded achenes, interesting fluffy seed head. Stem — slender, slightly downy.
Texture	Medium in foliage, but very fine with flowers and fruits.
Color	Foliage — bright green. Flower — white. Fruit — gray. Stem — gray.
Culture	Sun. Soil — good drainage; medium fertility. Moisture — high. Pruning — trim older stems to ground to promote foliage production. Annual pruning to thin out old wood. Pest Problems — spider mites and blister beetles. Growth Rate — rapid.
Notes	Valued for effect of flowers and fruits. Vigorous and easy to grow. Valuable as late blooming clematis for decorative screen. Will retain some leaves in winter. Blooms on current season's growth. Moderately resistant to salt spray. Grows well in cooler sections of Coastal Plains. Former botanical name *Clematis paniculata*.

Clematis (klem'a-tis)
    woody flowering vines

virginiana (vir-gin-i-a'-na)
    from Virginia

VIRGIN'S BOWER

Family Ranunculaceae

Size	Height 12-15 feet; spread indeterminate. Zones 6, 7, 8, 9.
Form	Climbs by twining stems and twining petioles; heavy at top with thin base. Foliage — very late spring to late fall; opposite, ovate leaflets 3-parted, some coarsely and unequally toothed. Flower — all summer; dioecious; small, profusely produced. Fruit — fall, persisting; achenes. Stem — younger growth ribbed, glabrous.
Texture	Medium in foliage, but very fine in bloom.
Color	Foliage — bright green; fall, purple. Flower — white. Fruit — gray. Stem — yellow-gray; young growth green.
Culture	Sun but will tolerate some shade. Soil — good drainage; medium fertility. Moisture — high. Pruning — train. Pest Problems — none. Growth Rate — moderate.
Notes	Commonly seen along creek banks and streams. Good for naturalized plantings. Valued for effect of fruit and flowers; also good foliage effect.

Decumaria (dek-ew-mah'ree-a)
    from Latin meaning ten,
    number of parts of
    flower

barbara (bar'ba-ra)
    foreign, originally thought
    to be introduced

WOOD VAMP

Family Hydrangeaceae

Size	Height to 30 feet; spread indeterminate.	Zones 6, 7, 8.
Form	Woody vine climbing by aerial rootlets. Foliage — opposite, petioled, mostly entire; 2-4 inches long, 1-2 inches wide. Flower — early summer; flat-headed clusters 3 inches across, fragrant. Fruit — winter; small capsules.	
Texture	Coarse.	
Color	Foliage — glossy green. Flower — white. Fruit — brown-green.	
Culture	Part shade to shade. Soil — tolerant; humus soil. Moisture — high. Pruning — maintain desired height. Pest Problems — none. Growth Rate — moderate to rapid.	
Notes	Attractive in naturalized areas; native to Southeast. Best in moist soils. Semi-evergreen. Good for covering tree trunks or rock outcroppings.	

Hydrangea (hy-dran'jee-a)
   hardy shrubs, vines

anomala (a-nom'a-la)
   unusual or out of ordinary

petiolaris (pet-i-o-la'ris)
   with leaf stalk

CLIMBING HYDRANGEA

Family Saxifragaceae

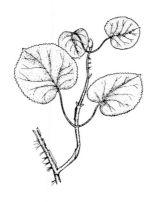

Size	Height to 50 feet; spread indeterminate.	Zones 6, 7, 8.
Form	High climbing and producing heavy laterals from supporting surface. Climbs by aerial roots. Foliage — opposite, 2-4 inches with long slender petioles. Flower — May; flat-topped clusters 6-10 inches wide, outer flowers of cluster sterile.	
Texture	Coarse.	
Color	Foliage — dark green, glabrous; fall, yellow. Flower — pure white. Bark — reddish, shredding.	
Culture	Part shade. Soil — medium drainage; medium to high fertility with humus added. Moisture — high. Pruning — none unless restriction is desired. Pest Problems — none. Growth Rate — slow.	
Notes	Clings to masonry and trees without support. Most suitable in rustic environments. Stems attractive in winter. Interesting effect on stone. Flowers only after mature. Does not bloom well in dense shade. Formerly named *H. petiolaris*.	

Parthenocissus (par-thenn-o-sis'sus)
　　Greek meaning virgin ivy

quinquefolia (kwin-kuh-fo'li-a)
　　with 5 leaves or 5 leaflets

VIRGINIA CREEPER

Family Vitaceae

Size	Height 10-20 feet; spread indeterminate.　　　　Zones 6, 7, 8, 9.
Form	Climbs by tendrils with adhesive discs. Foliage — alternate, palmately divided into 5 leaflets to 6 inches long. Flower — inconspicuous. Fruit — fall; small berries.
Texture	Coarse.
Color	Foliage — glossy green; fall, brilliant red. Flower — white. Fruit — bluish-black.
Culture	Sun to part shade. Soil — very tolerant; medium drainage; medium fertility. Moisture — medium. Pruning — none. Pest Problems — Japanese beetles. Growth Rate — rapid.
Notes	Native to woods in Southeast. Most useful for large-scale work. Small-leaved varieties more refined in appearance than species. Widely adapted. Produces quick screen. Grown for rich foliage effect in summer and outstanding fall color. Resistant to salt spray. Where no support is available, makes dense ground cover. Birds attracted to fruit.
Varieties	**engelmannii** — small leaflets; well-suited to city gardens. **saint-paulii** — small leaflets; clings well to stone walls.

Parthenocissus (par-thenn-o-sis'sus)
Greek meaning virgin ivy

tricuspidata (try-kus-pi-day'ta)
having 3 points

BOSTON IVY

Family Vitaceae

Size	Height up to 30 feet; spread indeterminate. Zones 6, 7, 8.
Form	Climbs by tendrils with adhesive discs. Foliage — alternate, 3-lobed to 8 inches wide. Flower — inconspicuous. Fruit — fall; small berries, inconspicuous.
Texture	Coarse.
Color	Foliage — glossy green; fall, red. Fruit — bluish-black.
Culture	Sun to part shade. Soil — tolerant; medium drainage; medium fertility. Moisture — medium. Pruning — needs periodic thinning. Pest Problems — scale, aphids on new shoots. Growth Rate — rapid.
Notes	Clings well on masonry work; small leaf varieties less vigorous. Withstands city conditions well. Cold hardy. Fall color not as outstanding as *P. quinquefolia*. Fruit attracts birds.
Varieties	**Beverly Brooks** — large leaves turning bright scarlet in fall. **Green Spring** — leaves broader than species; blue berries. **Lowii** — very small leaves; better suited to confined areas than species. **Minutifolia** — leaves 1-2 inches across. **Purpurea** — dark purple leaves throughout summer. **Veitchii** — very small leaves which are purple when young.

Rosa (ro'za)
old Latin name
for rose

hybrida (hy'brid-a)
hybrid

CLIMBING ROSE

Family Rosaceae

Size	Height 6-40 feet; spread indeterminate. Zones 6, 7, 8, 9.
Form	Vigorous growing canes incapable of climbing unless trained on support. Foliage — alternate, usually 5 leaflets. Flower — May to August; 1-3 inch diameter.
Texture	Medium to fine.
Color	Foliage — deep glossy green. Flower — white, yellow, orange, pink, red, lavender, or bicolor.
Culture	Sun or part shade. Soil — good drainage; high fertility. Moisture — medium. Pruning — annually to train growth and to maintain vigor of plant. Pest Problems — less susceptible to disease and pests than bush roses; use all-purpose rose spray when necessary. Growth Rate — rapid.
Notes	Train to cover walls, fences, or trellises. Excellent as cover for chain-link fence. Will bloom better if trained in horizontal plane. Grown for flower effect.
Varieties	**Blaze** — scarlet-red flowers; vigorous, everblooming. **Golden Showers** — yellow flowers; blooms almost continually. **New Dawn** — blush-pink flowers; everblooming. **Paul's Scarlet** — scarlet-red flowers; very hardy. **Peace** — cream to blush-pink flowers; fast-growing. **Silver Moon** — cream-white flowers with gold stamens; very vigorous. **Sparrieshoop** — single shell-pink flowers; exceptionally beautiful in form and color.

Vitis (vy'tis)
   woody vines, grape

rotundifolia (ro-tun-di-fo'li-a)
   round-leaved

MUSCADINE GRAPE

Family Vitaceae

Size	Height to 50 feet; spread indeterminate. Zones 6,7,8.
Form	Climbing by tendrils. Foliage — alternate, 3-6 inches wide, coarsely toothed. Flower — summer; inconspicuous. Fruit — early fall; small clusters, edible.
Texture	Coarse.
Color	Foliage — bright green; fall, green to lemon yellow depending on variety. Fruit — dull purple.
Culture	Sun. Soil — tolerant; good drainage; medium fertility. Moisture — medium. Pruning — annually. Pest Problems — spraying necessary for best fruit production. Growth Rate — rapid.
Notes	Plant perfect flowered varieties to insure pollination. Ideal summer screen. Fruit ripens in September and October. Grown for fruit, screening, and as ornament. Mildly tolerant to salt spray and sandy soil.
Varieties	**Albemarle** — black fruit; perfect flowered. **Carlos** — bronze fruit; perfect flowered. **Magnolia** — light bronze fruit; perfect flowered. **Magoon** — red-black fruit; perfect flowered. **Southland** — purple-black fruit; perfect flowered.

Wisteria (wis-ter'i-a)
   named for
   Casper Wistar

floribunda (flor-i-bun'da)
   blooming freely; floriferous

JAPANESE WISTERIA

Family Fabaceae

Size	Height to 30 feet or more; spread indeterminate. Zones 6, 7, 8, 9.
Form	Climbs by twining stems right to left, developing twisted woody trunk several inches in diameter. Foliage — early spring to fall; 13-19 pinnately compound leaflets. Flower — late spring; showy, pendent clusters 12-24 inches long, open from base to tip, fragrant. Fruit — fall; large velvety pods narrowed near base.
Texture	Medium.
Color	Foliage — bright green; fall, yellow. Flower — violet blue. Fruit — brown.
Culture	Sun. Soil — tolerant; medium drainage; medium fertility. Moisture — medium. Pruning — train. Pest Problems — aphids and scale. Growth Rate — moderate.
Notes	Large and very aggressive climber valued for flowers and foliage; useful on pergolas and trellises; may be trained as standard. Difficult to transplant. Rampant growth can girdle trees. Interesting trunk with age. Has longer blooming period than *W. sinensis*.
Varieties	**alba** — white flowers in dense clusters. Racemes 11 inches long. **Issai** — mild fragrance, blue-violet flowers. Racemes 12 inches long. **Kyushaki** — slight fragrance, reddish violet to violet flowers. Racemes 26 inches long. **Macrobotrys** — fragrant violet flowers in clusters 2-3 feet long; beautiful in containers. **Murasaki Noda** — slight fragrance, reddish violet flowers. Racemes 10 inches long. **Rosea** — fragrant pink flowers. Racemes about 18 inches long.

Wisteria (wis-ter'i-a)
   named for Casper Wistar

sinesis (sy-nen'sis)
   from China

CHINESE WISTERIA

Family Fabaceae

Size	Height to 30 feet or more; spread indeterminate. Zones 6, 7, 8, 9.
Form	Climbs by twining stems left to right; develops twisted woody trunk several inches in diameter. Foliage — early spring to midfall or late fall; 7-13 pinnately compound leaflets. Flower — early April before leaves; pendent clusters 6-12 inches long, showy. Fruit — fall, persisting; large pods, 1-3 seeded.
Texture	Medium.
Color	Foliage — light green. Flower — violet-blue. Fruit — brown.
Culture	Sun. Soil — tolerant; medium drainage; medium fertility. Moisture — medium. Pruning — regularly for restraint. Pest Problems — aphids and scale. Growth Rate — rapid.
Notes	Aggressive vine valued for flowers and foliage; useful on pergolas and trellises. Difficult to transplant. When planting, restrict roots and fertilize heavily. On small grounds best used trained in tree form. Interesting trunk and stems with age. Most popular and widely planted *Wisteria* species. Rampant growth can girdle trees.
Varieties	**Alba** — white flowers. **Black Dragon** — double dark purple flowers. **Caroline** — lavender flowers. **Jako** — extremely fragrant flowers. **Plena** — double lavender flowers.

Azaleas of harmonizing colors enhance spring beauty of dogwoods in roadside planting.

SHRUBS 1-4 FEET — EVERGREEN

Azalea (a-zay'lee-a)
   showy shrubs, botanically
   Rhododendrons

hybrida (hy'brid-a)
   hybrid

SATSUKI HYBRID AZALEA

Family Ericaceae

Size	Height 2-4 feet; spread 2-4 feet. Zones 6, 7, 8, 9.
Form	Compact and spreading. Foliage — alternate, simple, entire, 1-2 inches long. Flower — May to June.
Texture	Fine to medium.
Color	Foliage — dull green. Flower — red, white, orange, pink, purple, or variegated.
Culture	Part shade. Soil — medium to good drainage; medium to high fertility with humus added. Moisture — high. Pruning — remove dead or damaged wood. Pest Problems — lacebug, scale, spider mites, and root rot. Growth Rate — moderate.
Notes	Large, showy flowers late in season. Most useful for small-scale areas.
Varieties	**Amaghasa** — flowers between deep pink and strong red, 3½ inch diameter, single. Low spreading. **Beni-kirishima** — flowers orange red, double, 2 inch diameter. Height 2-3 feet. **Bunkwa** — large white flowers with salmon margins. **Gumpo** — flowers white, pink, salmon, or bicolor, single, 3 inch diameter. Dense dwarf. Some tolerance to direct sun. **Gunrei** — flowers pink with small flecks of rose, 2 inch diameter. **Higasa** — flowers deep rose pink, single, 4½ inch diameter. Low spreading. **Kikoshi** — lavender and white flowers.

Azalea (a-zay'lee-a)
　　showy shrubs, botanically
　　Rhododendrons

obtusum (ob-tew'sum)
　　blunt or rounded at end

KURUME AZALEA

Family Ericaceae

Size	Height 2-4 feet; spread 2-5 feet.　　　　　　Zones 6, 7, 8, 9.
Form	Dense and twiggy. Foliage — alternate, simple, entire, ½-1 inch long; shiny. Flower — mid-April; 1-2 inch diameter.
Texture	Medium.
Color	Foliage — dull green. Flower — white, lavender, pink, rose, or bright red.
Culture	Part shade. Soil — good drainage; medium fertility with humus added. Moisture — high. Pruning — remove dead or damaged wood. Pest Problems — lacebugs, scale, spider mites and root rot. Growth Rate — moderate.
Notes	Brilliant floral display with best color in light shade. Excellent for small gardens. Botanically *Rhododendron obtusum*.
Varieties	**Appleblossom** — flowers pink with white throat, single, 1¼ inch diameter. Upright growth. **Coral Bells** — flowers pink, single, hose-in-hose, 1 1/3 inch diameter. Low spreading growth. Good foliage. **Delaware Valley White** — flowers white, single, 2 inch diameter. Spreading growth. Very cold hardy. **Hexe** — flowers violet red, single, hose-in-hose, 1¾ inch diameter. Low, dense, spreading growth. **Hinode-giri** — flowers red, single, 1½ inch diameter. Very cold hardy plant of vivid color. **Salmon Beauty** — flowers salmon-pink, single, hose-in-hose, frilled, 1¾ inch diameter. Upright growth. **Snow** — flowers white, single, hose-in-hose, 1¾ inch diameter. Flowers not promptly shed. Upright growth.

Berberis (ber'ber-iss)
   Arabic name

verruculosa (vehr-rook-yew-loh'suh)
   warty

WARTY BARBERRY

Family Berberidaceae

Size	Height 3-4 feet; spread 3-4 feet.	Zones 6, 7.
Form	Compact and rounded with spreading branches. Foliage — alternate, simple, leathery, 1 inch long with spiny edges and margins rolled under. Flower — late April; ½ inch wide. Fruit — fall; 1/3 inch long, berrylike. Twig — thickly warty. Spines — ½ inch long.	
Texture	Fine.	
Color	Foliage — dark, shining green above, white beneath; winter, bronze. Flower — yellow. Fruit — violet-black.	
Culture	Sun to part shade. Soil — tolerant. Moisture — medium. Pruning — remove stray shoots and branches. Pest Problems — none. Growth Rate — slow.	
Notes	Excellent flowering; may be used as specimen plant or as clipped or unclipped hedge for public areas.	
Variety	**compacta** — very dwarf habit of growth.	

Buxus (bucks'us)
  classical Latin
  for box

harlandii (har-lan'di)
  from proper name

HARLAND BOXWOOD

Family Buxaceae

Size	Height 2-4 feet; spread 2-3 feet. Zones 7, 8, 9.
Form	Usually broad at top and narrow at base. Foliage — opposite, simple, oblanceolate to oblate, ¾ to 1¼ inches long, somewhat narrowed toward base, notched at tip. Flower — inconspicuous.
Texture	Fine.
Color	Foliage — bright green.
Culture	Sun to part shade. Soil — good drainage; medium fertility; requires mulch. Moisture — medium. Pruning — none. Pest Problems — root rot, nematodes, and spider mites. Growth Rate — moderate.
Notes	Not good as specimen but excellent in low hedges or as edging plant. Grows well in Coastal Plains. Of refined character, requiring extra care to look best. Untrimmed forms dense and rather top-heavy mound. Space 12 inches for hedge.
Variety	**Richardi** — larger leaves, rapid growth.

Buxus (bucks'us)
  classical Latin
  for box

microphylla (my-kro-fil'la)
  small-leaved

'Koreana' (kor-e-a'na)
  of Korea

KOREAN BOXWOOD

Family Buxaceae

Size	Height 3-4 feet; spread 4-6 feet.	Zones 6, 7, 8, 9.
Form	Open rounded mound. Foliage — opposite, simple, entire, ¾-1 inch long, narrow. Flower — inconspicuous.	
Texture	Fine.	
Color	Foliage — glossy yellowish-green; winter, bronze-green. Flower — white to green.	
Culture	Sun or shade. Soil — good drainage; medium to high fertility; requires mulching. Moisture — medium. Pruning — most attractive in informal growth habit; should not be sheared. Pest Problems — boxwood leaf miner, spider mites, and nematodes. Growth Rate — slow.	
Notes	Most hardy of boxwoods. Excellent in natural form as specimen, in groups, or in combination with other shrubs. Requires little care. Shallow root system.	
Varieties	**Tide Hill** — dense, spreading, slow-growing; dark green foliage all winter. Height 1 foot; spread 4 feet. **Wintergreen** — dark green foliage all year; height 1 foot; spread 4 feet.	

Buxus (bucks'us)
  classical Latin
  for box

sempervirens (sem-per-vy'renz)
  evergreen

'Suffruticosa' (suf-frew-ti-ko'sa)
  somewhat shrubby

DWARF BOXWOOD

Family Buxaceae

Size	Height 2-3 feet; spread 2-4 feet. Zones 6, 7, 8.
Form	Dense and compact. Assumes globular shape with billowy outline with age. Foliage — opposite, simple, entire, to ¾ inch long. Flower — inconspicuous.
Texture	Fine.
Color	Foliage — dark green.
Culture	Part shade. Soil — good drainage; medium fertility with high organic content; requires mulch. Moisture — medium. Pruning — none. Pest Problems — nematodes, spider mites, leaf miner, root rot, scale, and dogs. Growth Rate — extremely slow.
Notes	Ideal plant for edging flower beds or garden walks, space 12 inches apart when used for this purpose. Larger plants useful as specimens or accent.

Chamaecyparis (kam-ee-sip'a-ris)
    timber conifers used as
    ornamentals

obtusa (ob-tus'a)
    blunt or rounded at end

'Nana Gracilis' (nay'na gras'i-lis)
    small, dwarf; graceful, slender

DWARF HINOKI CYPRESS

Family Cupressaceae

Size	Height 2-4 feet; spread 2-3 feet.	Zones 6, 7, 8.
Form	Irregularly twisted and tufted. Central trunk usually leans. Foliage — scalelike, dense, somewhat twisted.	
Texture	Medium to fine.	
Color	Foliage — deep, shining green; aromatic.	
Culture	Sun to part shade. Soil — tolerant. Moisture — medium to low. Pruning — none. Pest Problems — juniper scale, spruce mites, and bark beetles. Growth Rate — very slow.	
Notes	Excellent as accent or specimen. Not for mass plantings. Loose but formal appearance with interesting character for oriental effects. Frequently sold in nurseries as *C. obtusa* 'Nana'. Grows well in containers.	

Cotoneaster (ko-to'nee-as-ter)
  Greek meaning like quince

horizontalis (hor-ri-zon-tay'lis)
  horizontal

ROCKSPRAY COTONEASTER

Family Rosaceae

Size	Height 2-3 feet; spread 5-8 feet. Zones 6, 7, 8, 9.
Form	Low, flat, and very dense with branches spreading almost horizontally, forming flat sprays. Foliage — alternate, simple, entire, ½ inch long, broad elliptic, lustrous and glabrous. Flower — mid-April; small. Fruit — early fall; abundant berries 1/5 inch wide.
Texture	Fine.
Color	Foliage — deep red-green; fall, deep red and orange. Flower — white tinged pink. Fruit — bright red.
Culture	Sun. Soil — tolerant; good drainage; medium fertility. Moisture — low. Pruning — thinning annually. Pest Problems — fire blight, scale, spider mites, and lacebug. Growth Rate — slow.
Notes	Charming plant with long season of handsome foliage and fruits; useful for rock gardens or as ground cover, or draping over low walls. Combines well with stone or wood. Difficult to transplant, sparse root system. Plant container-grown plants. Attractive specimen for balcony or terrace.
Varieties	**Little Gem** — dwarf form, height 12 inches. **Robusta** — upright and vigorous growth with abundant fruit. **Saxatilis** — compact and prostrate with distinct branching pattern. Small leaves; sparse fruiting. **Variegatus** — green and white leaves; compact, less vigorous than species.

Danae (dan'a-ee)
   named for Pierre Martin
   Dane, writer on plants
   of Piedmont

racemosa (ra-se-mo'sa)
   flowers in racemes

ALEXANDER LAUREL

Family Liliaceae

Size	Height 3 feet; spread 2-3 feet.	Zones 7, 8, 9.
Form	Unbranched stems arching gracefully, somewhat like dwarf bamboo. Foliage — minute, inconspicuous, apparent leaves being alternate flattened stems 3 inches long and ½-1 inch wide. Flower — spring; small in terminal racemes, not showy. Fruit — fall; berry about cherry size.	
Texture	Fine to medium.	
Color	Foliage — dark green. Flower — white. Fruit — orange-red.	
Culture	Shade. Soil — good drainage; high fertility with humus. Moisture — high. Pruning — none. Pest Problems — none. Growth Rate — moderate to slow.	
Notes	May be cut for winter display. Excellent selection for darker corners of patios and fenced gardens as filler or accent. Unique foliage and fruit.	

Daphne (daf'nee)
   Greek name for
   true laurel

odora (o-do'ra)
   fragrant

WINTER DAPHNE

Family Thymelaeaceae

Size	Height 3-4 feet; spread 3 feet.

Zones 7, 8, 9.

Form
Rounded, dense and twiggy. Foliage — alternate, simple, entire, 3 inches long, narrow, oval. Flower — January and February; small, terminal clusters, very fragrant, star-shaped.

Texture
Medium.

Color
Foliage — dark green. Flower — rosy-purple outside, white inside.

Culture
Sun or shade. Soil — good drainage; medium fertility. Moisture — medium. Pruning — none. Pest Problems — fungus diseases. Growth Rate — slow to moderate.

Notes
Rather expensive and temperamental but beautiful foliage plant for landscape use. Does not respond to fertilization or pruning and is difficult to establish. Most fragrant of all daphnes. Interesting in foreground of mixed shrub plantings, in rock gardens, or as edging material.

Varieties
Alba — white flowers. **Aureo-marginata** — leaves lightly bordered with yellow, surrounding rosettes of lavender-pink flowers. More hardy than species; loose form. Beautiful in containers. **Mazelii** — flowers borne in terminal clusters and in axils of leaves. **Rose Queen** — larger flowers than species.

Euonymus (you-on'i-mus)
   hardy shrubs and vines

fortunei (for-tu'nee-i)
   named for Robert Fortune

'Vegetus' (vej'e-tus)
   vigorous

EVERGREEN BITTERSWEET

Family Celastraceae

Size	Height 3-4 feet; spread indeterminate. Zones 6, 7, 8, 9.
Form	Irregular and open. Foliage — opposite, entire or serrate, petioled, 2 inches wide. Differs from variety *radicans* principally in orbicular-ovate coarsely toothed leathery leaves and large flowers and fruits. Fruit — fall; berries.
Texture	Medium.
Color	Foliage — glossy light green. Fruit — orange-red.
Culture	Sun to shade. Soil — tolerant. Moisture — medium to high. Pruning — none or train as vine. Pest Problems — scale and mildew. Growth Rate — moderate.
Notes	May be used as sheared low hedge, in planter boxes, as climber, or as cover when allowed to trail on ground. Requires spraying to prevent scale infestations. Grown for excellent fruit display and decorative foliage.
Variety	**E. f. Sarcoxie** — orange berries in fall; may be trained as dense wall-cover.

Euonymus (you-on'i-mus)
  hardy shrubs and vines

japonicus (ja-pon'i-kus)
  from Japan

'Microphyllus' (my-kro-fil'lus)
  small-leaved

DWARF JAPANESE EUONYMUS

Family Celastraceae

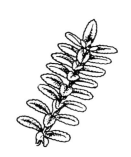

Size	Height 2-3 feet; spread 18-24 inches. Zones 7, 8, 9.
Form	Upright and rounded. Foliage — alternate, ½-1 inch long. Flower — inconspicuous. Fruit — inconspicuous.
Texture	Medium.
Color	Foliage — glossy, medium green.
Culture	Sun or shade. Soil — medium drainage; medium fertility with high organic content. Moisture — medium to high. Pruning — very little needed except for uniformity in edging use. Pest Problems — scale. Growth Rate — moderate.
Notes	Frequently used for edging, lawn border, or line definition; twigs break easily. Plant destroyed by Euonymus scale unless regularly sprayed. Easier to propagate and less expensive than boxwood.

Gardenia (gar-de'ni-a)
     named for Alexander Garden
     of Charleston, S.C.

jasminoides (jas-min-oy'deez)
     jasminelike

'Radicans' (rad'i-kanz)
     rooting, especially
     along stem

DWARF GARDENIA

Family Rubiaceae

Size	Height 1-2 feet; spread 2-3 feet.	Zones 8, 9.
Form	Dwarf with horizontal branching habit. Open and spreading. Foliage — opposite or in 3's, simple, entire, narrow, 2 inches long. Flower — May to June; 2 inches, fragrant.	
Texture	Medium to fine.	
Color	Foliage — dark lustrous green. Flower — white.	
Culture	Sun or part shade. Soil — medium drainage; medium fertility; prefers acid. Moisture — medium. Pruning — none. Pest Problems — white fly and aphids. Growth Rate — moderate to rapid.	
Notes	For Coastal Plain or warmer parts of Piedmont. Excellent in planter boxes. Charming as border or pot plant in sheltered areas.	

Hypericum (hy-per'i-kum)
   under, or among heather

patulum (pat'yew-lum)
   spreading

ST-JOHN'S-WORT

Family Hypericaceae

Size	Height 3 feet; spread 3 feet. Zones 6, 7, 8, 9.
Form	Spreading with arching branches. Foliage — opposite, simple, entire, 2-3 inches long; semi-evergreen. Flower — June; 2½ inches wide.
Texture	Medium.
Color	Foliage — dark green above, whitish beneath. Flower — golden yellow.
Culture	Sun. Soil — tolerant. Moisture — low. Pruning — remove dead or old wood. Pest Problems — none. Growth Rate — rapid.
Notes	More vigorous than species with handsome flower production. Excellent in foreground groupings or in shrub borders and foundation plantings.
Varieties	**grandiflorum** — flowers 3 inches wide. **henryi** — more vigorous than species; larger leaves and flowers. **Hidcote** — height 2½ feet; spread 2½ feet; fragrant golden yellow flowers. Often cold-damaged. **oblongifolium** — leaves 4 inches long, bluish beneath. **Sungold** — very hardy; similar to 'Hidcote' in form and flower. **uralum** — leaves 1 inch long; flowers 1 inch wide.

Ilex (eye'lecks)
  hollies

cornuta (kor-new'ta)
  horned

'Carissa' (ka-ris'a)
  tropical hedge plants

CARISSA HOLLY

Family Aquifoliaceae

Size	Height 3-4 feet; spread 4-6 feet.	Zones 6, 7, 8, 9.
Form	Compact and rounded. Foliage — alternate, single terminal spine, bullate shape leaf, thick, 2 inches long, 1 inch wide.	
Texture	Coarse.	
Color	Foliage — glossy dark green above; olive green beneath.	
Culture	Sun or part shade. Soil — tolerant. Moisture — medium. Pruning — none. Pest Problems — scale. Growth Rate — slow.	
Notes	Excellent formal shrub for grouping, accent or specimen use. May be used in foundation plantings; requires no care when established.	

Ilex (eye'lecks)
  hollies

cornuta (kor-new'ta)
  horned

'Rotunda' (roh-tun'da)
  nearly circular

DWARF HORNED HOLLY

Family Aquifoliaceae

Size	Height 2-3 feet; spread 3-4 feet. Zones 6, 7, 8, 9.
Form	Compact and rounded. Foliage — alternate, spiny, thick, 3 inches long. Flower — inconspicuous. Fruit — usually none.
Texture	Coarse.
Color	Foliage — glossy light green. Flower — white. Fruit — red.
Culture	Sun or part shade. Soil — tolerant. Moisture — medium. Pruning — none. Pest Problems — scale. Growth Rate — slow.
Notes	Excellent formal shrub for Piedmont and Coastal Plain. Requires no care when established. May be used as accent or foundation plant, unclipped hedge, or container plant.

Ilex (eye'lecks)
   hollies

crenata (kree-nay'ta)
   scalloped or with
   irregularly waved margin

'Carefree'

JAPANESE HOLLY

Family Aquifoliaceae

| Size | Height 3-4 feet; spread 3-4 feet. | Zones 6, 7, 8, 9. |

Size   Height 3-4 feet; spread 3-4 feet.   Zones 6, 7, 8, 9.

Form   Low dense mound. Foliage — alternate, simple, toothed, eliptical, ¾ inch
          long. Flower — inconspicuous. Fruit — late summer and fall; stalked
          berries ¼ inch diameter.

Texture   Medium.

Color   Foliage — dark green. Fruit — black.

Culture   Sun or part shade. Soil — medium drainage; medium fertility with high
          organic content. Moisture — medium. Pruning — none. Pest Problems —
          none. Growth Rate — slow.

Notes   Useful for small gardens, low growing foundation plant, and raised
          planter boxes. Dense but informal plant needing little maintenance.

Ilex (eye'lecks)
    hollies

crenata (kree-nay'ta)
    scalloped or with
    irregularly waved margin

'Helleri' (hell-er-ri')
    named for Joseph Heller

HELLER JAPANESE HOLLY

Family Aquifoliaceae

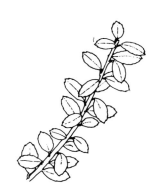

Size	Height 2-3 feet; spread 3-5 feet. Zones 6, 7.
Form	Spreading, compact and densely twiggy. Foliage — oval, alternate, ½ inch long. Flower — inconspicuous. Fruit — inconspicuous.
Texture	Medium to fine.
Color	Foliage — medium to dark green.
Culture	Sun or shade. Soil — medium drainage; high fertility. Moisture — medium to high. Pruning — none. Pest Problems — scale, spider mites, and nematodes. Growth Rate — slow.
Notes	Excellent substitute for Dwarf Boxwood. May be used as edging or accent plant. Not recommended for Coastal Plain. Resents droughts and sudden freezes until well-established, 4-6 years.

Ilex (eye'lecks)
hollies

crenata (kree-nay'ta)
scalloped or with
irregularly waved margin

'Kingsville'
named for Kingsville,
Maryland

KINGSVILLE JAPANESE HOLLY

Family Aquifoliaceae

Size	Height 3 feet; spread 5-6 feet. Zones 6, 7, 8.
Form	Loose and open mounds. Foliage — alternate, ½-¾ inch long with tip of leaf more pointed and larger than *I.c.* 'Helleri'. Flower — none. Fruit — none.
Texture	Medium to fine.
Color	Foliage — dark green.
Culture	Sun or shade. Soil — medium drainage; high fertility. Moisture — medium. Pruning — none. Pest Problems — scale and nematodes. Growth Rate — slow.
Notes	Excellent foliage; spreading habit useful for low mass plantings. Tolerant of city conditions. Considered superior to Heller Holly in color and form.

Ilex (eye'lecks)
  hollies

crenata (kre-nay'ta)
  scalloped or with
  irregularly waved
  margin

'Repandens' (ree-pan'denz)
  wavy-margined

REPANDEN JAPANESE HOLLY

Family Aquifoliaceae

Size	Height 2-3 feet; spread 5-6 feet. Zones 6, 7, 8.
Form	Spreading and dense. Foliage — alternate, ½-1 inch long. Flower — inconspicuous. Fruit — inconspicuous.
Texture	Medium to fine.
Color	Foliage — olive green.
Culture	Sun or shade. Soil — medium drainage; high fertility. Moisture — medium. Pruning — none. Pest Problems — scale and nematodes. Growth Rate — slow.
Notes	Selected for foliage color and low, compact growth. Good substitute for Dwarf Boxwood.

Ilex (eye'lecks)
  hollies

crenata (kree-nay'ta)
  scalloped or with
  irregularly waved margin

'Stokes' (stoks)
  named for Warren Stokes
  of Butler, Pennsylvania

STOKES JAPANESE HOLLY

Family Aquifoliaceae

Size	Height 1-3 feet; spread 3-4 feet.	Zones 6, 7, 8.
Form	Spreading, compact, and densely twiggy. Foliage — alternate, ¼-½ inch long; tip more rounded than *I.c.* 'Helleri'. Flower — inconspicuous. Fruit — inconspicuous.	
Texture	Fine to medium.	
Color	Foliage — medium to dark green.	
Culture	Sun or shade. Soil — medium drainage; high fertility. Moisture — medium. Pruning — none. Pest Problems — spider mites, scale, and nematodes. Growth Rate — slow.	
Notes	Less globose in form than *I.c.* 'Helleri'. Excellent as specimen, edging, or accent plant. Does well in city gardens. Considered superior to Heller Holly in color and form.	

Ilex (eye'lecks)
hollies

crenata (kree-nay'ta)
scalloped or with
irregularly waved margin

'Tiny Tim'

JAPANESE HOLLY

Family Aquifoliaceae

Size	Height 2-3 feet; spread 2-3 feet.	Zones 6, 7, 8.
Form	Dwarf, loose, open spreading form. Foliage — alternate, oval; ½ inch long.	
Texture	Fine.	
Color	Foliage — medium to dark green.	
Culture	Sun or shade. Soil — medium drainage; high fertility. Moisture — medium to high. Pruning — shape. Pest Problems — scale, spider mites and nematodes. Growth Rate — slow to moderate.	
Notes	Excellent informal growth habit for massing. May be used as accent, specimen, or foundation plant. More cold hardy than 'Helleri'.	

Ilex (eye'lecks)
   hollies

vomitoria (vom-i-tor'i-a)
   emetic

'**Nana**' (nay'na)
   small, dwarf

DWARF YAUPON

Family Aquifoliaceae

Size	Height 2-4 feet; spread 3-5 feet. Zones 7, 8, 9.
Form	Symmetrical and dense. Foliage — alternate, to 1 inch long. Flower — none. Fruit — none.
Texture	Fine.
Color	Foliage — gray-green. Bark — gray.
Culture	Sun or shade. Soil — medium drainage; medium fertility. Moisture — medium. Pruning — none. Pest Problems — none. Growth Rate — slow to moderate.
Notes	Excellent as low edging, specimen, or accent plant. Rather formal in character. Withstands drought when well-established. Useful as low growing foundation plant. Particularly valuable for Coastal Plains.
Variety	**Schelling's Dwarf (Stoke's Dwarf)** — more upright in form with dark green leaves.

Juniperus (jew-nip'er-us)
  juniperlike

communis (ko-mu'nis)
  common

depressa (de-pres'sa)
  depressed

PROSTRATE JUNIPER

Family Cupressaceae

Size	Height 2-4 feet; spread 3-5 feet. Zones 6, 7.
Form	Dwarf, spreading, prostrate shrub holding branchlets upwards at 60° from ground. Foliage — needlelike, prickly juvenile type leaves; ⅜ inch long. Fruit — fall, ¼ inch across, mostly 3 seeded.
Texture	Fine.
Color	Foliage — dark green with glaucous band on upper surface. Fruit — blue or black.
Culture	Sun to part shade. Soil — tolerates gravel and sandy soils; low fertility. Moisture — low. Pruning — none. Pest Problems — mites, bagworms, and scale. Growth Rate — moderate to rapid.
Notes	Hardy shrub or ground cover for adverse site conditions. Withstands heat and salt spray. Useful for undergrowth and naturalized plantings.

Juniperus (jew-nip'er-us)
  juniperlike

davurica (da-vur'i-ka)

'**Expansa**' ('**Parsoni**')

PARSONS JUNIPER

Family Cupressaceae

Size	Height 2-3 feet; spread 4-7 feet.	Zones 6, 7, 8, 9.
Form	Dense; long slender branches held rigidly horizontal, forms dome-shaped mound when mature. Foliage — scalelike, becoming linear-lanceolate. Flower — inconspicuous. Fruit — inconspicuous.	
Texture	Medium to fine.	
Color	Foliage — dark green.	
Culture	Sun. Soil — good drainage; medium to low fertility. Moisture — low. Pruning — none. Pest Problems — spider mites, juniper blight, bagworms. Growth Rate — moderate.	
Notes	Dignified and robust in appearance; useful as specimen or as large informal ground cover.	
Varieties	**Expansa Aureospicata** — butter yellow and dark green foliage. **Expansa Variegata** — cream-white and dark green foliage.	

Juniperus (jew-nip'er-us)
  juniperlike

sabina (sa-bi'na)
  from Latin name

'Tamariscifolia' (tam-a-ris-si-fo'li-a)
  leaves like tamarix

TAMARIX JUNIPER

Family Cupressaceae

Size	Height 2-4 feet; spread 4-6 feet. Zones 6, 7, 8, 9.
Form	Irregular and widespreading, strong horizontal and descending branches ascending at tips. Foliage — dense, tiny, needle-like, 4-ranked in pairs. Flower — inconspicuous. Fruit — inconspicuous.
Texture	Medium to fine.
Color	Foliage — rich dark green.
Culture	Sun. Soil — tolerant; very good drainage; medium fertility. Moisture — low. Pruning — tolerant. Pest Problems — bagworms, scale, spider mites. Growth Rate — slow.
Notes	Especially useful as specimen for exposed sites; excellent informal mass for large areas. Grows well in dry, windy areas and will tolerate most soils if well-drained.
Variety	**Tamariscifolia Glauca** — blue-green foliage.

Lavandula (la-van'dew-la)
   Latin to wash, in allusion
   to use in bath water

angustifolia (an-gus-tee-fo'li-a)
   narrow-leaved

angustifolia
   subspecies

ENGLISH LAVENDER

Family Labiatae

Size	Height 2½-3½ feet; spread 3-4 feet. Zones 6, 7, 8, 9.
Form	Irregular to semiglobe with vertical stem growth, medium to very dense. Foliage — opposite, fuzzy, aromatic, 1 inch long and ⅛ inch wide. Flower — May and June; fragrant small spikes 2 inches long on stems 4-8 inches long above foliage.
Texture	Medium to fine.
Color	Foliage — gray-green. Flower — lavender.
Culture	Sun. Soil — good drainage; medium fertility; prefers neutral to alkaline. Moisture — medium to low. Pruning — none. Pest Problems — none. Growth Rate — moderate.
Notes	Noted for fragrant leaves and flowers; dry seed heads very fragrant when crushed. Essential in herb gardens and may be clipped to form low hedge or border. Space 2 feet apart as hedging.
Varieties	**Gray Lady** — fragrant silver gray foliage; lavender flowers. **Hidcote** — dwarf and more compact; rich purple flowers. **Irene Doyle** — lavender blue flowers; may bloom twice each year. **Jean Davis** — abundant pink-white flowers; blue-green foliage. Forms mound 15 inches high; more vigorous than species. **Twickle Purple** — purple flowers; broad gray-green leaves.

Leucothoe (lew-ko'tho-ee)
  shrubs of heath family

axillaris (ak-si-ler'is)
  axil-flowering

COASTAL LEUCOTHOE

Family Ericaceae

Size	Height 3-4 feet; spread to 4-5 feet. Zones 6, 7, 8, 9.
Form	Graceful and informal with arching branches. Foliage — alternate, 3-5 inches long, finely toothed. Flower — April; bell-shaped on racemes in axils of leaves.
Texture	Medium.
Color	Foliage — dark glossy green; winter, purple-green. Flower — white or pinkish-white.
Culture	Part shade or shade. Soil — medium drainage; medium fertility; prefers acid woodland conditions. Moisture — high with high humidity. Pruning — remove 2 and 3 year old canes after bloom to stimulate new growth. Pest Problems — some leaf spot. Growth Rate — slow until established.
Notes	Excellent in masses. Arching habit contrasts with more upright shade plants such as rhododendrons. Good selection for enclosed city gardens or naturalized along stream banks and woodland trails. Mulch heavily. Best growth in sites with morning sunlight.

Leucothoe (lew-ko'tho-ee)
   shrubs of heath family

fontanesiana (fon-ta-nee'zi-a-na)
   named for R.L. Desfontaines,
   French botanist

DROOPING LEUCOTHOE

Family Ericaceae

Size	Height 3-4 feet; spread 4-6 feet.	Zones 6, 7, 8, 9.
Form	Graceful with long arching branches. Spreads by underground stems. Foliage — alternate, 3-5 inches long, leathery, lanceolate. Flower — late April; ¼ inch in 2-3 inch sprays or loose axillary racemes drooping below branches, waxy, fragrant. Fruit — fall; 5-lobed capsules.	
Texture	Medium to coarse.	
Color	Foliage — rich, lustrous dark green; winter, bronze-purple. Flower — white. Fruit — green turning brown. Bark — reddish.	
Culture	Part shade or shade. Soil — medium drainage; medium fertility; prefers acid loam. Moisture — high. Pruning — remove 2 and 3 year old canes after blooming to stimulate new growth. Pest Problems — leaf spot. Growth Rate — slow.	
Notes	Good color and habit; useful for massing and as undergrowth for naturalizing in woods. Good filler between other shrubs. Easy to transplant. Interesting in enclosed small city gardens. Requires heavy mulching. Formerly known as *L. catesbaei*.	
Varieties	**Girard's Rainbow** — new growth emerges white, pink, copper. **Nana** — dwarf form; height 2 feet, spread 4 feet; excellent selection. **Scarletta** — lustrous deep green foliage, becoming rich burgundy in winter. Height 18-20 inches.	

Ligustrum (ly-gus'trum)
   classical Latin name
   of privet

japonicum (ja-pon'i-kum)
   from Japan

'Rotundifolium' (ro-tun-di-fo'li-um)
   round-leaved

CURLYLEAF LIGUSTRUM

Family Oleaceae

Size	Height to 4 feet; spread 3 feet. Zones 7, 8, 9.
Form	Upright and columnar, dense. Foliage — opposite, thick, curved, 1-2½ inches long, crowded on short branches. Flower — inconspicuous panicles. Fruit — berrylike.
Texture	Medium.
Color	Foliage — glossy dark green. Flower — white. Fruit — black.
Culture	Sun or part shade. Soil — tolerant; medium drainage; medium fertility. Moisture — medium. Pruning — none. Pest Problems — white fly. Growth Rate — slow.
Notes	Useful as container specimen. Interesting twisted habit of leaf growth. Withstands adverse city conditions and drought fairly well. Also listed as *L. coriaceum*.

Lonicera (lon-iss'er-ra)
   honeysuckles

yunnanensis (yun-a-nen'sis)
   from Yunnan, China

YUNNAN HONEYSUCKLE

Family Caprifoliaceae

Size	Height 2-3 feet; spread 3-4 feet.	Zones 7, 8, 9.
Form	Low, creeping, arching, or twining. Foliage — opposite, 1 inch long. Flower — spring; 1 inch long.	
Texture	Fine.	
Color	Foliage — medium green. Flower — yellow.	
Culture	Sun. Soil — good drainage; medium fertility. Moisture — medium to low. Pruning — none. Pest Problems — none. Growth Rate — moderate.	
Notes	Useful as ground cover or in rock gardens. Good for quick and temporary effect.	

Mahonia (ma-ho'ni-a)
named for McMahon,
American horticulturist

aquifolium (a-kwi-fo'li-um)
holly-leaved

OREGON HOLLY-GRAPE

Family Berberidaceae

Size	Height 3-4 feet; spread 3-5 feet. Zones 6, 7, 8.
Form	Informal, irregular, becoming broadly clumped; upright stems with few branches. Foliage — alternate. Leathery, compound, with 5-9 spiny holly-like leaflets. Flower — late March to May; erect terminal clusters 3 inches long, fragrant. Fruit — early summer; grapelike clusters.
Texture	Coarse.
Color	Foliage — glossy dark green; fall and winter, reddish purple to bronze. Flower — yellow. Fruit — blue-black.
Culture	Part shade to shade. Soil — medium drainage; medium fertility. Moisture — medium. Pruning — remove 2-3 year old canes to stimulate new growth. Pest Problems — leaf miner and lacebug. Growth Rate — fairly slow.
Notes	Valued for foliage and flowers. Excellent for foundation plantings in part shade or for shrub borders. Avoid placing near red brick buildings. Not recommended for Coastal Plains. Withstands exposure to wind. Spreads slowly.
Varieties	**Atropurpureum** — leaves dark reddish purple in winter. **Compactum** — very glossy dark green leaves becoming bronze in winter. Height 1-2 feet. **Golden Abundance** — vigorous grower with profuse dense golden yellow flower clusters. **Mayhan Strain** — dwarf form with glossy foliage and fewer leaflets. **Moseri** — light bronze-red new leaves; turning light green and bronze-green in maturity. **Vicarii** — broad spreading; young leaves reddish turning green in summer through winter.

Pinus (py'nus)
old Latin name
for pine

mugo (mew'go)
native name in Alps
for Swiss mountain
pine

'Compacta' (kom-pack'ta)
compact, dense

MUGO PINE

Family Pinaceae

Size	Height 3-4 feet; spread 2-4 feet. Zones 6, 7, 8.
Form	Compact and globe-shaped. Foliage — needles in clusters of 2, 2 inches long and crowded. Attractive candlelike new growth in spring.
Texture	Fine.
Color	Foliage — deep green.
Culture	Sun. Soil — good drainage; medium to low fertility. Moisture — medium. Pruning — remove candles to create density. Pest Problems — pine root rot and scale. Growth Rate — slow.
Notes	Varies greatly from seed, some plants reaching height of 8 feet. Use only grafted plants for dwarf forms. Excellent planted in informal masses exposed to full sun and wind. Useful as specimen. Excellent container plant.
Varieties	**P.m. Gnome** — forms dense, globular, dark green mound less than 2 feet high and 3 feet wide. **P.m. mugo** — low growing form of species usually less than 5 feet high and about twice that in spread.

Prunus (proo'nus)
   classical Latin name
   of plum

laurocerasus (law-ro-se-ra'sus)
   classical name of Laurel

'Otto Luyken' (ot'toe lu'kin)

OTTO LAUREL

Family Rosaceae

Size	Height 3-4 feet; spread 5-7 feet. Zones 6, 7, 8, 9.
Form	Compact and broad spreading, moderately upright branching. Foliage — alternate, 4 inches long and 1 inch wide. Flower — spring; clusters of racemes 4 inches long. Fruit — summer; berrylike, 1/3-½ inch diameter.
Texture	Medium.
Color	Foliage — glossy dark green. Flower — white. Fruit — black.
Culture	Sun or shade. Soil — tolerant; good drainage; medium fertility with high organic content. Moisture — medium. Pruning — none. Pest Problems — shothole fungus, insects. Growth Rate — moderate.
Notes	Especially useful as foundation planting or low hedge; refined appearance. Excellent for masses. Interesting textural contrast with needleleaf evergreens.

Raphiolepis (raf-i-oll'ep-is)
Greek needle scale,
referring to bracts
in inflorescence

indica (in'di-ka)
from India

INDIA HAWTHORN

Family Rosaceae

Size	Height 3-4 feet; spread 4-5 feet. Zones 7, 8, 9.
Form	Spreading, open, irregularly branched. Foliage — alternate, thick and leathery, pointed with margins serrated, 1½-2½ inches long. Flower — April; terminal panicles. Fruit — fall; small berries, ½ inch diameter.
Texture	Medium to coarse.
Color	Foliage — dark green; winter, purplish if exposed. Flower — white or pink. Fruit — black.
Culture	Sun or shade. Soil — tolerant; medium drainage; medium fertility; prefers slightly alkaline. Moisture — medium. Pruning — none. Pest Problems — nematodes, scale, leaf spot, and blight. Growth Rate — slow.
Notes	Strong in character with dramatic appearance. Good informal hedge with excellent foliage and flower color combination. Ideal for coastal regions and warmer parts of Piedmont. Tolerates wind and salt spray.
Varieties	**Ballerina** — height 1½-2 feet; dark pink flowers. **Enchantress** — large flower clusters, large leaves; round form. **Fascination** — flower rose with white center, starlike in appearance. **Jack Evans** — compact, broad spreading growth habit; double pink flowers. **rosea** — pink flowers; more compact habit. Good replacement for azaleas in situations with hot sun and poor soil conditions. **Snow White** — white flower, light green foliage. **Springtime** — profuse pink flower clusters; graceful growth habit.

Rosmarinus (ros-ma-ry'nus)
  rosemary

officinalis (of-fish-i-na'lis)
  medicinal

ROSEMARY

Family Labiatae

Size	Height 2-4 feet; spread 2 feet. Zones 7, 8, 9.
Form	Irregular and loose with upright stems. Foliage — opposite, entire, narrow, to 1 inch long, aromatic . Flower — fall, winter and early spring; inconspicuous spikes.
Texture	Fine.
Color	Foliage — green to gray-green. Flower — pale violet-blue.
Culture	Sun. Soil — good drainage; low fertility. Moisture — low. Pruning — none, or as needed to maintain shape. Pest Problems — none. Growth Rate — slow until established.
Notes	For herb gardens and as accent or background for flowers. May be used as low hedge in warm areas with careful pruning. Grows well in containers.
Varieties	**Albus** — flowers white. **Arp** — height 3-4 feet; semi-upright growth habit. Hardy to -10°F. **Collingwood Ingram** — graceful curving branches; bright, blue-violet flowers. **Lockwood de Forest** — dark blue flowers; light green foliage. Prostrate form. **Prostratus** — trailing ground cover for zones 8 and 9. **Salem** — height 3 feet; dark green foliage. **Tuscan Blue** — taller and more upright than species with rigid stems. Blue-violet flowers.

Skimmia (skim'i-a)
   from skimmi, Japanese
   word signifying harmful
   fruit

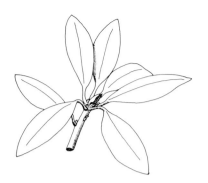

japonica (ja-pon'i-ca)
   from Japan

JAPANESE SKIMMIA

Family Rutaceae

Size	Height 4 feet; spread to 3 feet.	Zones 7, 8.

Form   Loose, rounded, moundlike. Foliage — alternate, simple, 3-5 inches long, 1½ inches wide. Flower — April; small in large terminal panicles, fragrant, sexes separate. Fruit — fall and winter; berry, 1/3 inch diameter in large clustered heads.

Texture   Coarse.

Color   Foliage — dark green. Flower — white. Fruit — scarlet.

Culture   Part shade or shade. Soil — good drainage; medium fertility with humus added. Moisture — low to medium. Pruning — remove cold damaged stems and dried berry stalks. Pest Problems — none. Growth Rate — slow.

Notes   Grown for excellent foliage, flowers, and fruit. Flowers on male plants larger and more fragrant. Useful in foundation plantings and foreground of mixed shrub plantings or in planter boxes.

Varieties **Formanii** — broad-leaved vigorous form with larger clusters of red fruit. **Nymans** — free fruiting form with large red berries. **Rubella** — male clone with red flower buds through winter; very fragrant in spring.

Skimmia (skim'i-a)
    from skimmi, Japanese word
    signifying harmful fruit

reevesiana (reevs'ee-an-na)
    named for R.G. Reeves of Texas

REEVES SKIMMIA

Family Rutaceae

Size	Height 1½-2 feet; spread 2-3 feet.	Zones 7, 8.
Form	Loose but more compact than *S. japonica*. Foliage — alternate, simple, 4 inches long. Flower — April; perfect, ½ inch long. Fruit — fall and winter; berry ½ inch thick.	
Texture	Medium to coarse.	
Color	Foliage — dark flat green. Flower — white. Fruit — red.	
Culture	Part shade. Soil — good drainage; medium fertility with acid humus added. Moisture — high. Pruning — remove cold damaged stems and dried berry stalks. Pest Problems — none. Growth Rate — slow.	
Notes	Grown for foliage, flowers, and fruits. Excellent for small gardens.	

Viburnum (vy-bur'num)
    classical Latin name
    of wayfaring tree

davidii (da-vid'i)
    from proper name

DAVID VIBURNUM

Family Caprifoliaceae

Size	Height 3-5 feet; spread 3-5 feet.	Zones 7, 8.
Form	Rounded, compact mound of medium density. Foliage — opposite, leathery, to 5½ inches long, slightly toothed at edges and deeply veined. Flower — early summer; clusters 2-3 inches wide. Fruit — early fall; berrylike.	
Texture	Medium to coarse.	
Color	Foliage — dark green. Flower — white. Fruit — light blue.	
Culture	Sun or part shade. Soil — tolerant; medium drainage; medium fertility. Moisture — medium. Pruning — none. Pest Problems — none. Growth Rate — moderate.	
Notes	Excellent low-growing foundation plant. Of dignified and rather formal character. Plant both male and female forms to obtain fruit.	
Variety	**Jermyn's Globe** — compact, roundish form.	

Yucca (yuk'ka)
Latinized version of
Spanish vernacular of
some other desert plant

filamentosa (fill-a-men-to'sa)
threadlike

ADAM'S NEEDLE YUCCA

Family Liliaceae

Size	Height 1½-4 feet; spread 2½-4 feet. Zones 6, 7, 8, 9.
Form	Fairly open. Foliage — stiff blades 2½ feet long, upright and outward from central crown, produces side shoots. Flower — late spring and summer; bell-shaped 2-3 inches wide on central stalk 3-5 feet high. Fruit — September and October; capsules 2 inches long.
Texture	Coarse.
Color	Foliage — medium green. Flower — greenish-white. Fruit — green to brown.
Culture	Sun or part shade. Soil — medium to good drainage; low fertility. Moisture — low. Pruning — annual removal of old flower stalks and unsightly foliage. Pest Problems — leaf spot or blight during rainy growing season. Growth Rate — moderate.
Notes	Very resistant to drought and adverse growing conditions. Hazardous near play areas because of sharp, pointed leaf blades. Very stiff visual effect; contrasts in texture and form with surrounding plant materials. Available in variegated leaf form. Also called *Y. smalliana.*
Variety	**concava** — spoonlike leaves which are broad and stiff.

Shore junipers, dogwoods, and Austrian pines soften formal entrance.

SHRUBS 1-4 FEET — DECIDUOUS

Callicarpa (kal-i-kar'pa)
   from Greek for beautiful
   and fruit

dichotoma (di-kot'o-ma)
   with forking

BEAUTYBERRY

Family Verbenaceae

Size	Height 3-4 feet; spread 4-6 feet. Zones 6, 7, 8.
Form	Graceful and rounded with long, slender, arching branches touching ground at tips. Foliage — opposite, borne in one plane along stems, elliptic and bluntly toothed near tip, 1-3 inches long. Flower — August; inconspicuous. Fruit — September through winter; berry-like drupes ⅛ inch diameter, borne in clusters in axils of leaves.
Texture	Medium.
Color	Foliage — medium green; fall; purple-green. Flower — pink. Fruit — violet-pink to purple.
Culture	Sun to part shade. Soil — medium drainage; medium fertility. Moisture — medium. Pruning — cut to ground in late winter. Pest Problems — none. Growth Rate — rapid.
Notes	Best planted in masses; textural and fruiting interest for shrub borders and naturalized areas.
Variety	**albifructus** — white berries.

Chaenomeles (kee-nom'e-lees)
  Greek meaning split apple

japonica (ja-pon'i-ka)
  from Japan

JAPANESE FLOWERING
QUINCE

Family Rosaceae

Size	Height 2-3 feet; spread 2-3 feet. Zones 6, 7, 8, 9.
Form	Open and spreading. Foliage — alternate, simple, long, coarsely toothed, base wedge-shaped. Flower — early spring; single, 1¼ inch diameter. Fruit — autumn; resembling miniature apples 1½ inches wide, fragrant, edible. Stem — thorny.
Texture	Medium.
Color	Foliage — medium green. Flower — red to light orange. Fruit — yellow.
Culture	Sun or part shade. Soil — very tolerant; medium drainage; low to medium fertility. Moisture — medium. Pruning — remove leggy, non-flowering shoots. Pest Problems — scale, fire blight, and aphids. Growth Rate — fairly rapid.
Notes	Withstands city conditions very well. Valued for showy flowers. Needs leafy background. Excellent for floral arrangement. Oriental in character.
Varieties	**alpina** — dense growth, height 1 foot, orange flowers. **Minerva** — velvety cherry red flowers; large and spreading growth. **Pink Beauty** — rose pink flower; tall, upright in growth. **Snow** — waxy, pure white flowers; large, upright growth.

Deutzia (doot'zi-a)
    named for Johan van
    der Deutz

gracilis (gras'i-lis)
    graceful, slender

SLENDER DEUTZIA

Family Saxifragaceae

Size	Height 3-4 feet; spread to 4 feet. Zones 6, 7, 8, 9.
Form	Graceful, rounded, and compact. Branches slender and arching. Foliage — opposite, simple, toothed, 2½ inches long. Flower — late April, on wood of previous season; single, ¾ inch wide in 2-4 inch upright clusters.
Texture	Medium to fine.
Color	Foliage — neutral, pale green. Flower — green.
Culture	Sun or part shade. Soil — tolerant; good drainage; low to medium fertility. Moisture — low to medium. Pruning — remove old stems annually after flowering. Pest Problems — none. Growth Rate — slow.
Notes	Excellent as filler in mixed shrub borders and flower gardens, or as low hedge around entrance, patio, or walk. Useful for small gardens or foundation plantings. Will tolerate neglect. Lacks vigor in warmer areas of Coastal Plain. Relatively neutral after flowering.
Varieties	**Carminea** — arching branches to 3 feet height. Large flower clusters with pale pink petals within, purplish outside. **Nikko** — height 2-3 feet; foliage becomes maroon in autumn.

Fothergilla (fo-thur-gil'a)
     after Dr. John Fothergill,
     English physician

gardenii (gar-de'ne-i)
     after Dr. Garden of
     Charleston, S.C.

DWARF FOTHERGILLA

Family Hamamelidaceae

Size	Height 2-3 feet; spread 3-4 feet.	Zones 6, 7, 8.
Form	Rounded with slender, spreading branches and informal open habit of growth. Foliage — leathery; obovate to oblong, rounded at base, 1½-2 inches long. Flower — April, before leaves; 1 inch spikes, fragrant. Fruit — capsule.	
Texture	Coarse.	
Color	Foliage — dark green, pale green beneath; fall, bright yellow and scarlet. Flower — cream-white.	
Culture	Sun or part shade. Soil — good drainage essential; medium fertility; prefers acid loam. Moisture — high to medium. Pruning — none. Pest Problems — none. Growth Rate — slow.	
Notes	Blooms for 3 weeks in early spring with redbud. Especially effective with evergreen ground-covers and in combination with evergreen shrubs such as azaleas and rhododendrons. Also useful in foundation and mass plantings.	
Variety	**Blue Mist** — soft light blue leaves.	

Hydrangea (hy-dran'jee-a)
  hardy shrubs, vines

arborescens (ar-bore-ress'ens)
  almost treelike

'Grandiflora' (grand-di-flo'ra)
  large or showy flowered

SNOWHILL HYDRANGEA

Family Saxifragaceae

Size	Height 3 feet; spread 3-5 feet.	Zones 6, 7, 8, 9.
Form	Upright, open and loose mounds with many branches suckering. Foliage — opposite, simple, toothed, oval, 3-6 inches long. Flower — June and July; rounded heads, 6 inch diameter; florets sterile.	
Texture	Coarse.	
Color	Foliage — light green. Flower — white turning green.	
Culture	Sun or part shade. Soil — good drainage; medium to high fertility. Moisture — medium. Pruning — cut back annually in late winter to encourage vigorous new growth. Pest Problems — none. Growth Rate — rapid.	
Notes	Best planted in generous drifts. Easy to grow and very hardy. Grown for summer flowers. Useful in foreground of shrub borders. Not recommended for Coastal Plain.	
Variety	**H.a. Annabelle** — superior cultivar of species; flowers 10-14 days later than 'Grandiflora'. Showy, globe-shaped flower heads, 12 inches diameter.	

Hypericum (hy-per'i-kum)
  under or among heather

kalmianum (kal-mee-ay'num)
  named for Peter Kalm
  of Sweden

KALM ST.-JOHN'S-WORT

Family Hypericaceae

Size	Height 3 feet; spread 3 feet. Zones 6, 7, 8.
Form	Rounded and loose. Foliage — opposite, 1-2½ inches long, ½ inch wide. Flower — early July; single, 1 inch diameter, cup-shaped, somewhat fragrant. Stem — 4-angled with peeling bark.
Texture	Fine.
Color	Foliage — blue-green above, whitish beneath. Flower — waxy, bright yellow.
Culture	Sun. Soil — tolerant. Moisture — low. Pruning — flowers produced on wood of current season, remove old wood in early spring. Pest Problems — none. Growth Rate — rapid.
Notes	Handsome summer flowers enhance value as edging for shrub border or foundation plantings. May be used to form low hedge along walks, drives, walls, or fences. Often evergreen in warmer areas.

Hypericum (hy-per'i-kum)
    under or among heather

x moseranum (mo-ze-ra'num)
    named for Moser of
    Versailles

GOLDFLOWER

Family Hypericaceae

Size	Height 2-3 feet; spread 3 feet or more. Zones 6, 7.
Form	Loose and rounded with arching stems, broader than tall. Foliage — opposite, 2 inches long. Flower — July and August; cup-shaped, single, 2 inch diameter; odorless. Fruit — fall, persisting through winter; capsules. Bark — peeling.
Texture	Medium to fine.
Color	Foliage — gray-green. Flower — yellow.
Culture	Sun. Soil — tolerant. Moisture — medium to high. Pruning — early spring; thin occasionally. Pest Problems — none. Growth Rate — fairly rapid.
Notes	Will thrive under poor growing conditions. Interesting small shrub valued for summer bloom; excellent for cover planting, facer shrub, or as undergrowth; may be used in rock gardens and in perennial borders. Not recommended for Coastal Plain.
Variety	**Tricolor** — foliage variegated cream and dark pink; not as hardy as species and not as vigorous.

Jasminum (jas'min-um)
    Arabic name for
    jasmine

nudiflorum (new-di-flo'rum)
    flowers without leaves

WINTER JASMINE

Family Oleaceae

Size	Height 2-4 feet; spread 3-5 feet. Zones 6, 7, 8, 9.
Form	Low spreading with pendulous 4-angled branches. Foliage — opposite, trifoliate leaflets 1 inch long. Flower — February; 1 inch diameter. Fruit — small berry.
Texture	Medium.
Color	Foliage — glossy green. Flower — yellow. Fruit — black. Stem — green.
Culture	Sun or shade. Soil — tolerant; medium drainage; low fertility. Moisture — medium. Pruning — heavy thinning every 3-4 years for rejuvenation. Pest Problems — spider mites. Growth Rate — moderate.
Notes	Twig tips root easily in contact with cultivated soil. Suitable for covering banks. Will survive in poor soil. Good for irregular, loose hedges. Attractive winter bloom. Little care required.

Potentilla (po-ten-till'a)
diminutive from *potens*,
powerful

fruticosa (fru-ti-ko'sa)
shrubby

BUSH CINQUEFOIL

Family Rosaceae

Size	Height 2-4 feet; spread 3-5 feet.	Zones 6, 7, 8, 9.

Form   Rounded and billowing, stems upright and much branched, dense. Foliage — alternate, pinnately compound with 3-7 leaflets ½-1½ inches long. Flower — mid-April and continuing all summer; single, ¾ inch diameter. Fruit — capsule.

Texture   Fine.

Color   Foliage — medium green above, whitish beneath. Flower — yellow or white. Fruit — brown.

Culture   Sun or part shade. Soil — tolerant; good drainage. Moisture — medium. Pruning — trim lightly in fall to remove dried fruit. Pest Problems — none. Growth Rate — moderate.

Notes   Valued for long flowering season. Excellent in rock gardens, over stone walls, or as ground cover. Interesting informal hedge or edging material. Grows well in containers.

Varieties   **Abbotswood** — large white flowers; dark blue-green foliage. **Coronation Triumph** — height 2-3 feet with more upright habit of growth; bright yellow flowers and fine-textured gray-green foliage. **Dakota Surprise** — light yellow flowers; dense growth. Suitable for mass planting. **Goldfinger** — compact shrub with 2 inch diameter bright yellow flowers. Finely divided dark green foliage, dense growth. **Primrose Beauty** — spreading habit of growth; silver gray foliage, pale yellow flowers. **Princess** — height and spread 2½ feet; flowers pink turning white in summer.

SHRUBS 4-6 FEET — EVERGREEN

Abelia (a-bee'li-a)
    named for Abel,
    physician and author

x grandiflora (gran-di-flo'ra)
    large or showy flowered

GLOSSY ABELIA

Family Caprifoliaceae

Size	Height 4-6 feet; spread 3-5 feet.	Zones 6, 7, 8, 9.

Form	Semiglobal; many canes from ground level; fairly open to medium density. Foliage — opposite, to 1½ inches long, glossy. Flower — summer; ¾ inch in clusters of 1-4.
Texture	Medium to fine.
Color	Foliage — purplish-green; winter, bronze-purple. Flower — pinkish-white with reddish bracts.
Culture	Sun or shade. Soil — medium to good drainage; medium fertility with organic content. Moisture — medium. Pruning — pinch new growth tips in spring for compactness; occasional thinning needed. Pest Problems — aphids. Growth Rate — moderate.
Notes	Good plant for medium height informal hedges or for background. Less expensive than most evergreens. Iron chlorosis common; not well adapted to deep sandy soils. Leaf drop from low temperatures, lack of pruning, and starvation.
Varieties	**Edward Goucher** — lighter and smaller in form than A. x grandiflora; arching branches, lavender purple flowers from June to October. **Prostrata** — white flowers; used as ground cover. **Sherwood** — excellent 2-3 feet trailing form with small white flowers.

Aucuba (aw-kew'ba)
Latinized from
Japanese name

japonica (ja-pon'i-ka)
from Japan

JAPANESE AUCUBA

Family Cornaceae

Size	Height 4-5 feet; spread 3-4 feet. Zones 7, 8, 9.
Form	Irregular with medium density. Foliage — opposite, 4-8 inches long. Flower — March; inconspicuous panicles 2-5 inches long. Fruit — winter; berries. Dioecious, plant both sexes to ensure fruiting.
Texture	Coarse.
Color	Foliage — deep green. Flower — brownish-white. Fruit — red.
Culture	Shade; sun causes burning of leaves. Soil — medium drainage; high fertility; prefers heavy soils. Moisture — medium to high. Pruning — keep plant low and compact. Pest Problems — spider mites and scale. Growth Rate — slow to moderate.
Notes	Excellent for dark corners or shady locations. May be grown in planter boxes. Foliage useful in flower arrangements.
Varieties	**borealis** — height 14 inches; hardier than species, very fruitful female plants. **Crassifolia** — male form with large dark green, leathery leaves. **Crotonifolia** — large leaves finely spotted with white and gold. **Longifolia** — vivid green willow-like leaves; female form. **Macrophylla** — broad, leathery dark green leaves; female form. **Nana** — dwarf form, about 2 feet in height. **variegata** — leaves marked with yellow spots. Use in moderation. Golddust Tree.

Azalea (a-zay'lee-a)
   showy shrubs, botanically
   Rhododendrons

hybrida (hy'brid-a)
   hybrid

GLENN DALE AZALEA

Family Ericaceae

Size	Height 4-6 feet; spread 3-4 feet.	Zones 6, 7, 8.

Form   Upright or spreading depending on variety. Foliage — alternate, simple, entire, 1-2 inches long. Flower — mid-April to May; 2-4 inches wide.

Texture   Medium.

Color   Foliage — dark green to medium green. Flower — white, rose, purple, salmon, red, or pink.

Culture   Part shade. Soil — medium drainage; medium fertility with high organic content. Moisture — high. Pruning — none. Pest Problems — lacebug, scale, spider mites, and root rot. Growth Rate — moderate.

Notes   Brilliant floral display with different varieties covering entire azalea blooming season. Somewhat more cold hardy than Kurume azalea.

Varieties **Aphrodite** — flowers rose-pink, single, 2 inch diameter. Upright growth with spreading branches. **Copperman** — flowers deep brick-red, single, 2¾-3 inch diameter. Dense, spreading. **Fashion** — flowers rose with darker blotch, 2 inch diameter. Erect, overarching habit; height 6-8 feet. **Festive** — flowers white with red striping, 2-2½ inch diameter. Spreading habit. **Glacier** — flowers white with faint green tone, 2½-3 inch diameter. Erect to spreading; height 3-6 feet. **Modesty** — flowers rose, semidouble, 2½-3 inch diameter. Erect habit. **Swansong** — flowers white with yellowish blotch, single, 3½-4 inch diameter. Dense habit. **Treasure** — upright white flowers with pink blotch.

Azalea (a-zay'lee-a)
  showy shrubs, botanically
  Rhododendrons

kaempferi (kamp'fer-i)
  named for Engelbert
  Kaempfer

KAEMPFERI AZALEA

Family Ericaceae

Size	Height 4-6 feet; spread 4-6 feet. Zones 6, 7, 8, 9.
Form	Upright and open. Foliage — alternate, simple, entire, pubescent, 1-2 inches long. Flower — late April and early May; 1½-2½ inches wide, single or hose-in-hose.
Texture	Medium.
Color	Foliage — medium green. Flower — red, pink, purple, or white.
Culture	Part shade. Soil — medium drainage; medium fertility with high organic content. Moisture — high. Pruning — none. Pest Problems — lacebug, scale, spider mites, and root rot. Growth Rate — moderate.
Notes	One of hardiest evergreen azaleas. Blooms late enough to escape frosts. Excellent for woodland plantings, especially under pines. Easier to grow and less demanding than Kurume azaleas. Botanically *Rhododendron kaempferi*.
Varieties	**albiforum** — white flowers. **angustisectum** — red flowers. **Anna Maria** — pure white flowers. **Cleopatra** — light pink flowers. **Lilac Time** — lavender flowers. **Monstrosum** — white hose-in-hose flowers. **tubiflorum** — small, tubular flowers with white throats and reddish pink margins.

Berberis (ber'ber-iss)
   Arabic name

julianae (jew-li-a'na)
   named for
   Mrs. C.K. Schneider

WINTERGREEN BARBERRY

Family Berberidaceae

Size	Height 4-6 feet; spread 2-5 feet. Zones 6, 7, 8.
Form	Dense and rounded with stiff thorns to 1½ inches long. Foliage — alternate in rosettes, sharply toothed, narrow-elliptic, 3 inches long. Flower — early April; ½ inch wide in clusters. Fruit — late fall; ovoid-oblong berries.
Texture	Fine to medium.
Color	Foliage — glossy deep green. Flower — yellow. Fruit — bluish-black. Bark — yellowish to brown.
Culture	Sun or part shade. Soil — very tolerant; medium drainage; medium fertility. Moisture — medium. Pruning — none. Pest Problems — none. Growth Rate — slow.
Notes	Very handsome shrub. Good as background material. May be used as specimen, hedge, border, or background material. Impenetrable because of thorns. Combines well with broadleaf evergreens.
Variety	**Nana** — 3-4 feet high; forms solid mound. Glossy dark green foliage becomes wine-red in winter; large spines.

Buxus (bucks'us)
   classical Latin
   for box

microphylla (my-kro-fil'la)
   small-leaved

japonica (ja-pon'i-ka)
   from Japan

JAPANESE BOXWOOD

Family Buxaceae

Size	Height 4-5 feet; spread 3-4 feet. Zones 7, 8, 9.
Form	Grows upright for first few years and then forms flattened globe. Foliage — opposite, simple, entire, 1¼ inches long. Flower — inconspicuous.
Texture	Medium.
Color	Foliage — glossy yellowish-green. Flower — white to green.
Culture	Sun or shade. Soil — good drainage; medium fertility. Moisture — medium. Pruning — needs frequent clipping to retain compactness in shade or part shade. Pest Problems — boxwood leaf miner, spider mites, and nematodes. Growth Rate — moderate.
Notes	Larger leaves than species. Excellent sheared or natural hedge. Good low specimen plant. Not as fast-growing as *B. sempervirens*, but better adapted to Coastal Plain areas. Not hardy in mountain area. Shallow root system. Requires mulch.
Varieties	**Compacta** — very slow-growing form with excellent dark green foliage. Less than one foot in height. **National** — narrower and more upright in form than *B. microphylla*; good winter color.

Buxus (bucks'us)
   classical Latin
   for box

sempervirens (sem-per-vy'renz)
   evergreen

AMERICAN BOXWOOD

Family Buxaceae

| Size | Height 3-6 feet; spread 3-4 feet. | Zones 6, 7, 8. |

Size   Height 3-6 feet; spread 3-4 feet.   Zones 6, 7, 8.

Form   Upright globe with many canes from crown; very dense. Foliage —
              opposite, simple, entire, pointed, to 1¼ inches long. Flower —
              inconspicuous.

Texture   Fine to medium.

Color   Foliage — lustrous dark green.

Culture   Part shade to shade. Soil — good drainage; medium fertility with high
              organic content. Moisture — medium. Pruning — occasional light
              shearing for compactness. Pest Problems — nematodes, boxwood leaf
              miner, spider mites, root rot, and dogs. Growth Rate — moderate to rapid.

Notes   Most dignified of shrubs lending elegance to any situation. Does well in
              cool sections of Piedmont. Shallow root system. Requires mulch.

Varieties   **Angustifolia** — treelike in habit with narrow leaves 1-1¼ inches long. **Hands-
              worthiensis** — wide and dense upright form with large dark green leaves; excel-
              lent for hedging. **Inglis** — dense branching, medium height, pyramidal in habit;
              dark green foliage; very hardy. **Myrtifolia** — 4-5 feet height; small narrow leaves.
              Vardar Valley — rounded, dense low-growing form; dark green foliage all winter.
              Hardiest variety. **Welleri** — dense, broad form; large lustrous leaves with good
              winter color.

Euonymus (you-on'i-mus)
   hardy shrubs and vines

kiautschovicus (ky-cho'va-kus)

SPREADING EUONYMUS

Family Celastraceae

Size	Height 4-6 feet; spread 4-6 feet. Zones 6, 7, 8.
Form	Informal and open with broad spread. Foliage — opposite, simple, thin, bluntly fine-toothed, 2-6 inches long. Flower — August; negligible size but very numerous, giving attractive filmy appearance. Fruit — fall; ½ inch diameter.
Texture	Medium to coarse.
Color	Foliage — bright green. Flower — greenish-white. Fruit — orange.
Culture	Sun or shade. Soil — very tolerant; medium drainage; medium fertility. Moisture — medium. Pruning — none. Pest Problems — scale. Growth Rate — rapid.
Notes	May be trained as vine on walls or fences; climbs by aerial roots. Lower branches sometimes prostrate and rooting. Useful as hedge, screen, border, or foundation planting. Not as susceptible to scale as some other Euonymus species. Often listed as *E. patens*. Varieties superior to species.
Varieties	**Dupont** — large leaves and vigorous growth habit. Height 4-5 feet. **Manhattan** — excellent dark green glossy foliage with leaves 2½ inches long. Forms dense upright shrub 4-6 feet in height. **Paulii** — upright form to 5 feet; glossy dark green leaves. **Sieboldiana** — excellent foliage; less suceptible to scale than species. **Vincifolia** — upright, spreading form with small leaves.

Fatsia (fat'si-a)
    derived from
    Japanese vernacular
    for plant

japonica (ja-pon'i-ka)
    from Japan

JAPANESE FATSIA

Family Araliaceae

Size	Height 4-6 feet; spread 4-6 feet. Zones 7, 8, 9.
Form	Rather globular and open. Foliage — alternate, leathery, 7-9 lobes, 8-12 inch diameter. Flower — fall; round heads 1-2 inches wide. Fruit — winter; berries ¼ inch diameter.
Texture	Coarse.
Color	Foliage — glossy dark green. Flower — white. Fruit — light blue.
Culture	Shade. Soil — tolerant; medium drainage; medium fertility; Moisture — medium. Pruning — remove older stems to maintain desired size. Pest Problems — none. Growth Rate — moderate.
Notes	Most useful for warmer parts of Piedmont and Coastal Plain. Prefers protected spot in deep shade. Excellent espaliered or in planter boxes; very tolerant of confined city conditions. Tropical in appearance. Tolerates salt spray. Ideal specimen for patios.
Varieties	**Moseri** — compact and vigorous form; larger leaves than species. **Variegata** — glossy leaves tipped and margined with white.

Gardenia (gar-de'ni-a)
   named for Alexander
   Garden of Charleston,
   South Carolina

jasminoides (jas-min-oy'deez)
   jasminelike

CAPE-JASMINE

Family Rubiaceae

Size	Height 4-6 feet; spread 4-5 feet.	Zones 8, 9.
Form	Rounded and open. Foliage — opposite or whorled in 2's or 3's, to 4 inches long. Flower — May and June; waxy, to 3 inches wide, fragrant.	
Texture	Medium.	
Color	Foliage — lustrous dark green. Flower — white.	
Culture	Sun or part shade. Soil — medium drainage; medium to high fertility with iron added. Moisture — medium. Pruning — none. Pest Problems — white fly, mealybug, sooty mold, and nematodes. Growth Rate — moderate.	
Notes	Should be used as specimen shrub; requires careful maintenance. Several forms with single or double flowers. Protect roots carefully during transplanting. Not cold hardy in mountain areas.	
Varieties	**August Beauty** — height 5 feet; small, narrow leaves and long blooming period. **fortuniana** — large flowers to 4 inches wide, double and camellia-like; larger leaves than species. **Mystery** — height 8 feet; large glossy leaves and large flowers. **Veitchii** — abundant small flowers, long blooming period.	

Ilex (eye'lecks)
  hollies

cornuta (kor-new'ta)
  horned

'Burfordii Nana' (burr'ferd-eye   nay'na)
  from Mr. Burford
  Atlanta, Georgia

DWARF BURFORD HOLLY

Family Aquifoliaceae

Size	Height 4-6 feet; spread 4-6 feet.	Zones 6, 7, 8, 9.
Form	Oval and upright with dense branches and foliage. Foliage — alternate, oblong, slightly recurved, 1-3 spines at tip, ¾-1 inch long. Flower — early spring; inconspicuous. Fruit — fall and winter; ⅛ inch diameter, sparsely produced.	
Texture	Medium to fine.	
Color	Foliage — glossy medium green. Fruit — red.	
Culture	Sun or part shade. Soil — good drainage; medium fertility. Moisture — medium. Pruning — tolerant. Pest Problems — usually none; mildew, leaf spot, scale, sooty mold occasionally. Growth Rate — moderate.	
Notes	Versatile and dependable as hedge, background, barrier, and medium-high foundation plant. Grows well in containers.	

Ilex (eye'lecks)
  hollies

crenata (kree-nay'ta)
  scalloped or with
  irregularly waved margin

'Convexa' (kon-vex'a)
  small, convex

CONVEXA JAPANESE HOLLY

Family Aquifoliaceae

Size	Height 4-6 feet; spread 3-5 feet. Zones 6, 7, 8, 9.
Form	Rounded, somewhat stiff and strawlike. Foliage — alternate, ½ inch long, oval, cupped and crowded on stems. Flower — inconspicuous. Fruit — fall; berries ¼ inch diameter.
Texture	Fine to medium.
Color	Foliage — glossy black-green. Fruit — dull black.
Culture	Sun or shade; part shade best in Coastal Plain. Soil — medium drainage; medium fertility with nitrogen and iron added. Moisture — medium. Pruning — snip back new branches in early summer to maintain compactness. Pest Problems — spider mites, usually scale-resistant. Growth Rate — moderate.
Notes	Useful broad-leaved evergreen, growing well throughout Southeast. Fine as foundation plant or in masses. Good substitute for boxwoods and may be developed into formal or informal hedge.

Ilex (eye'lecks)
    hollies

crenata (kree-nay'ta)
    scalloped or with
    irregularly waved margins

'Hetzi' (het-sy')
    from proper
    name

HETZI JAPANESE HOLLY

Family Aquifoliaceae

Size	Height 4-6 feet; spread 5-7 feet. Zones 6, 7, 8, 9.
Form	Spreading and rounded. Foliage — alternate, ¾ inch long, cupped. Flower — inconspicuous. Fruit — fall; berries ¼ inch diameter.
Texture	Medium to fine.
Color	Foliage — medium green. Fruit — black.
Culture	Sun or shade. Soil — medium drainage; medium fertility with high organic content. Moisture — medium. Pruning — maintain size. Pest Problems — scale, spider mites, and nematodes. Growth Rate — moderate.
Notes	Similar to *I.c.* 'Convexa' except in color. Vigorous, spreading habit of growth. Good background for azaleas. Needs part shade in Coastal Plain areas.

Ilex (eye'lecks)
    hollies

crenata (kree-nay'ta)
    scalloped or with
    irregularly waved margin

'Microphylla' (my-kro-fill'la)
    small-leaved

LITTLELEAF
JAPANESE HOLLY

Family Aquifoliaceae

Size	Height 4-6 feet; spread 5-7 feet. Zones 6, 7, 8, 9.
Form	Low but somewhat upright; open and slightly irregular branching. Foliage — alternate, oval to oblong, pointed, ¼-¾ inch long. Flower — inconspicuous. Fruit — fall; berries ¼ inch diameter.
Texture	Fine.
Color	Foliage — rich, dark green. Fruit — black.
Culture	Sun or shade. Soil — medium drainage; high fertility. Moisture — medium. Pruning — withstands shearing in late winter and again in June for formal hedges. Pest Problems — spider mites. Growth Rate — slow.
Notes	Excellent for hedges, specimen, or planter boxes. Picturesque in natural form. Good substitute for boxwood. Needs part shade in Coastal Plain.

Ilex (eye'lecks)
  hollies

crenata (kree-nay'ta)
  scalloped or with
  irregularly waved margin

'Rotundifolia' (ro-tun-di-fo'li-a)
  round-leaved

ROUNDLEAF
JAPANESE HOLLY

Family Aquifoliaceae

Size	Height 4-6 feet; spread 4-6 feet. Zones 6, 7, 8, 9.
Form	Rounded and irregular in outline. Foliage — alternate, 1 inch long with crenate margins. Flower — inconspicuous, sterile. Fruit — none.
Texture	Medium to fine.
Color	Foliage — dark green.
Culture	Sun or shade. Soil — medium drainage; medium fertility with high organic content. Moisture — medium. Pruning — maintain size. Pest Problems — scale, spider mites, and nematodes. Growth Rate — moderate.
Notes	Suitable for foundation plantings or grouped in masses as background. May be trimmed to form hedge or accent plant. Withstands city conditions well, requiring minimum care when established.

Ilex (eye'lecks)
  hollies

crenata (kree-nay'ta)
  scalloped or with
  irregularly waved margin

'Yellow Berry'

JAPANESE HOLLY

Family Aquifoliaceae

Size	Height 4-6 feet; spread 3-5 feet.	Zones 6, 7, 8.
Form	Upright and rounded; loose and open. Foliage — alternate, ½-¾ inch long. Flower — inconspicuous. Fruit — fall; berries ¼ inch diameter.	
Texture	Medium to fine.	
Color	Foliage — medium green. Fruit — yellow.	
Culture	Sun or shade. Soil — medium drainage; high fertility. Moisture — medium. Pruning — prune for best effect. Pest Problems — spider mites, scale and nematodes. Growth Rate — moderate.	
Notes	Good for masses. Can be used as foundation plant or as specimen. Heavy fruit set.	

Jasminum (jas'min-um)
   Arabic name for
   jasmine

floridum (flo'ri-dum)
   freely flowering

FLOWERING JASMINE

Family Oleaceae

Size	Height 4-6 feet; spread 5-7 feet.	Zones 7, 8, 9.
Form	Arching and rambling mound. Foliage — alternate, 3 leaflets ½-1½ inches long. Flower — May through June; ½ inch wide in clusters.	
Texture	Fine.	
Color	Foliage — medium green. Flower — yellow.	
Culture	Sun or part shade. Soil — tolerant; medium drainage; medium fertility. Moisture — low to medium. Pruning — none. Pest Problems — none. Growth Rate — moderate.	
Notes	May be trained as vine. Acts as large scale ground cover when used in plantings. Excellent on banks or over wall where graceful form shows to advantage. Useful for unclipped hedges or borders requiring little care once established. Interesting espaliered.	

Juniperus (jew-nip'er-us)
juniperlike

chinensis (chi-nen'sis)
from China

'Pfitzeriana' (fits-er-ee-ane'a)
named for E.H.H. Pfitzer
of Germany

PFITZER JUNIPER

Family Cupressaceae

Size	Height 5-7 feet; spread 8-10 feet. Zones 6, 7, 8, 9.
Form	Loose and graceful, medium density. Foliage — scalelike. Fruit — berries about ⅜ inch in diameter; sexes separate.
Texture	Medium to fine.
Color	Foliage — bright green. Fruit — green-gray.
Culture	Sun. Soil — tolerant; good drainage, medium fertility. Moisture — medium to low. Pruning — clip side branches for balance; allow adequate growing space. Pest Problems — bagworms, juniper scale, and spider mites. Growth Rate — fairly rapid.
Notes	Takes on rugged character with age. Best used in broad masses in large-scale areas. Exotic in appearance, does not mix well with other plants but blends nicely with rock or unpainted wood. Too large for residential foundation plantings. Grows well in Coastal Plain but is susceptible to salt burn.
Varieties	**Armstrongii** — dwarf form 3-4 feet in height with equal spread, branches horizontal; leaves scale-like and soft; yellowish green foliage. **Aurea** — light golden-yellow branch tips. **Glauca** — silvery blue foliage becoming purple-blue in winter; dense and prickly foliage. **Nana** — dwarf form. **Nick's Compact** — excellent compact form; gray-green foliage.

Kalmia (kal'mi-a)
　named for Peter
　Kalm, botanist

latifolia (la-ti-fo'li-a)
　broad-leaved

MOUNTAIN-LAUREL

Family Ericaceae

Size	Height 4-6 feet; spread 3-5 feet.　　　　　　Zones 6, 7, 8.
Form	Large and robust if not crowded, symmetrical and dense; in old age becomes open and loose with very picturesque trunks and limbs. Foliage — alternate, 3-5 inches long, glossy and leathery. Flower — May to June; large terminal corymbs. Fruit — fall and winter; 5-valved capsules.
Texture	Medium.
Color	Foliage — bright green. Flower — white to deep rose.
Culture	Shade or sun if moist; grows well in part shade on rocky sites near water. Soil — good drainage; medium fertility with acid humus added. Moisture — high. Pruning — none. Pest Problems — leaf miner, leaf spot, blight, aphids, borers, and lacebug. Growth Rate — slow.
Notes	Beautiful native shrub; mass on north of buildings or in dark nooks under trees. Used in foundation planting, informal borders, and on slopes. May be grown in Coastal Plain in moist cool sites.
Varieties	**Alba** — white flowers. **Myrtifolia** — dwarf form, less than 6 feet height. **Obtusata** — dwarf form with leathery oval leaves. **Ostbo Red** — deep red flower buds. Excellent form. **Pink Charm** — rich pink flowers. **Polypetala** — double feathery pink petals. **Quinnipiac** — pink flowers; dark green foliage. **Sharon Rose** — compact form; bright deep red buds, light pink flowers. **Silver Dollar** — large white flowers; dark green leaves. **Willowcrest** — blush pink flowers; narrow willow-like leaves.

Mahonia (ma-ho'ni-a)
  named for McMahon,
  American horticulturist

bealei (be-lea'i)
  named for T.C. Beale

LEATHERLEAF MAHONIA

Family Berberidaceae

Size	Height 5-6 feet; spread 3-4 feet. Zones 6, 7, 8, 9.
Form	Upright and open. Foliage — alternate, 5-9 leaflets of medium density, clustered at tops of stems. Flower — late March; small in clusters 6 inches long. Fruit — early summer; grapelike clusters.
Texture	Coarse.
Color	Foliage — bronze-green; fall, reddish-green. Flower — bright yellow. Fruit — blue.
Culture	Part shade or shade. Soil — medium drainage; medium fertility with high organic content. Moisture — medium. Pruning — heavy pruning of side branches on old or neglected plants. Pest Problems — leaf spot. Growth Rate — fairly slow.
Notes	Very dependable for use in shrub borders or as specimen. Winterburn if grown in sun. Interesting and exotic effect with contemporary structures.
Variety	**Arthur Menzies** — hybrid with *M. lomarifolia*. Spectacular upright panicles of yellow flowers in December and January. Height 4-6 feet.

Mahonia (ma-ho'ni-a)
named for McMahon, American
horticulturist

pinnata (pin-na'ta)
pinnate

CLUSTER MAHONIA

Family Berberidaceae

Size	Height 4-6 feet; spread 3 feet. Zones 6, 7, 8, 9.
Form	Thick and compact with vertical branching. Foliage — alternate, pinnately compound with 7-13 spiny leaflets. Flower — early April; terminal clusters. Fruit — summer; berry.
Texture	Medium to coarse.
Color	Foliage — dull green; winter, reddish-purple. Flower — yellow. Fruit — blue-black.
Culture	Sun to part shade. Resists cold, heat, and droughts. Soil — tolerant. Moisture — medium. Pruning — remove outer canes to promote foliage at base. Pest Problems — none. Growth Rate — slow to moderate.
Notes	Useful for border or specimen; not as limited in use as coarser textured species. Excellent vertical accent. Foliage and flowers interesting. One of few mahonias that will grow well in sun.

Myrica (mir-i'ka)
ancient Greek, possibly
name for Tamarisk

pensylvanica (pen-sel-va'nye-ca)
of Pennsylvania

NORTHERN BAYBERRY

Family Myricaceae

Size	Height 3-6 feet; spread 3-8 feet. Zones 6, 7, 8.
Form	Dense, mounded, and spreading. Foliage — alternate, leathery, oblong, 2-4 inches long, aromatic. Flower — spring; inconspicuous; sexes on separate plants. Fruit — late September, persisting through winter; ⅛ inch waxy berries on female plants.
Texture	Medium.
Color	Foliage — dark gray-green. Fruit — gray.
Culture	Sun or part shade. Soil — very tolerant. Moisture — medium to low. Pruning — tolerant. Pest Problems — none. Growth Rate — moderate.
Notes	Excellent for beach landscaping, particularly as salt wind barrier; plant 2-3 feet apart in row. May be naturalized in masses; effective in shrub borders and foundation plantings. Semi-evergreen in mountain areas. Fruit attracts birds.

Nandina (nan-dy'na)
Japanese name

domestica (do-mes'ti-ka)
domesticated, not wild

NANDINA

Family Berberidaceae

Size	Height 4-6 feet; spread 2-3 feet. Zones 7, 8, 9.
Form	Upright with many canes; becomes leggy at base unless special pruning practiced; non-branching stems. Foliage — alternate, twice or three times compound, with leaflets 1-1½ inches long. Flower — April; small and single, appearing in clusters on terminal growth. Fruit — fall and winter; terminal clusters about 12 inches long.
Texture	Medium to fine.
Color	Foliage — green; winter, greenish-maroon or red. Flower — creamy white. Fruit — red.
Culture	Sun or part shade. Soil — good drainage; medium fertility with high organic content. Moisture — medium. Pruning — light pinching of tips for compactness. Heading back of canes to varying lengths for rejuvenation of old plants. Renovation accomplished in 2 to 3 years on neglected plants. Pest Problems — none. Growth Rate — moderate.
Notes	Interesting used as facer shrub or planted in groups. Avoid placing near red brick buildings. Excellent vertical accent. Good for year-round interest.
Varieties	**Alba** — white berries. **Compacta** — height 4-5 feet; lacy foliage turns red in fall. **Fire Power** — height 18 inches; rounded form. Brilliant red non-twisting foliage. **Harbor Dwarf** — excellent graceful compact form; branches from ground to form dense mound 2-3 feet in height and spread. **Pygmaea** — reaches height of 18 inches, very few berries. Good for edging. **San Gabriel** — delicate, lacy foliage. Superior form.

Pieris (py-ee'ris)
  named for Greek muse

floribunda (flor-i-bun'da)
  free-flowering

MOUNTAIN ANDROMEDA

Family Ericaceae

Size	Height 4-6 feet; spread 4-5 feet. Zones 6, 7.
Form	Stems erect, with full rounded or oval habit. Foliage — alternate, toothed, 1-3 inches long. Flower — March and April; urn-shaped, ¼ inch long in upright terminal panicles 5 inches long. Fruit — fall; dry capsules 1/5 inch long.
Texture	Medium.
Color	Foliage — dark green; new growth, reddish green. Flower — white. Fruit — greenish-brown.
Culture	Part shade to full shade. Soil — good drainage; medium fertility with acid humus added. Moisture — medium to high. Pruning — infrequently remove older stems to encourage new growth. Pest Problems — lace bugs. Growth Rate — slow.
Notes	Hardiest of *Pieris* species to cold temperature. Flower buds formed in fall lend interest throughout winter months. Excellent as specimen or accent. Useful in foundation plantings for contemporary or traditional houses and with other evergreens in natural settings, mixed shrub borders, and groupings.
Varieties	**Grandiflora** — very large flower clusters. **Millstream** — flat-topped, mounded, slow growing form; excellent rock garden plant.

Pieris (py-ee'ris)
   named for
   Greek muse

japonica (ja-pon'i-ka)
   from Japan

JAPANESE ANDROMEDA

Family Ericaceae

Size	Height 4-6 feet; spread 4-6 feet. Zones 6, 7, 8.
Form	Upright and neat habit with stiff, spreading branches and dense rosette-like masses of foliage to ground. Foliage — alternate, in heavy whorls at ends of branches, leathery, 3 inches long. Flower — early April; terminal pendulous clusters 5 inches long, arranged to give effect of large panicles. Fruit — fall; 5-valved capsule.
Texture	Medium.
Color	Foliage — lustrous deep green; new growth rich bronze. Flower — white. Fruit — brownish.
Culture	Part shade. Soil — medium drainage; high fertility with acid humus added. Moisture — high. Pruning — dead twigs. Pest Problems — lace-bug and root rot in poorly drained soils. Growth Rate — slow.
Notes	Very beautiful and graceful early-blooming shrub. Useful among other broad-leaved evergreens, in shrub borders, or as specimen or mass. Needs morning sun for best flowering. Slow to reestablish when transplanted. Useful in city gardens. May be grown in Coastal Plain in moist cool sites.
Varieties	**Bisbee Dwarf** — glossy dark green leaves; compact, bushy plant. **Christmas Cheer** — early flowers, pink to deep pink; excellent grower. **Compacta** — small leaves, compact habit. **Crispa** — white flowers. **Dorothy Wycoff** — dark pink to red flowers; compact habit. **Flamingo** — foliage dark green; deep rose-red flowers. **Geisha** — slender leaves; white flowers. **John's Select** — compact form with dark green leaves. Red buds open to white flowers. **Mountain Fire** — new foliage bright red; flowers white. **Shojo** — dark red flowers. **Valley Rose** — deep green foliage; pastel pink flowers. **Variegata** — white margins on leaves. **Whitecaps** — long flower clusters lasting for 6 weeks. Pure white flowers. **White Cascade** — heavily flowering; pure white flowers lasting for 5 weeks.

Prunus (proo'nus)
    classical Latin name
    of plum

laurocerasus (law-ro-se-ra'sus)
    classical name of laurel

angustifolia (an-gus-ti-fo'li-a)
    narrow-leaved

NARROW-LEAVED
ENGLISH LAUREL

Family Rosaceae

Size	Height 4-6 feet; spread 5-6 feet.	Zones 6, 7, 8, 9.
Form	Low spreading with horizontal branches. Foliage — shiny and leathery; 3-4 inches long and 1 inch wide. Flower — spring; clusters. Fruit — summer; berrylike.	
Texture	Medium.	
Color	Foliage — medium green. Flower — white. Fruit — black.	
Culture	Sun or shade. Soil — tolerates acid or alkaline; good drainage; medium fertility with high organic content. Moisture — medium. Pruning — none. Pest Problems — wood borers, shothole fungus, and leaf spot. Growth Rate — moderate.	
Notes	Excellent for contemporary design. Good low growing foundation plant. Adapts well to city conditions. Often sheds foliage when transplanted.	
Variety	**P.l. Mount Vernon** — height 3-5 feet; spread 5-8 feet.	

Prunus (proo'nus)
    classical Latin name
    of plum

laurocerasus (law-ro-se-ra'sus)
    classical name of laurel

'Schipkaensis' (skip-ka-en'sis)
    of Schipka Pass,
    Bulgaria

SCHIPKA LAUREL

Family Rosaceae

Size	Height 4-5 feet; spread 5-8 feet. Zones 6, 7, 8, 9.
Form	Irregular and wide-spreading with horizontal branching. Foliage — alternate, oval and blunt pointed, 3-5½ inches long and ¾-1½ inches wide. Flower — spring; racemes 4 inches long. Fruit — summer; berrylike, ½ inch diameter.
Texture	Medium to coarse.
Color	Foliage — dark green. Flower — white. Fruit — black.
Culture	Sun or shade. Soil — tolerant; good drainage; medium fertility with high organic content. Moisture — medium. Pruning — none. Pest Problems — shothole fungus, and insects. Growth Rate — moderate.
Notes	Elegant foliage and refined appearance. Adapts to city conditions; useful as specimen, border, hedge or foundation plant. Hardy and vigorous in habit of growth.

Prunus (proo'nus)
  Latin name of plum

laurocerasus (law-ro-se-ra'sus)
  classical name of laurel

'Zabeliana'
  named for Hermann Zabel

ZABEL LAUREL

Family Rosaceae

Size	Height 4-5 feet; spread 5-8 feet.　　　　Zones 6, 7, 8, 9.
Form	Wide spreading with horizontal branching. Foliage — narrow, entire, willow-like, 1½-3½ inches long and ½-1 inch wide. Flower — April, May; ascending racemes 4 inches long. Fruit — summer; berrylike, ½ inch diameter.
Texture	Medium.
Color	Foliage — dark green. Flower — white. Fruit — black.
Culture	Sun or shade. Soil — good drainage; medium fertility with high organic content. Moisture — medium. Pruning — none. Pest Problems — shothole fungus, and insects. Growth Rate — moderate.
Notes	Elegant foliage; useful as foundation plant or specimen and as hedge or large-scale ground cover. Grows well in dense shade; adapts to city conditions.

Pyracantha (py-ra-kan'tha)
   from Greek for fire
   and thorn

coccinea (kok-sin'i-a)
   scarlet

SCARLET FIRETHORN

Family Rosaceae

Size	Height 5-6 feet; spread 6-8 feet.	Zones 6, 7, 8, 9.

Form   Upright and spreading; many trunks with thorns on branches. Foliage — alternate, 1½ inches long. Flower — early May; 1/3 inch wide in clusters. Fruit — fall and winter; ¼ inch berries in clusters distributed along branches.

Texture   Medium.

Color   Foliage — bronze-green. Flower — white. Fruit — red-orange.

Culture   Sun. Soil — medium to good drainage; medium fertility with high organic content. Moisture — medium. Pruning — shape; may be sheared for hedging. Pest Problems — scale, aphids, lacebug, scab, and fire blight. Growth Rate — moderate to rapid.

Notes   Needs 3 to 4 applications general purpose spray annually starting late March or early April. Large and showy varieties now available. Use as wall shrub, specimen, or foundation planting.

Varieties   **Aurea** — yellow fruit. **Chadwickii** — hardy form; abundant orange-red fruit. **Kasan** — outstanding for large orange-yellow berries which color in August and hold for 2 months. Leaves 1 inch long, elliptical and shiny. Spreading habit of growth. Branches to ground. Extremely cold hardy. Scab susceptible. **Lalandei** — hardy and widely grown. Orange fruit. Good for espalier. Scab susceptible. **Mohave** — hybrid with *P. koidzumii*; huge masses of orange-red berries. Resistant to scab and fire blight. Dense, upright branching.

Pyracantha (py-ra-kan'tha)
from Greek for fire
and thorn

koidzumii (kos-zu'me-i)
native name in Formosa

'Low-Dense'

LOWDENSE PYRACANTHA

Family Rosaceae

Size	Height 4-6 feet; spread 4-6 feet. Zones 7, 8, 9.
Form	Dense, mounded and twiggy. Foliage — alternate, oblanceolate, 1-1½ inches long. Flower — May; ¼ inch diameter. Fruit — fall; ¼ inch berries.
Texture	Fine.
Color	Foliage — dark green; new growth light green. Flower — white. Fruit — orange-red.
Culture	Sun. Soil — tolerant; good drainage; medium fertility. Moisture — medium. Pruning — maintain shape, remove long shoots. Pest Problems — fire blight, lacebug, and scale. Growth Rate — rapid.
Notes	Grows well in containers; useful as barrier or as cover for slopes in hot, dry areas.

Raphiolepis (raf-i-oll'ep-is)
    Greek needle scale, referring
    to bracts in inflorescence

umbellata (um-bel-lay'ta)
    with umbels

YEDDO-HAWTHORN

Family Rosaceae

Size	Height 4-6 feet; spread 6 feet. Zones 7, 8, 9.
Form	Upright and open with stout branches. Foliage — alternate, oval to almost round, leathery, 3 inches long. Flower — May; upright panicles, fragrant. Fruit — fall and winter; berries ⅜ inch diameter.
Texture	Medium to coarse.
Color	Foliage — dark green. Flower — white. Fruit — blue-black.
Culture	Sun or part shade. Soil — tolerant; medium drainage; medium fertility. Moisture — medium. Pruning — none. Pest Problems — nematodes, leaf spot, scale, and blight. Growth Rate — slow.
Notes	Inclined to legginess, may need facer shrubs to look best. Fairly drought resistant. Withstands salt spray and wind.
Varieties	**Majestic Beauty** — hybrid; resistant to leaf spot. **Springtime** — pink flowers; more vigorous growth.

Rhododendron (ro-do-den'dron)
Greek for rose and tree

carolinianum (ka-ro-lin-i-a'num)
from Carolinas

CAROLINA RHODODENDRON

Family Ericaceae

Size	Height 4-5 feet; spread 3-4 feet.	Zones 6, 7.
Form	Compact and global. Foliage — alternate, elliptic, leathery, 2-3 inches long. Flower — late April; about 1½ inches wide, fragrant.	
Texture	Medium.	
Color	Foliage — blue-green, brownish beneath. Flower — pink to white.	
Culture	Sun or part shade. Soil — very good drainage; medium fertility with high acid organic content. Moisture — medium to high. Pruning — promote denseness. Pest Problems — root rot. Growth Rate — moderate.	
Notes	Good for Western Carolina. Fine as individual specimen or in masses. Rugged and picturesque form with interesting twig structure. Pleasing but unspectacular flowering. Useful in foundation plantings and containers.	
Varieties	**album** — white flowers; popular and reliable. **Dora Amateis** — hybrid with R. *ciliatum*. Abundant white flowers lightly spotted with pale green. **lutem** — light yellow flowers.	

Rhododendron (ro-do-den'dron)
Greek for rose and tree

hybrida (hy'brid-a)
hybrid

HYBRID RHODODENDRON

Family Ericaceae

Size	Height 4-6 feet; spread 3-5 feet. Zones 6, 7, 8.
Form	Rounded or spreading depending on variety and exposure. Foliage — alternate, 3-5 inches, leathery, narrow-oblong to obovate, usually acute at tip. Flower — May; borne in trusses. Fruit — fall; capsules.
Texture	Medium to coarse.
Color	Foliage — medium to dark green. Flower — white, pink, red, purple.
Culture	Sun to part shade. Soil — very good drainage; medium fertility. Moisture — medium to high. Pruning — increase denseness. Pest Problems — root rot, lacebug, and spider mites. Growth Rate — slow to moderate.
Notes	Distinguished as specimen or in borders and foundation plantings; grows well under pines or oaks or with exposure to sun and wind. When established needs little care.
Varieties	**America** — dark red flowers. **Anna Rose Whitney** — pink flowers. Vigorous tall grower with large leaves. **Cheer** — flowers pink with conspicuous scarlet-red blotches. Compact low grower. **Chionoides** — white flowers. Low growing, bushy plant excellent for landscape use. **Doncaster** — orange-red flowers. Loose, low spreading growth. **Jean Marie De Montague** — bright red flowers and dark green foliage. Compact low grower. **Lord Roberts** — red flowers. Becomes leggy in shade. **Madame Masson** — white flowers. **Nova Zembla** — dark red flowers. Vigorous, upright growth. **Purple Splendour** — dark purple flowers with black blotch. Compact growth. **Roseum Elegans** — lavender pink flowers. Vigorous, tall grower. **Roseum Superbum** — purplish-rose flowers. Tall grower.

Siphonosmanthus (si-phon-os-man'thus)
  Greek for tube and
  osmanthus

delavayi (de-lay-vay'eye)
  named for Delavay,
  French missionary and botanist

DELAVAY TEA OLIVE

Family Oleaceae

Size	Height 4-6 feet; spread 3-5 feet. Zones 7, 8, 9.
Form	Upright, twiggy, branches arching. Foliage — opposite, toothed, ½-1 inch long. Flower — April; ½ inch long in axil of leaves, fragrant. Fruit — summer; berry ½ inch long.
Texture	Fine.
Color	Foliage — glossy, deep green. Flower — white. Fruit — blue-black.
Culture	Sun or part shade. Soil — good drainage; medium fertility with humus added. Moisture — medium. Pruning — none. Pest Problems — none. Growth Rate — slow.
Notes	Excellent specimen, accent, foundation planting, natural or sheared hedge. Attractive as espalier. Foliage handsome and fragrant flowers attractive. Excellent substitute for common boxwoood in lower Piedmont and Coastal Plain. Frequently listed as *Osmanthus delavayi*.

Taxus (tacks'us)
    classical Latin
    name of yew

cuspidata (kus-pi-day'ta)
    having sharp, stiff
    point

JAPANESE YEW

Family Taxaceae

Size	Height 4-6 feet; spread 5-7 feet. Zones 6, 7.
Form	Vase-shaped with open center. Foliage — needlelike, 1 inch long, loose. Flower — inconspicuous. Fruit — fall; ½ inch long, berrylike, on female plants, seed very poisonous.
Texture	Fine to medium.
Color	Foliage — light to dark green. Fruit — red.
Culture	Part shade or shade. Soil — tolerant; good drainage; medium fertility. Moisture — medium to high. Pruning — mid June; light shearing to maintain size. Pest Problems — spider mites. Growth Rate — slow.
Notes	Excellent shrub for hedges, screens, or foundation plantings; especially valuable for city gardens. Grows in variety of soils and tolerates poor growing conditions. Thrives in cool, moist sites.
Varieties	**Densa** — 2-3 feet in height, 6 feet in width; dark green leaves; excellent dwarf form. **Jeffrey's Pyramidal** — pyramidal form with heavy fruiting. **Nana** — smaller than species, 2-3 feet in height. **Pyramidalis** — pyramidal form with dark green leaves. **Thayerae** — wide-spreading form without open center of species.

Viburnum (vy-bur'num)
  classical Latin name
  of wayfaring tree

suspensum (sus-pen'sum)
  hung or suspended

SANDANKWA VIBURNUM

Family Caprifoliaceae

Size	Height 4-6 feet; spread 4-6 feet. Zones 8, 9.
Form	Erect shrub with arching branches. Foliage — opposite, rounded, leathery, 2-5 inches long. Flower — April; dense clusters 1½ inches wide, fragrant. Fruit — fall; drupe.
Texture	Coarse.
Color	Foliage — dark green. Flower — white tinged with rose. Fruit — red.
Culture	Sun or shade. Soil — sandy loam; medium drainage; medium fertility with high organic content. Moisture — medium to high. Pruning — none. Pest Problems — none. Growth Rate — moderate.
Notes	Excellent specimen or accent shrub. Suitable for foundation planting and shrub borders in formal or informal settings. Not hardy in mountain area.

Yucca (yuk'ka)
   Latinized version of
   Spanish vernacular for
   some other desert plant

gloriosa (glo-ri-o'sa)
   glory or climbing lily

MOUND-LILY YUCCA

Family Liliaceae

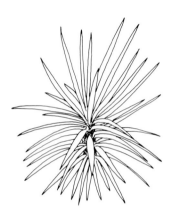

Size	Height 4-6 feet; spread 3-4 feet.	Zones 7, 8, 9.

Form   Short trunked or no trunk. Foliage — 2-2½ feet long, 2 inches wide, stiff points, smooth margin. Flower — September; 4 inches wide in large panicles on spikes of 6-8 feet, fragrant. Fruit — November and December; capsule.

Texture   Coarse.

Color   Foliage — dark green. Flower — greenish-white to reddish. Fruit — black.

Culture   Sun. Soil — good drainage; low fertility. Moisture — low. Pruning — remove dead leaves; lower leaves may be removed to form trunk. Pest Problems — none. Growth Rate — rapid after established.

Notes   Resistant to salt spray. Frequently seen grouped with smaller growing yuccas. Sharp, stiff leaves hazardous. Combines well with santolina.

Variety   **Nobilis** — improved form; dark green leaves.

SHRUBS 4-6 FEET — DECIDUOUS

Azalea (a-zay'lee-a)
   showy shrubs,
   botanically Rhododendrons

molle (mol'le)
   softly hairy

hybrida (hy'brid-a)
   hybrid

MOLLIS AZALEA

Family Ericaceae

Size	Height 3-5 feet; spread 3-5 feet. Zones 6, 7.
Form	Low spreading with well-shaped, symmetrical head resembling dwarf Rhododendron. Foliage — mid-spring to mid-fall; alternate, 2-4 inches long, white-hairy below, large and soft. Flower — early spring before leaves; large and showy, to 3½ inches, single. Fruit — late summer; dry dehiscent capsule.
Texture	Medium.
Color	Foliage — blue-green; fall, rich red or bronze. Flower — white, yellow, red, and many combinations.
Culture	Shade or part sun. Soil — good drainage; medium fertility with acid humus added; avoid manure. Moisture — high. Pruning — none. Pest Problems — spider mites, lacebug, and mildew. Growth Rate — slow.
Notes	Excellent habit and good foliage; useful in groups and mass. Not for Coastal Plain. Correct botanical name *Rhododendron molle*.
Varieties	**C.B. Van Nes** — fire-red flowers. **Dinie Metselaar** — pink flowers with faint yellow blotch; broad habit, very hardy. **Phidias** — yellow and pale pink flowers. **Red Perfection** — dark red flowers; vigorous, very hardy. **Snowdrift** — pale yellow flowers with green stripes and dots. **Speck's Brilliant** — flowers vivid red with yellow blotch; compact habit. **Susan Monyeen** — light pink flowers, blooms in mid-May. **Yellow Bouquet** — yellow flowers.

Berberis (ber'ber-iss)
Arabic name

x mentorensis (men-tor-en'sis)

MENTOR BARBERRY

Family Berberidaceae

Size	Height 4-6 feet; spread 5-7 feet. Zones 6, 7, 8.
Form	Rounded and upright with slender thorny branches. Foliage — leathery, ovate-elliptic, spiny, 1 inch long. Flower — March or April; ¼ inch diameter. Fruit — fall; berry.
Texture	Medium.
Color	Foliage — dark green; fall, yellow to red. Flower — yellow. Fruit — dull dark-red.
Culture	Sun to part shade. Soil — good drainage; medium fertility. Moisture — medium. Pruning — none. Pest Problems — none. Growth Rate — moderate to rapid.
Notes	May be evergreen in warm areas. Forms impenetrable barrier or hedge; requires no pruning or maintenance and withstands heat and drought. Attractive as foundation plant or in shrub borders.

Berberis (ber'ber-iss)
   Arabic name

thunbergii (thun-berg'ee-eye)
   named for C.P. Thunberg

JAPANESE BARBERRY

Family Berberidaceae

Size	Height 3-5 feet; spread 3-5 feet.	Zones 6, 7, 8.

Form   Globe; medium to very dense with many thorns. Foliage — alternate, simple, entire, ½-1½ inches long, without marginal teeth. Flower — mid-April; small, cup-shaped, ½ inch diameter. Fruit — fall; berry-shaped, ½ inch long. Twigs — deeply grooved with unbranched thorns.

Texture   Medium.

Color   Foliage — medium green; maroon red on red leaf varieties; fall, scarlet. Flower — creamy white. Fruit — orange-red.

Culture   Sun to part shade. Soil — tolerant; medium drainage; medium fertility. Moisture — medium. Pruning — none. Pest Problems — limited. Growth Rate — moderate.

Notes   Grows in any situation, particularly good for poor soil, shade, and exposed places. Good for use as impenetrable hedge. Tolerates exposure.

Varieties   **atropurpurea** — dark red leaves. Interesting background for pale roses. **Aurea** — vivid yellow foliage in sun; slow-growing, 3 feet in height. **Crimson Pygmy** — shrub to 1½ feet in height. Foliage red. Best color in full sun; as low hedge needs no clipping. Combines well with Shore Juniper. **Erecta** — forms excellent compact and erect hedge. **Kabold** — 2-2½ feet in height; forms perfect mound without pruning; dark green foliage; flowers and fruits sparsely produced. **Minor** — small, densely compact. **Thornless** — globe-like growth habit; mature size 4 feet by 6 feet.

Callicarpa (kal-i-kar'pa)
   from Greek for beautiful
   and fruit

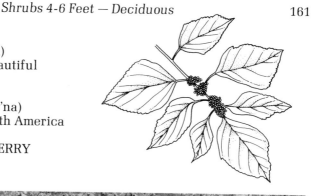

americana (a-me-ri-cay'na)
   from North or South America

AMERICAN BEAUTYBERRY

Family Verbenaceae

Size	Height 4-6 feet; spread 4-6 feet. Zones 7, 8, 9.
Form	Open and irregular with loose ascending or recurving branches. Foliage — opposite, ovate with narrow tip and toothed margins, 3-6 inches long; prominent veins; tomentose beneath. Flower — June to August; in clusters in leaf axils. Fruit — August through November; berry-like drupe ¼ inch diameter, borne in large clusters; conspicuous; berries encircle stem.
Texture	Medium to coarse.
Color	Foliage — yellow-green. Flower — blue-pink. Fruit — shiny rose-violet to purple-blue.
Culture	Sun to part shade. Soil — tolerant; medium drainage; medium fertility. Moisture — high. Pruning — cut to ground in late winter. Pest Problems — none. Growth Rate — moderate to rapid.
Notes	Best fruiting in sun. Striking planted in groups under pine trees; also useful as background for perennial beds or as specimen.
Varieties	**Lactea** — white berries; attractive foliage. **Russell Montgomery** — selection with especially effective white berries.

Callicarpa (kal-i-kar'pa)
> from Greek for beautiful
> and fruit

japonica (ja-pon'i-ka)
> from Japan

JAPANESE BEAUTYBERRY

Family Verbenaceae

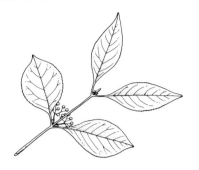

Size	Height 4-6 feet; spread 4-6 feet.	Zones 6, 7, 8.

Form   Rounded with upright and arching branches. Foliage — opposite, elliptic to ovate, finely toothed, 2-5 inches long. Flower — early July; inconspicuous. Fruit — fall; berry-like drupe ¼ inch diameter, borne on tips of new growth.

Texture   Medium.

Color   Foliage — medium green; fall, yellow. Flower — pink-white. Fruit — violet to dark purple.

Culture   Sun to part shade. Soil — medium drainage; medium fertility. Moisture — high to medium. Pruning — cut to ground in late winter. Pest Problems — none. Growth Rate — rapid.

Notes   Fruit lasts several weeks; effective planted in groups. For naturalized areas or specimen.

Varieties   **angustata** — narrow leaves. **Issai** — mounded form; violet-blue fruit in late summer and fall. **Leucocarpa** — white fruit. **Luxurians** — larger than species; large showy fruit clusters.

Chaenomeles (kee-nom'e-lees)
Greek meaning split apple

speciosa (spee-si-o'sa)
showy

FLOWERING QUINCE

Family Rosaceae

Size	Height 5-6 feet; spread 5-6 feet. Zones 6, 7, 8, 9.
Form	Semiglobe, dense. Foliage — alternate, 2-3 inches long, finely toothed. Flower — March, before leaves; 1½-2 inch diameter, single or double. Fruit — summer; applelike, 2 inches long.
Texture	Medium.
Color	Foliage — glossy green. Flower — rose-pink, scarlet, orange-red, and white. Fruit — greenish-yellow.
Culture	Sun or part shade. Soil — medium drainage; medium fertility. Moisture — medium. Pruning — annual thinning of old canes and sucker growth. Pest Problems — fire blight, scale, and aphids on new growth. Growth Rate — fairly rapid.
Notes	Splendid mass with fine foliage,showy flowers, and interesting winter color; excellent for borders,specimen, or hedges. Avoid using near orchards. Interesting espaliered. Formerly known as *C. lagenaria.*
Varieties	**Cameo** — semi-double apricot-pink flowers; few thorns. **Cardinalis** — bright red double flowers. **Jet Trail** — height and spread 1½ feet; white flowers. **Nivalis** — upright habit; pure white flowers. **Phyllis Moore** — semi-double pink flowers. **Snow** — single white flowers. **Spitfire** — red-flowered form of upright habit. **Texas Scarlet** — bright red flowers; spreading compact plant with profuse flowers. **Toyo-Nishiki** — upright habit; blends of pink, white, and dark rose flowers.

Cotoneaster (ko-to-nee-as'ter)
  Greek meaning like quince

divaricatus (di-vah-ri-kah'tus)
  spreading branches

SPREADING COTONEASTER

Family Rosaceae

Size	Height 5-6 feet; spread 6-7 feet. Zones 6, 7.
Form	Arching and spreading, multi-stemmed and heavily branched. Foliage — alternate, elliptic, acute at both ends, ¾ inch long and ½ inch wide. Flower — May; inconspicuous. Fruit — September through November; pome 1/3 inch long.
Texture	Fine.
Color	Foliage — lustrous dark green; fall, yellow, red, purple. Flower — pink. Fruit — bright red. Stem — purple to dark brown.
Culture	Sun or part shade. Soil — tolerant; good drainage; medium to low fertility. Moisture — medium to high. Pruning — very tolerant. Pest Problems — fire blight, scale, and lacebug. Growth Rate — moderate to rapid.
Notes	Blends well with other plants; excellent foliage color. Useful as hedge or foundation planting and as textural contrast with broadleaf evergreens. Often evergreen in warm areas.

Hamamelis (ham-am-ee'lis)
Greek for together and apple;
flowers and fruit are produced at
same time

vernalis (ver-nal'is)
of spring

VERNAL WITCH-HAZEL

Family Hamamelidaceae

Size	Height 4-6 feet; spread 2-3 feet. Zones 6, 7, 8.
Form	Dense with irregular horizontal branching. Foliage — alternate, 3-5 inches long. Flower — February to March; ½ inch wide with 4 petals, very fragrant. Fruit — dry capsule.
Texture	Coarse.
Color	Foliage — medium green; fall, bright yellow. Flower — yellow to red-brown. Fruit — brown with black seeds.
Culture	Sun or part shade. Soil — medium drainage; medium fertility with humus added. Moisture — medium to high. Pruning — none. Pest Problems — none. Growth Rate — rapid.
Notes	Useful for borders, low screens, and for naturalizing.
Varieties	**Carnea** — red flowers. **Lombart's Weeping** — orange-red flowers; low growing. **Squib** — yellow flowers. **Sandra** — new leaves plum-purple; fall foliage brilliant red.

Hydrangea (hy-dran'jee-a)
Greek meaning water
and jar

macrophylla (mak-ro-fil'la)
large leaf

BIGLEAF HYDRANGEA

Family Saxifragaceae

Size	Height 3-6 feet; spread 4-6 feet.	Zones 6, 7, 8, 9.

Form   Compact and rounded with crooked or erect unbranched stems. Foliage — opposite, ovate, 4-8 inches long with coarsely serrated margins. Flower — May, June; globe-shaped clusters 6-8 inches long and 4-6 inches wide. Fruit — inconspicuous.

Texture   Coarse.

Color   Foliage — lustrous medium green. Flower — pink, blue, red, lavender.

Culture   Part shade to shade. Soil — good drainage; high to medium fertility; pH of 5.0 to 5.5 for blue flowers, pH of 6.0 to 6.5 or more for pink flowers. Moisture — high. Pruning — remove old canes immediately after flowering; maintain natural form. Pest Problems — powdery mildew. Growth Rate — rapid.

Notes   Valued for flower display; particularly effective in containers or planted in mass. Excellent for coastal areas.

Varieties   **All Summer Beauty** — height 3-4 feet; cool blue flowers. **Alpengluhen** — large red flower heads. **Blue Billow** — compact growth habit to 3 feet height. Lace-cap flowers of intense blue; very hardy. **Nikko** — deep blue flowers; very hardy. **serrata Pink Lace Cap** — rare cultivar with exceptional beauty; height 3-4 feet; pure pink flowers. **Tosca** — beautiful pastel pink flower heads. **Variegated Mariesii** — height 4-5 feet; silver-edged deep green leaves; flat heads of soft blue flowers.

Hydrangea (hy-dran'jee-a)
 hardy shrubs, vines

quercifolia (quer-ki-fo'li-a)
 oaklike leaves

OAKLEAF HYDRANGEA

Family Saxifragaceae

Size	Height 4-6 feet; spread 3-5 feet. Zones 6, 7, 8, 9.
Form	Spreading and irregular in shape. Foliage — opposite, 3-8 inches long, 3-8 inches wide, 3-7 lobed. Flower — June; 4-12 inch erect panicles.
Texture	Coarse.
Color	Foliage — dark green above, light green beneath; fall, orange-red. Flower — white, purplish at maturity.
Culture	Part shade. Soil — medium drainage; high fertility with organic matter added. Moisture — high. Pruning — shape; remove old flower heads. Pest Problems — powdery mildew. Growth Rate — rapid.
Notes	Strong-textured accent or specimen for large scale gardens and parks. Excellent flowers and fall foliage color.
Varieties	**Harmony** — heavy white flower clusters, 12 inches long. **Snow Flake** — large double flowers. **Snow Queen** — large dense upright flowers.

Kerria (kerr'ia)
   named for William Kerr,
   Kew gardener and collector

japonica (ja-pon'i-ka)
   from Japan

KERRIA

Family Rosaceae

Size	Height 4-6 feet; spread 3-5 feet.	Zones 6, 7, 8, 9.

Form   Upright with slender, stems. Double flowered variety somewhat arching. Foliage — alternate, thin, 2 inches long, double-toothed. Flower — April; single, 1½-2 inches wide.

Texture   Medium.

Color   Foliage — light green; fall, yellow. Flower — yellow. Twig — green.

Culture   Sun or part shade. Single flowered varieties may fade in sun. Soil — tolerant; good drainage; medium fertility. Moisture — medium. Pruning — remove old stems and winterkilled parts. Pest Problems — Japanese beetle and leaf and twig blight. Growth Rate — moderate.

Notes   Useful in small groups in foreground of shrub border. Attractive against walls and fences that contrast in color and texture. Can be trained as vine and used in natural areas. Little care required.

Varieties **Aureo-variegata** — leaves edged with yellow, 2 inches long. **Aureo-vittata** — yellow twigs; interesting in winter landscape. **Picta** — leaves edged white; yellow flowers; good for massing. **Pleniflora** — Globe Flower. Abundant double flowers on arching branches.

Rosa (ro'za)
    old Latin name
    for rose

multiflora (mul-ti-flo'ra)
    many or profusely
    flowered

JAPANESE ROSE

Family Rosaceae

Size	Height 4-6 feet; spread 10-15 feet. Zones 6, 7, 8.
Form	Fountain with long, slender, curving branches scattered with slender prickles. Foliage — alternate, 5-9 leaflets, soft, finely wrinkled. Flower — late spring; ¾ inch in large panicles, very numerous. Fruit — summer and fall, lasting to spring; small ovoid hips ¼ inch diameter in large clusters.
Texture	Medium to fine.
Color	Foliage — bright green. Flower — white. Fruit — red. Bark — reddish.
Culture	Sun. Soil — good drainage; medium fertility. Moisture — medium. Pruning — occasionally remove old and weak wood. Pest Problems — aphids and mildew. Growth Rate — rapid.
Notes	May be used over fences and walls and on trellises but requires much space. Forms impenetrable wide hedge.
Varieties	**cathayensis** — pale pink flowers. **Inermis** — thornless branches. **Platyphylla** — deep pink flowers of various hues.

Rosa (ro'za)
old Latin name
for rose

rugosa (roo-go'sa)
rugose, rough

RUGOSE ROSE

Family Rosaceae

Size	Height 4-6 feet; spread 4-6 feet. Zones 6, 7, 8.
Form	Very sturdy with stout upright prickly stems covering ground and forming fairly dense mass. Foliage — alternate, 5-9 leaflets 1½-2 inches long, rough and thick with conspicuous veins. Flower — early summer through fall; 3½ inches wide, singly or in clusters, fragrant. Fruit — summer and fall; large, showy hips.
Texture	Medium.
Color	Foliage — bright green; fall, brilliant orange. Flower — purplish-rose to white. Fruit — orange-red.
Culture	Sun. Soil — good drainage; medium fertility. Moisture — medium. Pruning — remove old and dead branches and suckers. Pest Problems — borers. Growth Rate — rapid.
Notes	Handsome and useful in flower and shrub borders; numerous hybridizations. Especially suited for coastal and windy sites.
Varieties	**Alba** — single white flowers. **Albo-plena** — double white flowers. **Plena** — double purple flowers. **repens alba** — creeping form; excellent ground cover for coastal areas. White flowers; red fruit. **Rosea** — single Persian-rose flowers. **Rose Hips** — white flowers; fruit 1 inch long. Hardy in coastal areas, disease resistant. **Schneezwerg** — hybrid; height 4 feet; good for seaside or hedge plantings; white flowers.

Spiraea (spy'ree'a)
   Greek for wreath
   or garland

cantoniensis (kan-ton-i-en'sis)
   from China

REEVES SPIREA

Family Rosaceae

Size	Height 4-6 feet; spread 3-5 feet. Zones 6, 7, 8, 9.
Form	Upright branches flowing gracefully toward ground. Foliage — alternate, simple, 1-2½ inches long, wedge-shaped at base, deeply toothed. Flower — late May and early June; double, abundant in rounded clusters of 1-2 inch diameter.
Texture	Medium to fine.
Color	Foliage — slightly blue-green resembling S. *vanhouttei*; underside pale. Flower — pure white.
Culture	Sun or part shade. Soil — tolerant; medium drainage; medium fertility. Moisture — medium. Pruning — remove dead or injured canes. Pest Problems — aphids. Growth Rate — rapid.
Notes	Probably best spirea in Southeast. Excellent landscape plant. Easily transplanted. Use as specimen or accent plant or in shrub borders. Almost evergreen in warmer areas.
Variety	**Lanceata** — mounded with graceful, wispy, arching branches; abundant flowering; Double Reeves Spirea.

Spiraea (spy-ree'a)
    Greek for wreath
    or garland

nipponica (ni-pon'i-ka)
    of Japan

'Snow Mound'

SNOWMOUND NIPPON SPIREA

Family Rosaceae

Size	Height 4-5 feet; spread 4-5 feet. Zones 6, 7, 8.
Form	Rounded and dense with long, gracefully arching branches. Foliage — alternate, oval, ½-1½ inches long, toothed at tip with sides entire. Flower — May or June; in clusters covering upper surface of branches. Fruit — inconspicuous.
Texture	Medium to fine.
Color	Foliage — dark blue-green. Flower — white.
Culture	Sun or part shade. Soil — medium drainage; medium fertility. Moisture — medium. Pruning — none; remove old wood near ground. Pest Problems — aphids. Growth Rate — moderate.
Notes	Superior to *S. vanhouttei* in flower and foliage; withstands worst city conditions. Attractive as specimen or natural hedge. Good textural contrast in shrub borders.

Spiraea (spy-ree'a)
Greek for wreath
or garland

thunbergii (thun-berg'ee-eye)
named for C.P. Thunberg

THUNBERG SPIREA

Family Rosaceae

Size	Height 3-5 feet; spread 3-4 feet. Zones 6, 7, 8.
Form	Upright with thin branches recurving toward ground; fairly dense. Foliage — alternate, ¾-1½ inches long, linear and sharply toothed. Flower — February and March; single in profuse clusters 1-2 inches wide.
Texture	Very fine.
Color	Foliage — light yellow-green, pale beneath; fall, orange-red. Flower — white.
Culture	Sun or part shade. Soil — medium drainage; medium fertility. Moisture — medium. Pruning — annual thinning of old canes and weak growth to ground after flowering. Pest Problems — aphids. Growth Rate — rapid.
Notes	Earliest blooming of spireas. Graceful and delicate in appearance. Foliage retained until late November.
Variety	**Compacta** — height 2-4 feet.

Vaccinium (vak-sin'i-um)
    Latin for blueberry

ashei (ash'e-eye)
    named for W.W. Ashe,
    botanist

RABBITEYE BLUEBERRY

Family Ericaceae

Size	Height 4-6 feet; spread 3-5 feet.	Zones 7, 8.

Form   Globe to semiglobe with upright canes. Foliage — alternate, simple, 2-4 inches long. Flower — early spring; small but showy. Fruit — July to August; edible berries about ½ inch diameter.

Texture   Medium.

Color   Foliage — glossy green to powdery green; fall, dull green to bright red. Flower — white. Fruit — sky blue.

Culture   Sun. Soil — good drainage; medium fertility with low pH (5 or lower) and high organic matter; mulch with 4 inches sawdust, peat, or pine bark. Moisture — medium. Pruning — yearly or according to variety requirements. Pest Problems — spider mites, leafhoppers, and thrips. Growth Rate — moderate.

Notes   Excellent as informal hedge or border. Protect fruit from birds by enclosing plants. Highbush types (*V. corymbosum*) are not generally recommended for home plantings because of exacting soil requirements.

Varieties   **Bluebelle** — upright growth habit; early midseason ripening; large berries. **Brite-blue** — moderately vigorous and spreading growth habit; midseason ripening. **Delite** — upright growth habit; midseason ripening. **Southland** — compact upright growth habit; midseason to late ripening. Good ornamental qualities. **Tifblue** — midseason, large fruit; upright and vigorous. **Woodard** — early fruit; medium-sized plant.

SHRUBS 6-12 FEET — EVERGREEN

Azalea (a-zay'lee-a)
  showy shrubs, botanically
  Rhododendrons

indica (in'di-ka)
  from India

INDIAN AZALEA

Family Ericaceae

Size	Height 6-12 feet; spread 6-8 feet.	Zones 7, 8, 9.

Form   Spreading or upright depending on variety. Foliage — alternate, simple, pubescent, 1-2 inches long. Flower — late March to mid-April; 2-3 inch diameter. Stems — hairy.

Texture   Medium.

Color   Foliage — dark green. Flower — depends on variety.

Culture   Sun or shade. Soil — good drainage; medium fertility with high acid organic content. Moisture — high. Pruning — occasional thinning. Pest Problems — lacebug, spider mites, petal blight, and root rot. Growth Rate — moderate.

Notes   Best in Coastal Plain and warmer parts of Piedmont. Requires mulch. Easy to transplant. Botanically *Rhododendron indica*.

Varieties   **Fielder's White** — flowers white with faint chartreuse blotch, single, frilled, 2¾ inch diameter. Spreading growth. **Formosa** — flowers purple, single, 3 inch diameter. Upright growth. Not cold hardy in Piedmont. Excellent foliage. **George Lindley Tabor** — flowers white flushed violet-red, single, 3 inch diameter. Upright, medium height. Not cold hardy in Piedmont. **Judge Solomon** — flowers pink, single, 3 inch diameter. Upright growth. **Mrs. G.G. Gerbing** — flowers white, single, 3 inch diameter. Upright, medium height. **President Clay** — flowers orange-red, single, 2¼ inch diameter. Upright growth. **Pride of Mobile** — flowers deep rose-pink, single, 2¼ inch diameter. Upright growth. Not cold hardy in Piedmont.

Bambusa (bam-boo'sa)
    Latinized version
    of Malayan vernacular

glaucescens (gla-ses'enz)
    becoming glaucous

HEDGE BAMBOO

Family Poaceae

Size	Height 10-12 feet; spread 4-6 feet.	Zones 7, 8, 9.

Form
Slightly arching with many branches developing successively in year from crowded basal nodes of earlier branches. Foliage — alternate; 6 inches long, flat, glabrous.

Texture
Medium.

Color
Foliage — yellow-green; silver on underside. Stems — yellow-green.

Culture
Sun or shade. Soil — tolerant; medium drainage; medium fertility with organic matter added. Moisture — high. Pruning — none. Pest Problems — none. Growth Rate — rapid.

Notes
Clump bamboo which remains confined to limited area, unlike many bamboos which spread rapidly and require confinement of root system. Use in hedges, screens, and as tubbed specimen. Plant divisions only in spring, or from containers any time. Not hardy in mountain areas. Often listed as *B. multiplex*.

Varieties
Fernleaf — height 8 feet; narrow, feathery leaves. **Silverstripe Fernleaf** — white-striped fine-textured foliage.

Buxus (bucks'us)
    classical Latin
    for box

sempervirens (sem-per-vy'renz)
    evergreen

'Arborescens' (ar-bore-ress'ens)
    becoming treelike

TREE BOXWOOD

Family Buxaceae

Size	Height 8-12 feet; spread 8-10 feet. Zones 6, 7.
Form	Round and formal. Foliage — opposite, 1¼ inch, narrow and spaced well apart on twigs with leaf points forming rounded triangle. Flower — inconspicuous. Fruit — inconspicuous.
Texture	Fine.
Color	Foliage — dark green.
Culture	Part shade. Soil — fairly tolerant; medium drainage; medium fertility. Moisture — medium. Pruning — light shearing annually to promote compact growth; remove dead twigs and debris from center annually to prevent fungus growth. Pest Problems — leaf miner, nematodes, and scale insects. Growth Rate — medium.
Notes	Vigorous and hardy shrub for cooler sections. Best used as tall screen for parks or large properties. Requires little care when established except for mulching and shelter from wind and winter sun.

Callistemon (kal-iss-tee'mon)
  Greek for *kalos*, beauty, and
  stemon, stamen

citrinus (si-tri'nus)
  lemon-scented leaves

BOTTLEBRUSH

Family Myrtaceae

Size	Height 6-12 feet; spread to 8 feet. Zones 8, 9.
Form	Dense with upright branching. Foliage — alternate, simple, entire, 3 inches long, leathery, lanceolate. Flower — April to May; 2-4 inch spikes with numerous stamens 1 inch long. Fruit — woody capsule.
Texture	Fine.
Color	Foliage — medium to light green. Flower — bright red. Fruit — light brown.
Culture	Sun. Soil — tolerant; withstands drought. Moisture — low. Pruning — none. Pest Problems — none. Growth Rate — moderate.
Notes	Grown primarily for floral display. Best placed in front of evergreen background. Fruit useful in dried arrangements. In very warm areas may be trained as specimen tree. Good screening material for protected beach properties. Formerly named *C. lanceolatus*.
Varieties	**Jeffers** — upright form; height 8 feet. **splendens** — leaves linear-lanceolate; flower spikes cylindrical; dense branching.

Camellia (ka-me'li-a)
  named for
  George J. Kamel

japonica (ja-pon'i-ka)
  from Japan

CAMELLIA

Family Theaceae

Size	Height 7-12 feet; spread 5-7 feet.	Zones 7, 8, 9.

Form
Usually upright with slightly pyramidal form. Foliage — alternate, to 4 inches long. Flower — late August to May, depending on variety; 2-6 inches across.

Texture
Medium.

Color
Foliage — glossy dark green. Flower — white, pink, red, or variegated.

Culture
Part shade; plant on northern exposure if in full sun. Soil — good drainage; medium fertility with humus added. Moisture — medium. Pruning — shape. Remove faded flowers. Pest Problems — scale, dieback, and root rot. Growth Rate — rapid.

Notes
Easily grown but very formal in character, suitable as specimen in large gardens. Hundreds of varieties available. Requires protection from winter wind. Mulch. May be used as background or espalier. Subject to chlorosis from iron deficiency. Grows well in large containers.

Varieties
Bernice Boddy — flowers light pink, deep pink under petals, semidouble, 3-4 inch diameter. Vigorous compact upright growth. **Betty Sheffield Supreme** — flowers white with deep pink to red border on each petal, 3-5 inch diameter. Medium, compact growth. **Elegans** — flowers rose pink, 4-6 inch diameter. Slow, spreading growth. Very cold hardy. **Finlandia White** — flowers white, 3-4 inch diameter. Medium, compact growth. Very cold hardy. **Frau Minna Seidel** — pink double flowers; suitable for small gardens. **Imura** — semidouble white flowers; reliable. **Lady Clare** — deep pink flowers; loose, vigorous growth. **Magnoliaeflora** — blush-pink single flowers; medium and compact. **R.L. Wheeler** — flowers rose pink, 5-6 inch diameter. Vigorous, upright growth. **Vulcan** — flowers deep fiery red, 4-6 inch diameter. Vigorous, upright growth. Very cold hardy.

Camellia (ka-mee'li-a)
named for
George J. Kamel

sasanqua (sass-ann'qua)
from Japanese
vernacular name

SASANQUA CAMELLIA

Family Theaceae

Size	Height 7-12 feet; spread 5-7 feet.

Zones 7, 8, 9.

Form	Upright, columnar, compact or open and spreading. Foliage — alternate, to 2 inches long. Flower — October through January depending on variety; single or double, 2-3½ inches wide.
Texture	Medium.
Color	Foliage — lustrous dark green. Flower — depends on variety.
Culture	Sun to part shade. Soil — good drainage; low to medium fertility, slightly acid. Moisture — medium. Pruning — none. Pest Problems — scale and root rot. Growth Rate — rapid.
Notes	Excellent for informal borders, specimen, accent, and sheared or natural hedges. If not planted in shade, should be planted where morning sun does not strike foliage. Overgrown specimens may be trimmed to multi-trunk small tree.
Varieties	**Appleblossom** — flowers white edged pink, single. Upright rapid growth; excellent for tall hedges and screens. **Cleopatra** — flowers rose-pink, semidouble. Rapid compact growth, excellent for hedges. **Dauphine** — flowers pink, single. Slow, compact, upright growth; excellent for foundation planting. **Jean May** — flowers shell pink, double. **Mino-no-yuki** — flowers white, peony form. Low and spreading growth habit. Buds often killed by cold weather. **Oleifera** — flowers white with deep pink margins and crinkled petals. Rapid, erect growth. **Rosea** — flowers deep rose-pink, single. Rapid, upright growth; excellent for hedges and screens. **Yuletide** — flowers orange-red, single, small. Compact upright growth.

Camellia (ka-me'li-a)
   named for
   George J. Kamel

sinensis (sy-nen'sis)
   from China

TEA PLANT

Family Theaceae

Size	Height 6-12 feet; spread 5-7 feet.	Zones 7, 8, 9.
Form	Rounded and rather open and informal in appearance. Foliage — alternate, elliptic, 2-5 inches long and 1-2 inches wide with shallow teeth; leathery. Flower — autumn; fragrant; 1½ inches diameter, single or in 2-5 flowered clusters.	
Texture	Medium.	
Color	Foliage — glossy dark green. Flower — cream-white.	
Culture	Part shade or shade. Soil — good drainage; medium fertility with humus added. Moisture — medium. Pruning — shape. Pest Problems — scale and root rot. Growth Rate — rapid.	
Notes	For informal shrub borders, sheared or natural hedges and screens; background for herb gardens or perennial borders. Grows well in shady situations, of great value as understory shrub.	

Cleyera (clay'er-a)
   named for
   Andrew Cleyer

japonica (ja-pon'i-ka)
   from Japan

CLEYERA

Family Theaceae

Size	Height 8-10 feet; spread 5-6 feet. Zones 7, 8, 9.
Form	Upright and billowing. Foliage — alternate, 2-6 inches long, oblong, veinless, and minutely serrate at apex. Flower — spring; fragrant, about ½ inch across. Fruit — fall; globose to ovoid berry.
Texture	Medium.
Color	Foliage — glossy reddish-bronze to green. Flower — white. Fruit — red.
Culture	Part shade. Soil — very good drainage; medium to low fertility with organic matter added. Moisture — medium to high. Pruning — shape. Pest Problems — none. Growth Rate — moderate.
Notes	Hardy through Piedmont and Coastal Plain. Highly shade tolerant; withstands city conditions. Excellent for large shrub borders and screens or as specimen or patio planting when trimmed to multi-trunk tree form. Ideal for narrow places and formal or informal hedge. Excellent along coast but must be protected from salt spray. Often listed as *Eurya ochnacea*.
Variety	**variegata** — leaves thinner, bright green, variegated with golden-yellow and rose toward margins. Not as vigorous as species.

Cotoneaster (ko-to'nee-as-ter)
Greek meaning like quince

franchetii (fron-shay'tee-ee)
after Adrian Franchet,
French botanist

FRANCHET COTONEASTER

Family Rosaceae

Size	Height 6-10 feet; spread 6-8 feet.	Zones 7, 8, 9.

Form	Upright and fountain-like with arching branches. Foliage — alternate, elliptic, ¾-1½ inches long. Flower — spring; in clusters of 5-15. Fruit — fall through winter; berries ¼ inch long, abundantly produced.
Texture	Fine.
Color	Foliage — shiny gray-green, silvery beneath. Flower — white. Fruit — orange-red or red.
Culture	Sun to part shade. Soil — good drainage; medium fertility. Moisture — medium. Pruning — maintain soft arching form. Pest Problems — blight, scale, mites, lacebug occasionally; usually clean. Growth Rate — moderate.
Notes	Elegant gray foliage effect for sunny situations; graceful background shrub or hedge. Excellent evergreen cotoneaster for southern areas.
Variety	**cinerascens** — height 10-12 feet; abundant flowers and fruit.

Elaeagnus (eel-ee-ag'nus)
from Greek for olive
and chaste tree

pungens (pun'jenz)
piercing, sharp pointed

THORNY ELAEAGNUS

Family Elaeagnaceae

Size	Height 8-11 feet; spread 6-10 feet. Zones 7, 8, 9.
Form	Spreading and dense with pendulous branches. Readily trimmed to compact, ovate or globose form. Foliage — alternate, 1½-3 inches long, oblong-ovate. Flower — October; ½ inch long, inconspicuous, very fragrant. Fruit — April; elliptical, inconspicuous.
Texture	Medium.
Color	Foliage — glossy, bright green, silvery beneath. Flower — silvery-white. Fruit — rusty-brown.
Culture	Sun. Soil — very tolerant; medium drainage; low to medium fertility. Moisture — low. Pruning — tolerant. Pest Problems — spider mites during summer. Growth Rate — rapid.
Notes	Effective as large scale specimen, natural hedge, shrub border, covering on banks. One of few plants having winter flowering and spring fruiting. Gardenia scented flowers. Tolerant of many adverse conditions such as salt spray. Espaliers well against dark background. Fruit attracts birds.
Varieties	**Aurea** — leaves bordered with bright yellow. **Frederici** — small narrow leaves with yellow center bordered with thin margin of green. **Fruitland** — symmetrical in habit; leaves slightly larger than species, wavy, silvery beneath. **Maculata** — glossy leaves with yellow centers; dense form to 8 feet in height. Brilliant winter color. **Simonii** — large leaves with silvery undersides, sometimes variegated yellow and pinkish-white.

Euonymus (you-on'i-mus)
  hardy shrubs and vines

japonica (ja-pon'i-ka)
  from Japan

EVERGREEN EUONYMUS

Family Celastraceae

Size	Height 6-7 feet; spread 3-5 feet.	Zones 7, 8, 9.

Form   Compact in sun, spreading in shade. Foliage — opposite, thick, slightly serrated, 1-3 inches long, waxy. Flower — early summer; clusters, inconspicuous. Fruit — late summer and fall, often failing to develop; capsule with 4 seeds.

Texture   Medium.

Color   Foliage — dark green. Flower — white. Fruit — pink to red. Stem — green.

Culture   Sun or shade. Soil — medium drainage; medium fertility with high organic content. Moisture — medium. Pruning — none. Pest Problems — anthracnose, crown gall, leaf spots, aphids, and scale. Growth Rate — rapid.

Notes   Formerly used widely as specimen shrub and in hedges. Prevention and control of insects and disease limits desirability. Tolerates salt spray.

Varieties **Albo-marginata** — white margins on leaves. **Chollipo** — fastigiate columnar growth habit; height 12-14 feet; spread 4-5 feet. **Grandifolia** — upright; leaves large, glossy deep green. **Mediopicta** — leaves with large yellow blotch in center. **Microphylla** — small leaves. **Picta** — dwarf; leaves dark green. **Variegata** — dense; leaves small variegated with silver. **Viridi-variegata** — leaves bright green, variegated with yellow and green.

Feijoa (fy-ho'a)
   subtropical fruit;
   pineapple guava

sellowiana (sel-lo-wi-a'na)
   named for Friedrich Sello,
   German traveler in South
   America

PINEAPPLE GUAVA

Family Myrtaceae

Size	Height 10-18 feet; spread to 10 feet. Zones 8, 9.
Form	Loose and open with spreading or slightly horizontal branching. Foliage — opposite, entire, 2-3 inches long, oval-oblong. Flower — May; 1¼ inch diameter. Fruit — fall; 1-3 inches long, egg-shaped, edible.
Texture	Medium.
Color	Foliage — gray-green with silver beneath. Flower — white to reddish. Fruit — green, tinged red, turning pale yellow.
Culture	Sun. Soil — good drainage; medium fertility with humus added. Moisture — low. Pruning — maintain shape. Pest Problems — none. Growth Rate — rapid.
Notes	Valuable for loose, open appearance in screens and borders or clipped as hedge. Subject to cold damage in mountain areas and Piedmont, hardy to 10°.
Varieties	**Coolidgei** — self-fruiting selection. **Pineapple Gem** — self-fruiting selection. **Variegata** — leaves with white variegation.

Ilex (eye'lecks)
   hollies

aquifolium (a-kwi-fo'li-um)
   holly-leaved

ENGLISH HOLLY

Family Aquifoliaceae

Size	Height 8-12 feet; spread 7-12 feet.	Zones 6, 7, 8.
Form	Conical in youth, becoming more irregular and loose with age, more dense than *I. opaca*. Branches to ground. Foliage — alternate, 1½-3 inches long, wavy-margined with large triangular teeth, inclined to curl and very spiny. Flower — spring; on previous year's wood; fragrant, inconspicuous. Fruit — fall; ¼ inch globose drupes in large clusters.	
Texture	Medium.	
Color	Foliage — shiny dark green. Flower — dull-whitish. Fruit — bright red. Bark — pale gray.	
Culture	Sun or part shade. Soil — medium drainage; medium fertility. Moisture — medium. Pruning — tolerant when mature. Pest Problems — cottony cushion scale. Growth Rate — slow.	
Notes	Both male and female plants necessary for fruiting. Handsome foliage; useful as specimen, mass, or hedge in areas having moist atmosphere. Susceptible to cold injury in mountains. Foliage with long-lasting fruit excellent for Christmas decorations.	
Varieties	**Angustifolia** — small narrow leaves. **argentea marginata** — dark green leaves with silver margins; female. **Aurea Mediopicta** — leaves yellow in center with green margins; male and female. **Aurea Regina** — leaves variegated with deep golden-yellow; male. **Balkans** — glossy dark green leaves; upright habit; male and female. Hardiest English Holly. **Boulder Creek** — large glossy black-green leaves; female. Upright habit; hardy. **Hastata** — dwarf; leaves small, spines toward base; male. **Pendula** — leaves dark green, spiny; female. Weeping habit. **Scotia** — erect, densely leafy; leaves deep green, slightly twisted and spineless. **Sparkler** — free-fruiting form, sets heavy crops early. Fast-growing, upright habit.	

Ilex (eye'lecks)
  hollies

cornuta (kor-new'ta)
  horned

CHINESE HOLLY

Family Aquifoliaceae

Size	Height 8-10 feet; spread 5-7 feet. Zones 7, 8, 9.
Form	Rounded and upright with medium density. Foliage — alternate, 1½-5 inches long with 4-5 spines. Flower — inconspicuous. Fruit — late summer and fall; ⅜ inch diameter in large clusters.
Texture	Medium to slightly coarse.
Color	Foliage — medium green. Fruit — red or yellow.
Culture	Sun or part shade. Soil — medium to good drainage; medium fertility with high organic content. Moisture — medium. Pruning — sometimes needed for control of form. Pest Problems — scale. Growth Rate — moderate.
Notes	Partly self-fruitful; transplants with some degree of difficulty. Useful as hedge or massive foundation plant. Ragged appearance when sheared.
Varieties	**Berries Jubilee** — height 6-10 feet with large leaves; large fruit clusters inside foliage canopy. **Hume** — large leaves with 5 spines; female. **National** — leaves spineless except at apex; female. **Pendula** — weeping form. **Shangri-la** — spiny dark green glossy leaves; female. **Shrie-ying** — slow-growing and compact; glossy dark leaves, strongly spined. Tree form.

Ilex (eye'lecks)
  hollies

cornuta (kor-new'ta)
  horned

'Burfordii' (burr'ferd-eye)
  from Mr. Burford,
  Atlanta, Georgia

BURFORD HOLLY

Family Aquifoliaceae

Size	Height 8-15 feet; spread 6-8 feet. Zones 6, 7, 8, 9.
Form	Large, globose, dense and bushy; branches drooping. Foliage — alternate, 1½-4 inches, cupped with no or few spines, usually one on tip. Flower — inconspicuous. Fruit — fall and winter; heavily fruiting, ⅜ inch diameter berry.
Texture	Medium.
Color	Foliage — dark green with waxy sheen. Fruit — orange-red.
Culture	Sun or part shade. Soil — tolerant. Moisture — medium. Pruning — none. Pest Problems — usually none; black mildew, leaf spot, scale, and holly leaf miner occasionally. Growth Rate — rapid.
Notes	Widely used in landscaping. Excellent plant for formal and informal hedge or specimen for spacious areas and large buildings. Attractive as multi-stem small tree. Tolerates salt spray.
Variety	**O'Spring** — selection with variegated cream-colored and green foliage; new growth purple-green. Best foliage color in part shade.

Ilex (eye'lecks)
   hollies

crenata (kree-nay'ta)
   scalloped or with
   irregularly waved
   margin

JAPANESE HOLLY

Family Aquifoliaceae

Size	Height 10-12 feet; spread 3-5 feet. Zones 6, 7, 8.
Form	Semiglobular. Foliage — alternate, simple, toothed, ⅝ to 1¼ inches long. Flower — inconspicuous. Fruit — late summer and fall; stalked berries ¼ inch diameter.
Texture	Medium.
Color	Foliage — dark green. Fruit — black.
Culture	Sun or part shade. Soil — medium drainage; medium fertility with high organic content. Moisture — medium. Pruning — none. Pest Problems — scale, spider mites, and nematodes. Growth Rate — fairly slow.
Notes	Male and female plants necessary to produce berries. Suitable for screening or hedging. Dozens of variations in form and foliage from this species. Useful as background material.
Varieties	**Black Beauty** — lustrous dark green foliage; compact habit. Very cold hardy. **Buxifolia** — 12-15 feet in height; pyramidal form. **Compacta** — 5-6 feet in height; compact form. Lustrous dark green leaves. **Green Island** — loose and open shrub form; less than 5 feet in height. Spreading form to 8 feet. **Highlander** — tall, pyramidal, rather loose form to 6-8 feet in height. **latifolia** — glossy leaves 1½ inches long and ½ inch wide. Vigorous upright growth to 12-16 feet. **Petit Point** — pyramidal growth habit; very small leaves. **Sentinel** — tall upright form with glossy foliage; male.

Ilex (eye'lecks)
  hollies

glabra (glay'bra)
  smooth

INKBERRY HOLLY

Family Aquifoliaceae

Size	Height 6-9 feet; spread 4-7 feet. Zones 6, 7, 8, 9.
Form	Upright, semiglobular. Foliage — alternate, simple, entire or with few obtuse teeth toward apex, glabrous, 1-2 inches long. Flower — May; inconspicuous. Fruit — late summer and fall; ¼ inch single berries on female plants.
Texture	Medium.
Color	Foliage — lustrous dark green. Fruit — black.
Culture	Sun or shade. Soil — medium drainage; medium fertility with high organic content. Moisture — medium. Pruning — none. Pest Problems — scale. Growth Rate — slow to moderate.
Notes	Select male plants for best winter color. Native to coastal regions of Southeast. Most useful as background plant. Excellent material for naturalizing.
Varieties	**Compacta** — dwarf female clone; height 3-3½ feet; spread 3½-4 feet. Excellent foundation or informal hedge plant. May be used as filler with flowering shrubs. **Ivory Queen** — 6-8 feet in height; white fruit. **Viridis** — leaves green through winter.

Ilex (eye'lecks)
   hollies

latifolia (la-ti-fo'li-a)
   broad-leaved

LUSTERLEAF HOLLY

Family Aquifoliaceae

Size	Height 8-12 feet; spread 7-11 feet. Zones 7, 8.
Form	Dense and rounded. Foliage — alternate, 4-8 inches long, thick and leathery with serrated margins. Flower — inconspicuous; sexes separate. Fruit — fall and winter; berries 1/3 inch diameter in crowded clusters.
Texture	Coarse.
Color	Foliage — lustrous dark green. Fruit — dull red.
Culture	Part shade. Soil — good drainage; medium fertility with high organic content. Moisture — medium to high. Pruning — maintain desired size. Pest Problems — none. Growth Rate — moderate.
Notes	Handsome evergreen. Use in large scale shrub borders; excellent for industrial or park sites or as specimen or screening plant for large areas. Small tree at maturity.
Variety	**Wirt L. Winn** — excellent form and foliage color.

Ilex (eye'lecks)
   hollies

pedunculosa (pe-dunk-u-low'sa)
   stalked flowers

LONGSTALK HOLLY

Family Aquifoliaceae

Size	Height 8-15 feet; spread 6-15 feet. Zones 6, 7, 8.
Form	Multi-stemmed, rounded and pyramidal with branching to ground. Loose and graceful in form. Foliage — spineless, ovate or oblong-elliptic; 1½-3 inches long and ¾-1¼ inch wide. Flower — mid-June; inconspicuous; male and female flowers on separate plants. Fruit — early fall; ¼ inch diameter on peduncles 1½ inch long.
Texture	Medium.
Color	Foliage — glossy medium or dark green. Fruit — shiny red.
Culture	Part shade. Soil — good drainage; medium fertility with high organic content. Moisture — medium to high. Pruning — maintain desired size. Pest Problems — none. Growth Rate — moderate.
Notes	Beautiful background for witch hazel or low-growing deciduous shrubs. Excellent informal hedge or screen; may be trained as espalier. Withstands dry winds and summer heat.
Variety	**Variegata** — white variegated leaves.

Ilex (eye'lecks)
  hollies

pernyi (pern'ee-i)
  named for Paul Perny

PERNY HOLLY

Family Aquifoliaceae

Size	Height 9-12 feet; spread 4-6 feet. Zones 6, 7, 8, 9.
Form	Pyramidal outline with twigs drooping and graceful, rare for hollies. Foliage — alternate, ½-1 inch long with irregular spines. Fruit — fall and winter; clusters of berries ¼ inch diameter.
Texture	Medium.
Color	Foliage — light green. Fruit — red.
Culture	Sun or part shade. Soil — tolerant; medium drainage; medium fertility. Moisture — medium. Pruning — none. Pest Problems — none. Growth Rate — slow.
Notes	Taller growing than many shrub hollies. Valued for showy red fruit.
Varieties	**Compacta** — compact habit of growth. **veitchii** — leaves 2 inches long.

Ilex (eye'lecks)
   hollies

vomitoria (vom-i-tor'i-a)
   emetic

YAUPON HOLLY

Family Aquifoliaceae

Size	Height 5-15 feet; spread 6-12 feet.	Zones 7, 8, 9.

Form   Upright, irregular large shrub to small tree. Foliage — alternate, to 1 inch long, leathery, similar to *I. crenata*. Flower — inconspicuous, separate sexes. Fruit — fall and winter; small single berries.

Texture   Medium to fine.

Color   Foliage — gray-green. Fruit — translucent red. Bark — whitish-gray.

Culture   Sun or shade. Soil — tolerant; medium drainage; medium fertility. Moisture — medium. Pruning — may be shaped for special growth habits; picturesque with multiple trunk; tolerates shearing. Pest Problems — none. Growth Rate — slow to moderate.

Notes   Highly versatile shrub or small tree which adapts to most adverse conditions. Useful as border, screen, specimen, or barrier for large properties. May be clipped to form low or high hedge or multi-trunk small tree. Susceptible to salt burn. Fruit attracts birds.

Varieties   **Jewel** — heavy fruit production. **Otis Miley** — small leaves; yellow fruit. **Pride of Houston** — medium-sized shrub with heavy fruiting. **Wiggins' Yellow** — yellow fruit.

Ilex (eye'lecks)
   hollies

vomitoria (vom-i-tor'i-a)
   emetic

'Pendula' (pen'du-la)
   weeping

WEEPING YAUPON HOLLY

Family Aquifoliaceae

Size	Height 10-12 feet; spread 8-10 feet. Zones 7, 8, 9.
Form	Upright with straight trunk and slender pendulous branches. Foliage — alternate, narrow oval to ovate, 1 inch long. Flower — inconspicuous, male and female flowers on separate plants. Fruit — fall, winter; abundant small single berries.
Texture	Medium to fine.
Color	Foliage — gray-green. Fruit — translucent red. Stems — gray.
Culture	Sun or part shade. Soil — tolerant; medium drainage; medium to high fertility. Moisture — medium. Pruning — maintain shape. Pest Problems — none. Growth Rate — moderate.
Notes	Unique specimen or accent plant with spectacular fruit display in fall and winter. Easily transplanted; adapts to most soil conditions.
Variety	**Folsom's Weeping** — similar to 'Pendula' (Grey's Weeping).

Illicium (il-li'si-um)
   Latin for something
   enticing, in allusion
   to pleasant aroma

anisatum (a-ni-say'tum)
   anise-scented

ANISETREE

Family Magnoliaceae

Size	Height 8-12 feet; spread 8-10 feet.	Zones 7, 8, 9.

Form	Open and rounded. Foliage — alternate, 2-3 inches long, held upright, leathery and aromatic. Flower — July; 1 inch diameter, fragrant. Fruit — fall; follicles arranged in star shape.
Texture	Medium to coarse.
Color	Foliage — olive green. Flower — white. Fruit — brown.
Culture	Sun or part shade. Soil — medium drainage; high fertility. Moisture — medium to high. Pruning — none. Pest Problems — usually none. Growth Rate — moderate.
Notes	Excellent as enclosure and foundation plant for large buildings or as large specimen. Attractive form and foliage; rarely produces flowers.

Illicium (il-li'si-um)
Latin for something
enticing, in allusion
to pleasant aroma

floridanum (flo-ri-dah'num)
of Florida

FLORIDA ANISETREE

Family Magnoliaceae

Size	Height 6-10 feet; spread 5-8 feet. Zones 8, 9.
Form	Pyramidal or oval, compact and upright with many branches. Foliage — alternate, elliptic, 2-6 inches long and 1-3 inches wide, aromatic when crushed. Flower — April, May; 1-2 inches diameter with 20-30 narrow petals. Fruit — August, September; star-like follicles 1 inch diameter.
Texture	Medium to coarse.
Color	Foliage — olive green with red-purple petioles. Flower — maroon. Fruit — yellow to brown.
Culture	Sun or shade. Soil — good drainage; medium fertility with high organic content. Moisture — high. Pruning — none. Pest Problems — none. Growth Rate — moderate.
Notes	Attractive as specimen or in grouping and shrub borders. Ideal for shady natural areas; good contrast with dark needle-leaf evergreen shrubs. Begins flowering when young.
Variety	**Album** — white flowers; very hardy.

Juniperus (jew-nip'er-us)
  juniperlike

chinensis (chi-nen'sis)
  from China

'Hetzii' (het'sy)
  from proper name

HETZI JUNIPER

Family Cupressaceae

Size	Height 10-12 feet; spread 10-12 feet. Zones 6, 7, 8, 9.
Form	Upright and spreading with vertical, horizontal, and drooping branches. Foliage — scalelike, glaucous. Fruit — cones (berries) about ½ inch diameter, profuse.
Texture	Medium to fine.
Color	Foliage — blue-green. Fruit — blue-gray.
Culture	Sun. Soil — very tolerant; good drainage; medium fertility. Moisture — medium to low. Pruning — very tolerant; Pest Problems — blight, bagworms, juniper scale, and spider mites. Growth Rate — rapid.
Notes	Tolerates worst city conditions. Useful as specimen, hedge or windbreak; foliage color difficult to blend with other shrubs.
Varieties	**Hetzii Columnaris** — upright form; bright green needles. **Hetzii Glauca** — semi-erect growth habit; very dense light blue foliage.

Juniperus (jew-nip'er-us)
  juniperlike

chinensis (chi-nen'sis)
  from China

'Kaizuka' (ka-zu'ka)

HOLLYWOOD JUNIPER

Family Cupressaceae

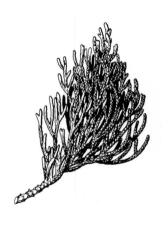

Size	Height 10-12 feet; spread 6-8 feet. Zones 6, 7, 8, 9.
Form	Loose upright branches slightly twisted; oriental effect. Foliage — scale-like.
Texture	Medium to fine.
Color	Foliage — green.
Culture	Sun. Soil — tolerant; good drainage, medium fertility. Moisture — medium to low. Pruning — clip for balance. Pest Problems — bagworms, juniper scale and spider mites. Growth Rate — rapid.
Notes	Use as specimen. Exotic in appearance. Does not mix well with other plants.

Laurus (law'rus)
   classical name
   of laurel

nobilis (no'bil-lis)
   noble, famous,
   renowned

LAUREL

Family Lauraceae

Size	Height 10-12 feet; spread 8-10 feet.	Zones 7, 8, 9.
Form	Irregular and upright. Foliage — alternate, simple, 2-4 inches long, aromatic. Flower — inconspicuous. Fruit — fall; berries ½ inch diameter.	
Texture	Medium to coarse.	
Color	Foliage — bright green. Fruit — dark green becoming black.	
Culture	Sun. Soil — good drainage; high fertility. Moisture — high. Pruning — none required but may be sheared to any desired form. Pest Problems — none. Growth Rate — moderate.	
Notes	Ancient and famous plant. Dried leaves used as seasoning; essential for herb gardens. Grows well in tubs if pruned rigorously. Often used as screen or informal hedge. Grows well in Coastal Plain and Piedmont.	
Varieties	**Angustifolia** — leaves narrowly lanceolate. **Aurea** — golden-green leaves. **Undulata** — leaf margins wavy.	

Leucothoe (lew-ko'tho-ee)
   shrubs of heath family

populifolia (pop-u-li-fo'li-a)

FLORIDA LEUCOTHOE

Family Ericaceae

Size	Height 8-12 feet; spread 6-8 feet. Zones 6, 7, 8, 9.
Form	Multi-stemmed with lax arching branches. Foliage — alternate, ovate-lanceolate, 1½-4 inches long. Flower — May; borne in axillary racemes, profuse. Fruit — fall; capsules.
Texture	Medium.
Color	Foliage — glossy rich green; new leaves tinged red. Flower — cream-white. Fruit — brown.
Culture	Part shade or shade. Soil — medium drainage; medium fertility; prefers acid loam. Moisture — high. Pruning — tolerant. Pest Problems — none; resistant to leaf spot. Growth Rate — slow.
Notes	Combines well with rhododendron and mountain laurel; gives textural contrast and natural effect in shade gardens. Very hardy; better for southern areas than *L. fontanesiana*.

Ligustrum (ly-gus'trum)
    classical Latin name
    of privet

japonicum (ja-pon'i-kum)
    from Japan

JAPANESE PRIVET

Family Oleaceae

Size	Height 6-10 feet; spread 5-6 feet.	Zones 7, 8, 9.

Form	Erect with ovate head on short trunk. Foliage — opposite, simple, entire, to 4 inches long and rather leathery with veins on underside raised. Flower — May; 4-6 inch terminal racemes of small conspicuous blossoms with very strong odor. Fruit — fall; berry about ¼ inch long, racemose, conspicuous.
Texture	Coarse.
Color	Foliage — dark green. Flower — white. Fruit — blue-black.
Culture	Sun or shade. Soil — medium drainage; medium fertility. Moisture — medium. Pruning — none. Pest Problems — white flies and scale. Growth Rate — rapid.
Notes	Good for formal or informal hedge or shrub border. Adapted to adverse conditions of drought, heat, cold, and salt spray. Effective trained as topiary. Use in foundation plantings only for large structures and sites. Excellent background material.
Varieties	**Fraseri** — new growth yellow to yellow-green, turning green with maturity. **Jack Frost** — glossy green leaves with thin cream-white margins. **Lake Tresca** — small leaves; lower branches droop to form mound. **Lusterleaf** — large, thick leaves. **Suwanee River** — compact erect branches. Cold hardy.

Ligustrum (ly-gus'trum)
   classical Latin name
   of privet

lucidum (lew'si-dum)
   bright or shining

TALL GLOSSY PRIVET

Family Oleaceae

Size	Height 8-12 feet; spread 5-10 feet. Zones 7, 8, 9.
Form	Spreading, irregular, and slightly horizontal. Foliage — opposite, simple, entire, to 6 inches long, and rather thin with veins on underside sunken. Flower — June; clusters 8-9 inches long. Fruit — fall; clusters of berries.
Texture	Coarse.
Color	Foliage — dark green. Flower — white. Fruit — dark purple-blue.
Culture	Sun or shade. Soil — medium drainage; medium fertility. Moisture — medium. Pruning — occasional corrective training for shape, avoid heavy pruning. Pest Problems — white flies and scale. Growth Rate — very rapid.
Notes	Does well in adverse conditions. Excellent as tall screen or windbreak. Mature specimens easily trimmed to multitrunk tree forms.
Varieties	**Compactum** — dense leaves of dark waxy green. **Davidson Hardy** — exceptionally hardy; excellent foliage. **Gracile** — closely spaced erect branches. **Macrophyllum** — large leaves. **Nigrifolium** — leaves very dark green. **Nobile** — branches strongly ascending, fastigiate. **Pyramidale** — narrowly conical in form. **Repandum** — narrow leaves with waxy edges. **Tricolor** — leaves variegated with white, pink when young.

Ligustrum (ly-gus'trum)
    classical Latin name
    of privet

sinense (sy-nen'se)
    from China

'Variegatum'

VARIEGATED CHINESE
PRIVET

Family Oleaceae

Size	Height 4-6 feet; spread 4-6 feet.	Zones 7, 8, 9.

Form   Upright oval. Foliage — opposite, simple, entire, 2 inches long. Flower — July; small racemes 3 inches long. Fruit — fall; berries.

Texture   Medium.

Color   Foliage — gray-green with white margins. Flower — white. Fruit — blue-black.

Culture   Sun. Soil — medium drainage; medium fertility. Moisture — medium. Pruning — none. Pest Problems — none. Growth Rate — moderate.

Notes   Good color constancy; branches reverting to green should be removed. May be used as specimen or in group plantings. Has hardiness of other privets. Good against dark background. Deciduous in cool climates.

Loropetalum (lor-o-pet'a-lum)
   Greek for strap and petal,
   in allusion to shape of
   petals

chinense (chi-nen'see)
   from China

LOROPETALUM

Family Hamamelidaceae

Size	Height 6-10 feet; spread 8-9 feet. Zones 7, 8, 9.
Form	Irregular and rounded with horizontal twigs giving flat foliage effect. Foliage — alternate, entire, 1-2 inches long, oval, with rough surface. Flower — March; feathery petals 1 inch long. Fruit — summer; woody capsule.
Texture	Medium to fine.
Color	Foliage — dark green. Flower — white or cream. Fruit — brown.
Culture	Sun or part shade. Soil — good drainage; high fertility (acid pH). Moisture — high. Pruning — none. Pest Problems — none. Growth Rate — rapid.
Notes	Showy flowers in early spring. Useful as screen, border, or foundation shrub; should be more widely planted. Excellent espaliered.

Magnolia (mag-no'li-a)
   named for Pierre Magnol

virginiana (vir-gin-i-a'na)
   from Virginia

SWEET BAY

Family Magnoliaceae

Size	Height 10-12 feet; spread 8-10 feet. Zones 6, 7, 8, 9.
Form	Rounded with irregular branching and open crown; in native areas, larger, more regular, and more dense. Foliage — alternate, simple, entire, 3-5 inches long, oblong and thick with slender petioles. Flower — early summer; terminal, like small magnolia, 2-3 inch diameter, very fragrant. Fruit — late summer or early fall; conelike, conspicuous. Bark — smooth.
Texture	Medium.
Color	Foliage — gray-green, white beneath. Flower — creamy-white. Fruit — red. Bark — yellow-gray, twig glaucous green.
Culture	Sun or part shade. Soil — low to medium drainage; high fertility. Moisture — high. Pruning — tolerant. Pest Problems — scale. Growth Rate — slow to moderate.
Notes	Native to coastal areas and sometimes reaches treelike proportions. Becomes deciduous farther north. Light and airy effect. Use against architectural or evergreen background. Not easy to transplant; move when actively beginning growth. May be trained as multi-trunk specimen.
Varieties	**australis** — large shrub or small tree; more pubescent stalks. **Havener** — large flowers with many petals. **Henry Hicks** — very cold hardy.

Michelia (me-chel'i-a)
    named for P.A. Micheli,
    Florentine botanist

figo (fy'go)

BANANA SHRUB

Family Magnoliaceae

Size	Height 6-8 feet; spread 6-8 feet. Zones 7, 8, 9.
Form	Rounded, dense, and massive; rich and refined in character. Foliage — alternate, 3 inches long, narrow-oval. Flower — April through June; magnolia-type, 1½ inch diameter, fragrant.
Texture	Medium.
Color	Foliage — glossy dark green. Flower — yellowish-white, edged with maroon.
Culture	Sun or light shade. Soil — good drainage; medium fertility in sandy loam with high organic content. Moisture — medium. Pruning — none. Pest Problems — none. Growth Rate — slow.
Notes	Handsome foliage and pleasant banana fragrance from flowers in evening. Foliage may freeze in severe winters. Needs no care after established. Choice specimen plant for Coastal Plain. Often listed as *M. fuscata*.
Variety	**Stubbs' Purple** — very fragrant purple flowers.

Myrica (mir-i'ka)
    ancient Greek,
    possibly name
    for tamarisk

cerifera (se-rif'fer-ra)
    wax-bearing

WAX-MYRTLE

Family Myricaceae

Size	Height 10-12 feet; spread 8-10 feet. Zones 7, 8, 9.
Form	Irregular. Foliage — alternate, 3 inches long, leathery, lanceolate to oblong-lanceolate, aromatic. Flower — early spring; inconspicuous. Fruit — late summer through winter; clusters of ⅛ inch globular berries covered with whitish resin; only on female plants.
Texture	Fine to medium.
Color	Foliage — yellow-green. Fruit — gray-green.
Culture	Sun or part shade. Soil — tolerant; medium drainage; medium fertility. Moisture — high. Pruning — none. Pest Problems — none. Growth Rate — rapid.
Notes	Will thrive in practically any situation. Good background material; combines well with junipers. May be used in borders or trimmed to tree-form for planter boxes. Provides good foliage texture and color contrast in borders. Plentiful in Carolina coastal area. Useful on coast but will not tolerate direct exposure to salt spray. Not for mountain areas. Fruit attracts birds.

Myrtus (mir'tus)
  ancient Greek name

communis (cahm-myoon'iss)
  growing in common or
  community

MYRTLE

Family Myrtaceae

Size	Height 5-10 feet; spread 4-7 feet.	Zones 8, 9.

Form   Open and upright. Foliage — opposite, entire, 2 inches long, aromatic. Flower — spring; ¾ inch diameter in axils; stamens prominent. Fruit — fall; berry ½ inch long.

Texture   Fine.

Color   Foliage — dark green. Flower — clear white. Fruit — blue-black.

Culture   Sun. Soil — tolerant. Moisture — medium. Pruning — withstands shearing. Pest Problems — mites, scales, and mushroom root rot. Growth Rate — moderate.

Notes   Excellent specimen or for sheared or natural hedges. Useful for foundation plantings for large buildings. Transplants poorly and is difficult to establish. Will grow in containers; abundant fragrant flowers.

Varieties   **Albocarpa** — white fruit. **Compacta** — to 3 feet in height with compact, rounded form. Excellent for edging and small specimen. Slightly more cold hardy than species. **Microphylla** — leaves overlapping and less than 1 inch long; height 2 feet. **Microphylla Variegata** — small bright green and silver-white leaves. **tarentina** — to 6 feet in height, dense and compact; narrow leaves less than 1 inch long on downy stems. White berries. **tarentina Jenny Reitenbach** — abundant flowers; white berries. **Variegata Romana** — large leaves variegated cream and green.

Nerium (neer'i-um)
   Greek name of
   oleander

oleander (oh-lee-ann'der)
   with leaves like olive

OLEANDER

Family Apocynaceae

Size	Height 7-10 feet; spread 6-9 feet. Zones 8, 9.
Form	Upright and rounded. Foliage — in whorls of 3, rarely in 4's or opposite, 5-7 inches long, narrow-oblong, leathery. Flower — spring and summer; 3 inch diameter in terminal cymes, fragrant, single or double. Fruit — summer; pods 7 inches long.
Texture	Fine to medium.
Color	Foliage — gray-green. Flower — red, pink, yellow, or white. Fruit — green turning black.
Culture	Sun. Soil — very tolerant; medium drainage; medium fertility. Moisture — medium to low. Pruning — remove old wood occasionally. Pest Problems — scale and mealybugs. Growth Rate — rapid.
Notes	Grows very well in coastal areas with little care. Showy clusters of fragrant flowers all summer; excellent as specimen and in shrub borders. Excellent tub or container plant. High salt and wind tolerance. All parts of plant very toxic. Hardy in zone 7 with heavy protection in winter.
Varieties	**Calypso** — single cherry red flowers; very hardy. **Cardinal** — single red flowers. **Compte Barthelemy** — double red flowers. **Hardy Pink** — single salmon pink flowers. **Mrs. Roeding** — double pink flowers. **Petite Pink** — single shell pink flowers; dwarf form. **Sister Agnes** — single pure white flowers. **Variegata** — leaves with cream-white margins. **Variegatum Plenum** — large double flowers and variegated leaves.

Osmanthus (oz-man'thus)
 Greek for fragrance
 and flower

x fortunei (for-too'nee-i)
 named for Robert Fortune

FORTUNE TEA OLIVE

Family Oleaceae

Size	Height 9-12 feet; spread 5-7 feet.　　　　　　　　　　　Zones 7, 8, 9.
Form	Rounded and compact. Foliage — opposite, 4 inches long, spiny. Flower — fall; very small and fragrant axillary clusters.
Texture	Medium.
Color	Foliage — dark green. Flower — white.
Culture	Sun. Soil — tolerant; medium drainage; medium fertility. Moisture — medium. Pruning — none. Pest Problems — none. Growth Rate — moderate.
Notes	Excellent in large borders and screens or as clipped hedge. May be used as formal specimen. Hybrid of *O. fragrans* and *O. heterophyllus*.
Varieties	**Aurea** — variegated foliage. **San Jose** — excellent foliage.

Osmanthus (oz-man'thus)
　　Greek for fragrance
　　and flower

fragrans (fray'granz)
　　fragrant

FRAGRANT TEA OLIVE

Family Oleaceae

Size	Height 10-12 feet; spread 10-14 feet.	Zones 7, 8, 9.

Form	Upright and rounded. Foliage — opposite, to 4 inches long, no spines. Flower — October through January; small, very sweet fragrance.
Texture	Medium.
Color	Foliage — deep green. Flower — white.
Culture	Sun or part shade. Soil — tolerant; medium drainage; medium fertility. Moisture — medium to high. Pruning — intolerant of shearing. Pest Problems — none. Growth Rate — moderate.
Notes	May become treelike in Coastal Plain. Use as large specimen near porch or walkway where delightful fragrance can be appreciated. Less hardy than O. x fortunei and may be killed to ground in Western Carolina in severe winters.
Variety	**aurantiacus** — showy yellow-orange flowers and large leaves; not as hardy as species.

Osmanthus (oz-man'thus)
    Greek for fragrance
    and flower

heterophyllus (het-er-o-fill'us)
    with variously shaped leaves

HOLLY OSMANTHUS

Family Oleaceae

Size	Height 6-10 feet; spread 3-5 feet. Zones 7, 8, 9.
Form	Upright with irregular shape. Foliage — opposite, to 2½ inches long, usually spiny. Flower — July and August; small, very fragrant.
Texture	Medium.
Color	Foliage — deep green. Flower — white.
Culture	Sun or part shade. Soil — tolerant; medium drainage; medium fertility. Moisture — medium. Pruning — none. Pest Problems — none. Growth Rate — moderate.
Notes	May be used as formal specimen or hedge. Useful as background planting. Varieties with small leaves occasionally offered. Formerly listed as *O. ilicifolius*.
Varieties	**Aureus** — leaves margined with yellow. **Gulftide** — glossy green spiny leaves; compact, upright form. **Myrtifolius** — leaves entire, some with spine-tipped apex; 1-2 inches long. **Purpureus** — mature leaves on dark green with purple tinge. Very cold hardy. **Variegatus** — white margins on leaves. Slower growing than species and more upright.

Osmanthus (oz-man'thus)
  Greek for fragrance
  and flower

heterophyllus (het-er-o-fill'us)
  with variously shaped leaves

'Rotundifolius' (ro-tun-di-fol'li-us)
  round-leaved

CURLYLEAF TEA OLIVE

Family Oleaceae

Size	Height 6-10 feet; spread to 6 feet. Zones 6, 7, 8, 9.
Form	Rounded, spreading, and irregular. Foliage — opposite, about 1 inch long, wavy margins, thick and leathery, no spines. Flower — fall; inconspicuous, very fragrant.
Texture	Medium.
Color	Foliage — dark green. Flower — white.
Culture	Sun or part shade. Soil — tolerant; prefers loam. Moisture — medium. Pruning — shape. Pest Problems — none. Growth Rate — moderate.
Notes	Excellent holly substitute. May be used as irregular hedge, specimen, or accent plant.

Photinia (fo-tin'i-a)
Greek for shining,
in allusion to glossy
leaves

x fraseri (fra'ser-i)
named for John
Fraser, English
botanist

FRASER PHOTINIA

Family Rosaceae

Size	Height 7-12 feet; spread 5-8 feet. Zones 7, 8, 9.
Form	Upright, slightly rounded. Foliage — alternate, 5 inches long, few or no teeth on margins. Flower — April; small clusters. Fruit — fall; berrylike.
Texture	Coarse.
Color	Foliage — medium to dark green; copper-red with bright red stems when immature. Flower — white. Fruit — red.
Culture	Sun. Soil — medium drainage; medium fertility with high organic content. Moisture — medium. Pruning — very tolerant. Pest Problems — none. Growth Rate — rapid.
Notes	Hybrid between *P. glabra* and *P. serrulata* having good characteristics of both parents. Resistant to mildew which disfigures *P. serrulata*. Best used for hedge in full sun or where color harmonizies. May be trained as multi-trunk specimen.

Photinia (fo-tin'i-a)
  Greek for shining
  in allusion to glossy
  leaves

glabra (glay'bra)
  smooth

RED PHOTINIA

Family Rosaceae

Size	Height 6-10 feet; spread 4-5 feet. Zones 7, 8, 9.
Form	Upright, rather loose. Foliage — alternate, to 3 inches long, smooth edged or very finely toothed. Flower — summer; flat 4 inch clusters. Fruit — fall; fleshy pea-size berries in clusters.
Texture	Medium.
Color	Foliage — young leaves, bright red; mature leaves, medium dull green. Flower — white. Fruit — red.
Culture	Sun. Soil — medium drainage; medium fertility with high organic content. Moisture — medium. Pruning — very tolerant. Pest Problems — none. Growth Rate — rapid.
Notes	Best used for hedges in full sun or where color harmonizes. Avoid placing against red brick walls.
Variety	**Rubens** — bright bronze-red young leaves.

Photinia (fo-tin'i-a)
  Greek for shining,
  in allusion to glossy
  leaves

serrulata (sir-roo-lay'ta)
  serrulate

CHINESE PHOTINIA

Family Rosaceae

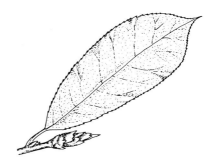

Size	Height 7-12 feet; spread 5-12 feet. Zones 7, 8.
Form	Broadly oval, occasionally becoming multiple trunked small tree. Foliage — alternate, to 8 inches long, usually with serrate edge. Flower — May; 6 inch heads on terminal growth. Fruit — late summer; clusters of berries ¼ inch in diameter.
Texture	Coarse.
Color	Foliage — green with slight maroon coloration in early spring, young foliage coppery-red. Flower — white. Fruit — red.
Culture	Sun. Soil — good drainage; medium fertility with high organic content. Moisture — low to medium. Pruning — very tolerant. Pest Problems — scale, European fruit-tip moth, leaf spot, and mildew. Growth Rate — rapid.
Notes	Limited landscape use because of color and susceptibility to mildew. Large specimen or accent plant for unlimited areas requiring mass. Container grown stock easier to transplant.
Varieties	**Aculeata** — young stems reddish; leaves more serrated than species; height 10 feet. **Nova** — height 10 feet; spread 7-8 feet.

Pittosporum (pit-o-spor'um)
Greek for pitch and seed
referring to resinous
coating of seeds

tobira (toe-by'ra)
native Japanese name

PITTOSPORUM

Family Pittosporaceae

Size	Height 8-10 feet; spread 6-9 feet. Zones 8, 9.
Form	Stiff bushy growth with interesting branching habit. Foliage — alternate, blunt, leathery, thick, to 4 inches long. Flower — April through May; about 1 inch diameter in clusters; fragrance similar to orange blossoms. Fruit — October and November; 4 angled-capsule.
Texture	Medium.
Color	Foliage — dark green. Flower — creamy-white. Fruit — brown.
Culture	Sun in Coastal Plains, requires some shade in Piedmont. Soil — good drainage; medium fertility. Moisture — medium. Pruning — may be sheared if started when young. Pest Problems — cottony cushion scale. Growth Rate — moderate to rapid.
Notes	Excellent as specimen plant or for natural or clipped hedges, screens, and planter boxes. Very popular for beach landscaping.
Varieties	**Nana** — compact spreading form; height and spread 2 feet. Grows well in containers. **Variegata** — attractive white and green leaves; smaller than the species; less hardy. **Wheeler's Dwarf** — height 3-4 feet; dark green foliage; less cold hardy than species.

Podocarpus (po-do-kar'pus)
Greek for foot and fruit,
in allusion to prominent
stalk of fruit

macrophyllus (mak-ro-fil'lus)
large-leaved

maki (mac'e)
Japanese name

PODOCARPUS

Family Podocarpaceae

Size	Height 8-10 feet; spread 3-5 feet. Zones 7, 8, 9.

Size   Height 8-10 feet; spread 3-5 feet.   Zones 7, 8, 9.

Form   Pyramidal branches upright and dense. Foliage — alternate, simple, 2-3 inches long and 1/3 inch wide, with distinct midrib. Flower — catkins. Fruit — ¼ -½ inch long.

Texture   Fine.

Color   Foliage — lustrous medium green above, paler beneath. Fruit — greenish or purplish.

Culture   Sun or shade. Soil — medium drainage; medium fertility in sandy loam. Moisture — medium to high. Pruning — easily clipped to form many different and interesting shapes. Pest Problems — none. Growth Rate — slow.

Notes   Excellent specimen, hedge, or screening material for large or small gardens. Withstands city conditions. Useful to contrast foliage and form in mixed plantings and for espalier. Particularly good for Coastal Plains; tips sometimes winter-kill in Piedmont areas.

Varieties   **P.m. angustifolius** — narrow tree with dense foliage, leaves 2-4½ inches long.
P.m. appressus — low shrub with small leaves.

Prunus (proo'nuss)
   classical Latin
   name of plum

laurocerasus (law-ro-se'ra-sus)
   classical name of laurel

ENGLISH LAUREL

Family Rosaceae

Size	Height 10-12 feet; spread 8-11 feet. Zones 6, 7, 8, 9.
Form	Upright, semiconical to slightly open. Foliage — alternate, 4-6 inches long. Flower — spring; racemes 2-5 inches long. Fruit — summer; berry-like. ¼ -½ inch diameter.
Texture	Medium to coarse.
Color	Foliage — glossy light green. Flower — white. Fruit — black.
Culture	Sun or shade. Soil — good drainage; medium fertility with high organic content. Moisture — medium. Pruning — sometimes needs training for central leader; old plants occasionally need severe renovation. Pest Problems — wood borers and leaf spot. Growth Rate — moderate.
Notes	Sometimes has scorched foliage appearance, especially in winter. Often sheds foliage when transplanted. May be used for tall hedges, wind-breaks, or foundation planting for large buildings.
Varieties	**Magnoliifolia** — large shiny leaves, very hardy. May be trained as tree form. **Variegata** — leaves marked with cream-white.

Pyracantha (py-ra-kan'tha)
   from Greek for fire
   and thorn

koidzumii (kos-zu'me-i)
   native name in Formosa

FORMOSA FIRETHORN

Family Rosaceae

Size	Height 6-10 feet; spread 6-10 feet. Zones 7, 8, 9.
Form	Dense and irregularly spreading. Foliage — alternate, 1-2 inches long, wedge-shaped with notch at tip, pubescent beneath. Flower — May; ¼ inch diameter in 1 inch clusters, fragrant. Fruit — fall; ¼ inch berries.
Texture	Medium.
Color	Foliage — grayish-green. Flower — white. Fruit — orange to dark red.
Culture	Sun or part shade. Soil — good drainage; medium fertility. Moisture — medium. Pruning — prevent legginess and train. Pest Problems — scab, fire blight, lacebug, and scale. Growth Rate — rapid.
Notes	Heavy clusters of bright red fruit in fall and winter. Hardy through Coastal Plain and warmer parts of Piedmont. Interesting as specimen, border, or screen plant. Often seen espaliered or trained on trellis.
Varieties	**San Jose** — widely spreading form, highly scab resistant. **Santa Cruz** — prostrate form; red berries, highly scab resistant. **Victory** — upright arching form; dark red berries; very showy, scab resistant. **Walderi Prostrata** — height 3-4 feet with prostrate habit of growth; large red berries. **Watereri** — height and spread 6-8 feet; dark red berries on thornless stems.

Taxus (tack'sus)
    classical Latin name
    of yew

x media (me'di-a)
    intermediate

INTERMEDIATE YEW

Family Taxaceae

Size	Height 6-12 feet; spread 8-10 feet.	Zones 6, 7.

Form   Spreading and widely pyramidal, may have central leader. Foliage —
          very narrow, needle-like, ½-1 inch long. Flower — inconspicuous;
          dioecious. Fruit — fall; fleshy aril ½ inch diameter.

Texture   Medium.

Color   Foliage — shiny dark green above, light green beneath; new growth soft
          yellow-green. Fruit — red. Bark — red-brown.

Culture   Sun or shade. Soil — good drainage essential; medium fertility.
          Moisture — high. Pruning — very tolerant. Pest Problems — spider
          mites. Growth Rate — slow.

Notes   Attractive as background contrast and as hedge, foundation or terrace
          planting. Use as bank covering; tolerant of pollution. Also named Anglo-
          japanese Yew.

Varieties **Hatfieldii** — broad pyramidal growth habit with dense branching; dark green
          foliage. Superior selection. **Hicksii** — height 20 feet; columnar growth habit; very
          hardy. **Sentinalis** — height 8 feet; spread 1½ feet; very narrow columnar form.
          Tauntonii — height 3-4 feet; spreading form. Extremely cold hardy, also grows
          well in zone 8. **Wardii** — height 6-7 feet; spread 18-20 feet; very wide-spreading
          form.

Thuja (thew'ya)
    Greek name of
    juniper

orientalis (or-i-en-tay'lis)
    Oriental, eastern

ORIENTAL ARBORVITAE

Family Cupressaceae

Size	Height 10-12 feet; spread 8-10 feet. Zones 6, 7, 8, 9.
Form	Dense and compact with slender branches growing in conical or columnar pattern; flattened branchlets held vertically. Foliage — triangular, 1/12 inch long, arranged in vertical plane on branchlet. Flower — inconspicuous. Fruit — egg-shaped cone ½-¾ inch long with 6-8 scales, each with hook.
Texture	Medium to fine.
Color	Foliage — dark green; yellow-green when young. Fruit — dull green.
Culture	Sun. Soil — tolerant; good drainage; medium fertility. Moisture — low to medium. Pruning — tolerant only when young. Pest Problems — spider mites and bagworms. Growth Rate — slow to moderate.
Notes	For screen or hedge or as background for contrasting broadleaf evergreens; too exotic in character for natural or informal areas. Occasionally useful as specimen, but becomes unsightly with age. New botanical name may be *Platycladus orientalis* or *Biota orientalis*.
Varieties	**Baker** — height 7-9 feet; broad conical form with bright pale-green foliage; hardy in hot, dry areas. **Berckmanii** — height 4-6 feet; compact and globe-shaped with golden-tipped branchlets. Slow growing. **Sieboldii** — height 4-6 feet; mounded form with dense bright green foliage.

Viburnum (vy-bur'num)
　classical Latin name
　of wayfaring tree

japonicum (ja-pon'i-kum)
　from Japan

JAPANESE VIBURNUM

Family Caprifoliaceae

Size	Height 10-12 feet; spread 8-10 feet.　　　　　　　　　Zones 8, 9.
Form	Upright with stiff branches, broader with age, multi-trunked. Foliage — opposite, ovate to rounded, 3-6 inches long and 1½-3 inches wide. Flower — spring; fragrant; ⅜ inch wide in cymes 3-4 inches wide. Fruit — late summer; oval drupe.
Texture	Coarse.
Color	Foliage — lustrous dark blue-green above, pale green beneath. Flower — white. Fruit — red.
Culture	Sun. Soil — tolerant; good drainage; medium to high fertility. Moisture — high. Pruning — tolerant. Pest Problems — none. Growth Rate — moderate to rapid.
Notes	Foliage attractive all year; excellent as screen or as mass planting. May be trained as multi-trunked specimen.

Viburnum (vy-bur'num)
  classical Latin name of
  wayfaring tree

odoratissimum (o-do-ra-tis'i-mum)
  very fragrant

SWEET VIBURNUM

Family Caprifoliaceae

Size	Height 6-10 feet; spread 5-8 feet. Zones 8, 9.
Form	Broadly oval and dense with upright stout branches. Foliage — opposite, elliptic to oval, 4-6 inches long and 2 inches wide. Flower — early spring; in pyramidal panicles 3-6 inches high; fragrant. Fruit — drupe.
Texture	Medium to coarse.
Color	Foliage — glossy bright green, pale green beneath. Flower — white. Fruit — red becoming black.
Culture	Part shade. Soil — medium to low drainage; medium to high fertility. Moisture — high. Pruning — none. Pest Problems — white fly and sooty mold. Growth Rate — rapid.
Notes	Handsome foliage for background hedge or screen; may be damaged by freezes and winter wind. Attractive trained as multi-trunk small tree.
Varieties	**Awabuki** — height 12 feet; large glossy green leaves and large flower panicles. **Nanum** — dwarf form.

Viburnum (vy-bur'num)
  classical Latin name
  of wayfaring tree

rhytidophyllum (rit-i-do-fill'um)
  wrinkle-leaved

LEATHERLEAF VIBURNUM

Family Caprifoliaceae

Size	Height 6-10 feet; spread 5-7 feet.	Zones 6, 7, 8.
Form	Upright and inclined to legginess. Foliage — opposite, entire, 3-7 inches long with prominent veins beneath. Flower — May; cymes 4-8 inch diameter. Fruit — autumn; berries ¼-½ inch long.	
Texture	Coarse.	
Color	Foliage — lustrous dark green above, rusty tomentose beneath. Flower — yellowish-white, not attractive. Fruit — red turning black.	
Culture	Shade or part shade with shelter from excessive wind exposure. Soil — medium drainage; medium fertility. Moisture — medium. Pruning — none. Pest Problems — none. Growth Rate — moderate.	
Notes	Dignified shrub of architectural character; excellent foliage and fruit. Used as specimen and foundation plant especially for narrow wall spots. Grown for interesting form and foliage texture.	
Varieties	**Allegheny** — hybrid with V. *lantana*. Abundant flowers; brilliant red fruit in September. Height 10 feet; spread 11 feet. Extremely hardy. **roseum** — pink flower buds.	

Viburnum (vy-bur'num)
   classical Latin name
   of wayfaring tree

tinus (ty'nus)
   pre-Linnean name
   for laurestinus

LAURESTINUS VIBURNUM

Family Caprifoliaceae

Size	Height 10-12 feet; spread 10-12 feet. Zones 7, 8, 9.
Form	Globe-shaped. Foliage — opposite, 2-3 inches long, shiny above, pubescent beneath on veins. Flower — early spring; fragrant cyme 2-3 inch diameter. Fruit — summer; ovoid, partially dry.
Texture	Coarse.
Color	Foliage — dark green. Flower — white to pinkish. Fruit — blue-black.
Culture	Sun or part shade. Soil — tolerant; medium drainage; medium fertility. Moisture — medium to high. Pruning — none. Pest Problems — mildew. Growth Rate — moderate.
Notes	Valuable evergreen for barrier, specimen, clipped or unclipped hedge. Bears luxuriant masses of leaves. Avoid watering in fall or planting on very fertile soils. Good background material. Often flowers in winter.
Varieties	**Eve Price** — compact form with small leaves and pink flowers. **Lucidum** — large leaves. **Strictum** — upright habit of growth. **Variegatum** — variegated leaves of green and cream-white with pink leaf-stalks.

Yucca (yuk'ka)
Latinized version of
Spanish vernacular for
some other desert plant

aloifolia (alo-i-fol'ia)
with leaves like aloe

SPANISH-BAYONET

Family Liliaceae

| Size | Height 6-15 feet; spread 4-5 feet. | Zones 8, 9. |

Form   Trunk tall, usually leaning, sometimes branched. Bottom leaves die off
           as trunk lengthens. Foliage — stiff and pointed, 2-2½ feet long, 2 inches
           wide with toothed margins. Flower — early summer; waxy, 4 inches
           wide in clusters 2 feet long, opening and fragrant at night. Fruit —
           October through December; 3½ inches long.

Texture   Coarse.

Color   Foliage — dark green. Flower — white, often tinged with purple. Fruit —
           purplish-black.

Culture   Sun or part shade. Soil — good drainage; low fertility; prefers sandy
           loam. Moisture — low. Pruning — remove dead or damaged leaves. Pest
           Problems — none. Growth Rate — moderate.

Notes   Excellent texture or form contrast against architectural features.
           Effective massed in large areas. May be used in city gardens or in pro-
           tected beach plantings. Combines well with santolina.

Varieties **draconis** — trunk branched, leaves more flexible and recurved, not as rigid as
           species. **Tricolor** — leaves white in center.

SHRUBS 6-12 FEET — DECIDUOUS

Azalea (a-zay'lee-a)
  showy shrubs, botanically
  Rhododendrons

calendulacea (ka-len-dew-lay'see-a)
  like marigold in its
  brilliant color

FLAME AZALEA

Family Ericaceae

Size	Height 8-12 feet; spread 5-8 feet.

Zones 6, 7, 8.

Form
  Loosely open with broad spreading top. Foliage — midspring to midfall; alternate, entire, 1½-3½ inches long. Flower — early May with developing leaves; 2 inches wide in large clusters, very showy, glandular pubescent outside.

Texture
  Medium.

Color
  Foliage — light green. Flower — yellow, orange, and orange-red.

Culture
  Sun to part shade; does not flower as profusely when shaded. Soil — medium drainage; medium fertility; slightly acid with 6 inch mulch of leaves or bark. Moisture — high. Pruning — tolerant. Pest Problems — usually none. Growth Rate — moderate.

Notes
  Handsome and showy native azalea. Best in woodland plantings. Good fall color. Transplants easily when dormant. Grows wild through mountainous sections. Correct botanical name is *Rhododendron calendulaceum.*

Variety
  Croceum — corolla yellow.

Azalea (a-zay'lee-a)
    showy shrubs, botanically
    Rhododendrons

hybrida (hy'brid-a)
    hybrid

'Exbury' (ecks'berry)
    named for Exbury,
    Southhampton, England

EXBURY HYBRID AZALEA

Family Ericaceae

Size	Height 6-8 feet; spread 5-7 feet. Zones 6, 7, 8.

Form   Upright and loose. Foliage — alternate, simple, entire, ½ inch wide, 2½ inches long, lanceolate. Flower — mid-April and May; 2-3 inches wide, mostly single, 6-18 in cluster.

Texture   Medium.

Color   Foliage — light green. Flower — white, cream, pink, orange, yellow, red, and intermediate colors, usually with gold blotches.

Culture   Part shade. Soil — good drainage; medium to high fertility with humus added. Moisture — high. Pruning — tolerant; shape and remove dead flowers and dead wood. Pest Problems — none. Growth Rate — moderate.

Notes   Excellent for naturalizing or in mass for color accent in spring. Effective in combination with evergreen azaleas and camellias. Often called Rothschild Azalea.

Varieties   **Attair** — pale yellow flowers with yellow blotch. **Ballerina** — white flowers. **Crimson Tide** — deep pink flowers; vigorous growth. **Fireball** — deep red flowers; reddish foliage. **Gibraltar** — vivid orange flowers; 2½ inches, diameter. **Hotspur White** — white flowers with deep yellow blotch. **Yellow Giant** — brilliant yellow flowers, 3½ inches diameter; large shrubs.

Azalea (a-zay'lee-a)
   showy shrubs, botanically
   Rhododendrons

periclymenoides (per-i-cli-men-oy'dez)

PINXTERBLOOM AZALEA

Family Ericaceae

Size	Height 5-8 feet; spread 2-6 feet. Zones 6, 7, 8.
Form	Usually low with spreading branches. Foliage — early spring to late fall; alternate, entire, 1½-3 inches long, crowded toward end of branches. Flower — mid-April; 1½ inches wide in large clusters, fragrant, corolla hairy.
Texture	Medium.
Color	Foliage — bright green above and downy, paler beneath. Flower — pink to white.
Culture	Part shade. Soil — very good drainage; medium fertility; slightly acid. Moisture — high. Pruning — tolerant. Pest Problems — usually none. Growth Rate — slow.
Notes	Native to southeastern areas. Self layering. Transplants easily when dormant. Useful in masses for naturalistic areas. Correct botanical name is *Rhododendron periclymenoides*. Previously known as *R. nudiflorum*.
Variety	**roseum** — flowers more deeply colored.

Buddleja (bud-lee'ja)
  named for Adam Buddle

davidii (da'vid-eye)
  named for Armand David

BUTTERFLY-BUSH

Family Loganiaceae

Size | Height 5-8 feet; spread 3-6 feet.   Zones 6, 7, 8, 9.

Form | Open, irregular, and rambling with arching branches. Foliage — late spring to very late fall; opposite, 6-9 inches long. Flower — July and August; spikes 5-12 inches long, fragrant, attracting butterflies. Fruit — late fall; 2-celled capsules.

Texture | Coarse.

Color | Foliage — dull green. Flower — white, pink, red, or purple. Fruit — brownish-green.

Culture | Sun. Soil — good drainage; high fertility. Moisture — low. Pruning — cut to ground in fall. Pest Problems — nematodes. Growth Rate — rapid after established.

Notes | Valued for summer flowering and usually treated as perennial. Useful scattered through large shrub borders or as accent for flower beds. Formerly named *Buddleia*.

Varieties | **Black Knight** — dark purple flowers; vigorous grower. **Charming** — pink flowers in panicles 1-2 feet long. **Dubonnet** — dark purple flowers. **Empire Blue** — deep blue flowers in panicles ½-1 foot long. **Fascination** — panicles of soft orchid pink. **Harlequin** — leaves variegated with cream-white; red-purple flowers. **Royal Red** — purple-red flowers. **White Bouquet** — white flowers. **Wilsonii** — flowers rose-lilac, spikes drooping.

Calycanthus (kal-ee-kan'thus)
　　Greek for calyx and flower,
　　referring to colored calyx

floridus (flo'ri-dus)
　　freely flowering

SWEETSHRUB

Family Calycanthaceae

Size	Height 6-9 feet; spread 5-8 feet.	Zones 6, 7, 8, 9.

Form　Coarse, rounded, often straggling and open when mature. Foliage — early spring to early fall; opposite, to 6 inches long, aromatic when crushed. Flower — mid-April after leaves; 1½ inches wide, strawberry odor. Fruit — midsummer, long persistent; fig-shaped capsule, fragrant when crushed.

Texture　Rather coarse.

Color　Foliage — yellow-green; fall, yellow. Flower — dark reddish-brown. Fruit — tan-brown.

Culture　Sun or shade. Soil — tolerant; medium drainage; medium fertility. Moisture — medium. Pruning — occasional thinning and removing of dead wood. Pest Problems — none. Growth Rate — moderate.

Notes　Native to southeastern areas. Valued for fragrance of flowers and fruit; useful in unclipped borders and moist areas. Easily transplanted.

Varieties　**Edith Wilder** — superior selection with clear strawberry fragrance. **Katherine** — rare yellow-flowered form with exceptional fragrance and dark green foliage; dense, rounded growth habit. **Purpureus** — purple leaves.

Chimonanthus (ky-mo-nan'thus)
Greek for snow and flower

praecox (pre'koks)
precocious, very early

WINTERSWEET

Family Calycanthaceae

Size	Height 10-15 feet; spread 10 feet or more.　　Zones 6, 7, 8, 9.
Form	Loose and upright. Foliage — opposite, 3-6 inches long. Flower — December on leafless branches, continues all winter; about 1 inch diameter, very fragrant.
Texture	Coarse.
Color	Foliage — lustrous rich green above, glabrous beneath; fall, clear yellow. Flower — yellow-striped with purplish-brown.
Culture	Sun to part shade. Soil — tolerant; good drainage; medium fertility. Moisture — medium. Pruning — remove old wood occasionally. Pest Problems — none. Growth Rate — slow.
Notes	Valuable for fragrant flowering and fall color in screens and borders. Flowering branches useful for floral arrangements. May be trained as multi-trunk specimen.
Varieties	**grandiflorus** — large leaves; large pure yellow flowers, less fragrant than species. **Mangetsu** — double bright yellow flowers.

Chionanthus (ki-o-nan'thus)
  Greek for snow and flower

virginicus (vir-gin'i-cus)
  from Virginia

FRINGETREE

Family Oleaceae

Size	Height 10-12 feet; spread 8-10 feet. Zones 6, 7, 8, 9.
Form	Large shrub or small tree with somewhat stiff, spreading branches, round-topped, usually taller than broad. Foliage — very late to leaf out in spring, drops in midfall; opposite, entire, to 8 inches long. Flower — early May on previous year's wood; pendulous, panicles often unisexual, 1 inch long in clusters to 8 inches long. Fruit — late summer and early fall; drupes.
Texture	Coarse.
Color	Foliage — bright green; fall, yellow. Flower — white. Fruit — dark blue.
Culture	Sun. Soil — medium drainage; medium fertility in sandy loam. Moisture — medium. Pruning — thin occasionally to stimulate new growth. Pest Problems — none. Growth Rate — slow.
Notes	Valued for fragrance and beauty of flowers; used generally as specimen; good in cities, will endure smoke and dust. Difficult to transplant, very slow to grow roots. Flowers on male plants larger and more showy, fruit only on female plants. May be trained as small tree. *C. retusus* — smaller in height (6 feet) with flower clusters 4 inches long borne on current year's wood.

Cortaderia (kor-ta-deer'ia)
from *Cortadero*, native
name in Argentina

selloana (sel-lo-a'na)
named for Friedrich Sello,
German traveler in
South America

PAMPAS GRASS

Family Poaceae

Size	Height 6-10 feet; spread to 6 feet.	Zones 7, 8, 9.
Form	Perennial grass; upright and open to upright-narrow. Foliage — 3-10 feet arching to ground, ¾inch wide. Flower — September to late October; panicles 20-36 inches long; silky and hairy.	
Texture	Fine.	
Color	Foliage — medium green; fall, beige. Flower — white.	
Culture	Sun or part shade. Soil — good drainage; medium to high fertility. Moisture — low to medium. Pruning — trim to ground yearly for new growth. Pest Problems — none. Growth Rate — rapid.	
Notes	Excellent as specimen in larger areas with flowers and foliage giving striking effect. Limited in use by large size. Use female plants for best flower display.	
Varieties	**Argenteum** — height 9-12 feet; silvery flower panicles. **Gold Band** — leaves with broad yellow stripe along outer edge. **Pumila** — dwarf form, 4-6 feet in height. **Rendatleri** — height 8-10 feet; pink flower panicles. **Rosa Feder** — height 9-12 feet; pink flower panicles. **Sunningdale Silver** — height 6-9 feet; silver-white flower panicles.	

Cotoneaster (ko-to'nee-as-ter)
  Greek meaning like quince

salicifolius (sal-is-i-fo'li-us)
  leaves like willow

floccosus (flok-ko'sus)
  woolly

WILLOWLEAF COTONEASTER

Family Rosaceae

Size	Height 7-12 feet; spread 7-12 feet. Zones 6, 7, 8.
Form	Upright branches arching gracefully. Foliage — alternate, narrow, 2-4 inches long with red veins, woolly beneath. Flower — spring; small clusters. Fruit — fall and winter; clusters of ¼ inch berries.
Texture	Medium.
Color	Foliage — dark green; fall, purple-red. Flower — white. Fruit — red.
Culture	Part shade. Soil — good drainage; medium to low fertility. Moisture — medium to high. Pruning — none. Pest Problems — fire blight, mites, scale, and lacebug. Growth Rate — slow.
Notes	Semi-evergreen in cool areas. Outstanding in form, foliage, and fruit. For parks or large gardens as specimen or background.
Varieties	**C.s. Autumn Fire** — height 2-3 feet; glossy leaves and scarlet berries. **C.s. Scarlet Leader** — fast growing low ground cover, 6-12 inches in height. Dark glossy green leaves.

Cytisus (sit'i-sus)
    Greek for some cloverlike
    plant, in allusion to
    3 leaflets

scoparius (sko-pair'i-us)
    broomlike

SCOTCH BROOM

Family Fabaceae

Size	Height 5-7 feet; spread 3-5 feet. Zones 6, 7, 8.
Form	Upright, fan-shaped, fairly open. Foliage — alternate, compound, usually 3 leaflets 1/3 inch long. Flower — late April and early May; pealike, 1 inch long. Fruit — summer; pod 1½-2 inches long. Twigs — ridged.
Texture	Fine.
Color	Foliage — medium green. Flower — yellow or pink. Twigs — green.
Culture	Sun to part shade. Soil — very tolerant; medium to good drainage; medium fertility. Moisture — medium. Pruning — remove dead wood. Pest Problems — none. Growth Rate — rapid.
Notes	Form derived from vertical twig growth rather than foliage effect; somewhat unpredictable in survival. Numerous seedlings replace old plants. Has become naturalized in spots all over Southeastern United States. Will grow on clay banks.
Varieties	**Andreanus** — yellow flowers, dark crimson wing petals. **Burkwoodii** — upright in habit; crimson flowers. **Hollandia** — height 5-6 feet, robust growth. Rose-pink flowers. **Lilac Time** — dwarf form; dark red-purple flowers. **Nova Scotia** — bright yellow flowers; very hardy. **Pink Beauty** — pink flowers. **St. Mary's** — cream white flowers.

Deutzia (doot'zi-a)
   named for Johann
   van der Deutz

scabra (skay'bra)
   rough

PRIDE OF ROCHESTER

Family Saxifragaceae

Size	Height 6-10 feet; spread 4-8 feet. Zones 6, 7, 8, 9.
Form	Tall and erect. Foliage — late spring to midfall; opposite, simple, 2 inches long, ovate, covered with minute, roughish hairs like sandpaper. Flower — late May; 1 inch diameter, double. Fruit — early fall, persisting through winter; capsules.
Texture	Coarse.
Color	Foliage — dull green; fall, yellow. Flower — white or tinged pink. Fruit — brown. Bark — dark brown, golden brown inner bark.
Culture	Sun or part shade. Soil — tolerant; good drainage; medium fertility. Moisture — medium. Pruning — not tolerant but needs occasional thinning and removal of dead wood. Pest Problems — aphids. Growth Rate — moderate.
Notes	Handsome mass useful in shrub borders or as specimen. Very showy in flower. Useful as background or accent for flower beds.
Varieties	**Candidissima** — pure white double flowers. **Mirabilis** — vigorous form with large panicles of flowers. **Pride of Rochester** — double white flowers with pink tinge. **Rosea** — flowers rose-pink. **Staphyleoides** — very large flowers in drooping panicles. **Watereri** — single white flowers, petals tinged rose outside.

Elaeagnus (eel-ee-ag'nus)
   from Greek for olive
   and chaste tree

commutata (kom-ew-tah'ta)
   changeable

SILVERBERRY

Family Elaeagnaceae

Size	Height 10-12 feet; spread 12-15 feet. Zones 6, 7, 8, 9.
Form	Erect and wide spreading with slender branches. Foliage — oval to narrowly ovate, 1½-3½ inches long and ¾-1½ inches wide, surfaces covered with silver white scales. Flower — May; tubular, ½ inch long, produced in leaf axils, fragrant. Fruit — September, October; drupe 1/3 inch long.
Texture	Medium.
Color	Foliage — silver-white. Flower — pale silver yellow. Fruit — silver-yellow.
Culture	Sun. Soil — very tolerant; medium drainage; low to medium fertility. Moisture — low. Pruning — tolerant; maintain shape and size. Pest Problems — occasional spider mites, scale. Growth Rate — rapid.
Notes	Attractive foliage for natural hedges and windbreaks; useful as accent plant in large shrub borders. Tolerant of adverse conditions and will thrive in coastal regions. Spreads by suckering to form large-scale ground cover for banks and road-cuts.

Elaeagnus (eel-ee-ag'nus)
   from Greek for olive
   and chaste tree

multiflora (mul-ti-flo'ra)
   many or profusely flowered

'Crispa' (kris'pa)
   curled

CHERRY ELAEAGNUS

Family Elaeagnaceae

Size	Height 6-10 feet; spread 6-10 feet. Zones 6, 7, 8.
Form	Wide spreading and dense with pendulous branches. Foliage — alternate, 1½-3 inches long. Flower — April-May; ½ inch long, fragrant. Fruit — June-July; scaly, ¾ inch diameter, acid flavor.
Texture	Medium.
Color	Foliage — silvery green. Flower — brownish white. Fruit — red.
Culture	Sun. Soil — very tolerant; medium drainage; low to medium fertility. Moisture — low. Pruning — control size. Pest Problems — spider mites. Growth Rate — rapid.
Notes	Good as large scale specimen. Tolerant of adverse conditions. Fruit attracts birds.

Elaeagnus (eel-ee-ag'nus)
from Greek for olive
and chaste tree

umbellata (um-bel-lay'ta)
with umbels

AUTUMN ELAEAGNUS

Family Elaeagnaceae

Size	Height 8-12 feet; spread 10-15 feet. Zones 6, 7, 8.
Form	Upright and broad-spreading branching; often multi-stemmed. Foliage — alternate, elliptic to ovate, 2-4 inches long and ¾-1½ inches wide. Flower — spring; fragrant, inconspicuous. Fruit — fall; drupe 1/3 inch long, abundantly produced.
Texture	Medium.
Color	Foliage — bright green, silvery beneath. Flower — yellow. Fruit — silver-tan becoming scarlet in fall.
Culture	Sun or shade. Soil — very tolerant; medium drainage; medium to low fertility. Moisture — low to medium. Pruning — very tolerant. Pest Problems — none. Growth Rate — rapid.
Notes	For rapid growing windbreak, hedge or screen along highways or in natural areas. Will grow near seashore; drought resistant. Withstands worst city conditions.
Varieties	**Cardinal** — profuse silver-brown berries turning bright red in fall; for large parks or highway plantings. **Jazbo** — very large red fruit in summer. **Titan** — upright form with dense branching; olive green foliage, soft gold flowers; red fruit. Excellent barrier, hedge or screen.

Euonymus (you-on'i-mus)
  hardy shrubs and vines

alatus (a-lay'tus)
  winged

WINGED EUONYMUS

Family Celastraceae

Size	Height 5-8 feet; spread 3-5 feet. Zones 6, 7, 8.
Form	Upright with horizontal branching and rugged twig structures. Foliage — opposite, 1½-3 inches long. Flower — inconspicuous. Fruit — fall, persisting; capsules opening to expose brightly colored interior.
Texture	Medium.
Color	Foliage — green, slightly mottled; fall, scarlet. Fruit — pink to scarlet. Twigs — green with corky ridges.
Culture	Sun to part shade. Soil — medium drainage; medium fertility. Moisture — medium to high. Pruning — shape and maintain density. Pest Problems — scale. Growth Rate — moderate.
Notes	Excellent for parks or industrial sites. Flamboyant coloring and rank growth limit use to large-scale properties. Grown for fall color and interesting twig structure in winter. Foliage remains green in shade.
Varieties	**Compactus** — dwarf form to 6 feet tall; corky wings not as pronounced. **Monstrosa** — very vigorous growth; spectacular fall color. **Nordine Strain** — compact with branching close to ground. Very hardy. **Rudy Haag** — 4-5 feet height and spread; excellent fall color.

Euonymus (you-on'i-mus)
hardy shrubs and vines

americanus (a-me-ri-cay'nus)
from North or
South America

STRAWBERRY-BUSH

Family Celastraceae

Size	Height 7-8 feet; spread 6-7 feet.	Zones 6, 7, 8, 9.

Form
: Spreading and irregular with rounded crown and sparse upright or trailing branches. Foliage — opposite, 1-3 inches long. Flower — May to June; ½ inch wide, inconspicuous. Fruit — early fall; capsules 1-2 inches wide with warty covering that cracks to expose seeds, pendulous.

Texture
: Medium.

Color
: Foliage — dark green; fall, bright red. Flower — reddish-green. Fruit — orange-red covering with scarlet seeds inside. Stem — green.

Culture
: Shade. Soil — good drainage; medium fertility. Moisture — medium. Pruning — shape. Pest Problems — euonymus scale and crown gall. Growth Rate — rapid if in fertile soil.

Notes
: Useful for naturalizing. Fall color and fruit interesting. Gives striking effect massed with water in foreground.

Exochorda (ecks-o-kor'da)
  Greek external cord,
  referring to internal
  structures in carpels

racemosa (ra-see-mo'sa)
  flowers in racemes

PEARLBUSH

Family Rosaceae

Size	Height 10-12 feet; spread 8-10 feet. Zones 6, 7, 8.
Form	Loose and irregular in growth, becoming open and picturesque; may become straggly; occasionally treelike. Foliage — mid-spring to midfall; alternate, simple, toothed, thin, 2 inches long, oblong-ovate. Flower — early April with leaves; buds pearl-like; loose terminal racemes, 2 inch diameter, odorless. Fruit — early summer; 5-lobed capsules.
Texture	Medium.
Color	Foliage — bluish-green. Flower — buds white, flowers white with green centers. Fruit — brown.
Culture	Sun or part shade. Soil — good drainage; medium fertility, slightly acid. Moisture — medium. Pruning — shape and maintain compact form. Pest Problems — none. Growth Rate — moderate.
Notes	Delicate appearance in bloom; attractive foliage. Grows leggy with age, requiring facer shrubs. Valuable as light mass or specimen for large areas. Sometimes difficult to transplant.

Ficus (fy'kus)
  classical Latin
  for fig

carica (kar'i-ka)
  tropical fruit

COMMON FIG TREE

Family Moraceae

Size	Height 8-12 feet; spread 8-12 feet.	Zones 8, 9.
Form	Broadly rounded with spreading low branches; multi-trunked. Foliage — alternate, orbicular, 3-5 deeply cut lobes, 4-8 inches long and wide; pubescent on both sides. Flower — within fleshy receptacle. Fruit — receptacle 1½-3 inches long (edible fruit).	
Texture	Coarse.	
Color	Foliage — dark green with lighter veins. Fruit — yellow-green to purple-brown. Bark — gray.	
Culture	Sun. Soil — good drainage; low fertility. Moisture — high to medium. Pruning — very tolerant. Pest Problems — scale, spider mites, rust, and leaf spot. Growth Rate — moderate to rapid.	
Notes	Interesting winter branching pattern. May be trained as espalier. Use at edges of plant groupings in large borders or as container specimen in protected areas.	
Varieties	**Alma** — light yellow figs; requires long, warm summer to ripen figs. **Black Jack** — very large figs; small spreading plant. Grows well in containers. **Brown Turkey** — small sweet brown-purple figs; usually produces fruit first year planted; hardy in zone 7. **Brunswick** — large red-brown figs; ornamental foliage. **Celeste** — small violet-brown figs; hardy in zone 7. **Marseilles** — large yellow-green figs; attractive espaliered.	

Forsythia (for-sith'i-a)
   named for William Forsyth

x intermedia (in-ter-mee'di-a)
   intermediate

BORDER FORSYTHIA

Family Oleaceae

Size	Height 8-10 feet; spread 7-10 feet. Zones 6, 7, 8, 9.
Form	Erect with arching branches. Foliage — midspring to late fall; opposite, 3-5 inches long, often 3-parted. Flower — early March, before leaves; 1¼ inches long, bell-like, profusely produced in clusters. Fruit — late summer, more or less persisting; dry capsule.
Texture	Medium.
Color	Foliage — deep green. Flower — yellow. Fruit — brown.
Culture	Sun. Soil — tolerant; good drainage; medium fertility. Moisture — low to medium. Pruning — tolerant (prune after flowering); thin and renew occasionally, cutting 3-year old wood at ground. Pest Problems — none. Growth Rate — rapid.
Notes	Good foliage mass but most beautiful in flower; useful as large accent, dense mass or screen, and in border with spring bulbs. Withstands city conditions. Transplants well, roots quickly. Hybrid between *F. suspensa* and *F. viridissima*.
Varieties	**Arnold Dwarf** — wide-spreading and low growing, useful as ground cover; flowers pale greenish-yellow. **Beatrix Farrand** — vivid yellow flowers, 2 inch diameter; upright growth. **Densiflora** — flowers pale, profuse; spreading habit of growth with pendulous branches. **Karl Sax** — large deep yellow flowers; very hardy. **Lynwood** — deep yellow flowers; upright in habit. **Spectabilis** — large deep yellow flowers, 2 inch diameter. **Spring Glory** — height 6 feet; pale sulphur yellow flowers covering branches.

Hamamelis (ham-am-ee'lis)
Greek for together and apple;
flowers and fruit are produced
at same time

virginiana (vir-gin-i-a'na)
from Virginia

COMMON WITCH-HAZEL

Family Hamamelidaceae

Size	Height 8-15 feet; spread 7-14 feet.	Zones 6, 7.

Size — Height 8-15 feet; spread 7-14 feet.   Zones 6, 7.

Form — Round to vase-shaped with open horizontal branching. Foliage — alternate, 4-6 inches long. Flower — October to November; ¾ inch wide with 4 petals, fragrant. Fruit — December; dry capsule.

Texture — Coarse.

Color — Foliage — medium green; fall, golden yellow. Flower — bright yellow. Fruit — brown with black seeds.

Culture — Sun to shade. Soil — medium drainage; low to medium fertility with humus added. Moisture — medium to high. Pruning — none. Pest Problems — galls. Growth Rate — moderate to rapid.

Notes — Excellent for naturalizing in shady areas. Blooms after leaves have fallen. Most useful for large estates and parks. May be trained as multi-trunk specimen.

Hibiscus (hi-bis'kus)
   Greek name for mallow

syriacus (si-ree-ah'kus)
   of Syria

ROSE OF SHARON

Family Malvaceae

Size	Height 8-12 feet; spread 6-8 feet.	Zones 6, 7, 8, 9.

Form   Erect and stately with upright branches. Foliage — alternate, 3-lobed, ovate, 2-4 inches long, usually coarsely toothed. Flower — July-September; 2-4 inches wide with 5 petals. Fruit — winter; 5-valved capsule.

Texture   Medium.

Color   Foliage — lustrous medium green. Flower — white, pink, red, lavender, or blue. Fruit — gray-brown.

Culture   Sun to part shade. Soil — good drainage; medium fertility. Moisture — high to medium. Pruning — shape heavily in winter, blooms on new growth. Pest Problems — aphids, leaf spot. Growth Rate — moderate to rapid.

Notes   Valuable for screening, hedges, shrub borders, and in parks and street plantings. Grows well in containers and as espaliered small tree with careful pruning. Blooms almost all summer. Tolerates poor soil conditions.

Varieties   **Blue Bird** — large azure blue flowers. **Diana** — dense branching and compact, graceful form; glossy green foliage. Abundant large single white flowers 6 inches diameter, remaining open at night; usually seedless. **Hamabo** — large single flowers, white with red stripes. **Helene** — large white flowers with red eye; usually seedless. **Paeoniflora** — excellent double pale pink flowers from June to September. **Woodbridge** — large rose-pink flowers summer to fall.

Hydrangea (hy-dran'ji-a)
   hardy shrubs, vines

paniculata (pan-ick-kew-lay'ta)
   compound raceme

'Grandiflora' (gran-di-flo'ra)
   large or showy flowered

PEEGEE HYDRANGEA

Family Saxifragaceae

Size	Height 8-20 feet; spread 6-8 feet. Zones 6, 7, 8.
Form	Rounded, loose; occasionally treelike. Foliage — opposite, oval, 3-5 inches long with toothed margin. Flower — July; small in pyramidal clusters to 12 inches; most florets sterile. Fruit — usually none.
Texture	Coarse.
Color	Foliage — medium green. Flower — white, turning pink at maturity.
Culture	Part shade. Soil — tolerant. Moisture — medium. Pruning — cut back old wood in late winter or early spring to encourage shrubby form and flowering. Pest Problems — powdery mildew. Growth Rate — rapid.
Notes	Grows well in seaside gardens; tolerant of city conditions. May be trimmed to form small tree.
Varieties	**H.p. Praecox** — height 10-15 feet; flowers in June; hardier than 'Grandiflora'. **H.p. Tardiva** — flowers in August and September.

Ilex (eye'lecks)
   hollies

decidua (de-sid'ua)
   deciduous

POSSUMHAW

Family Aquifoliaceae

Size	Height 10-15 feet; spread 7-10 feet.	Zones 6, 7, 8, 9.

Form   Multi-trunked with spreading horizontal branching. Foliage — alternate, obovate, 1½-3 inches long and ½-¾ inch wide. Flower — spring; inconspicuous, male and female flowers on separate plants. Fruit — September to March; berry-like drupe, ⅜ inch diameter, singly and in clusters.

Texture Medium.

Color   Foliage — lustrous dark green; fall, yellow. Flower — white. Fruit — bright orange-red. Bark — light gray.

Culture Sun to part shade. Soil — very tolerant; medium drainage; medium fertility. Moisture — medium to high. Pruning — none. Pest Problems — none. Growth Rate — slow to moderate.

Notes   Ideal patio specimen, useful as screen or border filler. Attractive berries persist all winter. Good for naturalizing.

Varieties **Byer's Golden** — yellow fruit; dark green foliage. **Council Fire** — tolerant of wide variety of soil conditions; bright red berries. Height 7-12 feet. **Pocohantas** — height 7-12 feet; tolerant of most soil conditions; red berries. **Warren's Red** — height 7-12 feet; shiny dark green foliage; fall color yellow. Abundant scarlet berries.

Ilex (eye'lecks)
  hollies

verticillata (ver-ti-si-la'ta)
  in circles around stem

WINTERBERRY

Family Aquifoliaceae

Size	Height 6-12 feet; spread 6-10 feet. Zones 6, 7, 8, 9.
Form	Oval or round with dense twiggy branching. Foliage — alternate, elliptic to oblong-lanceolate, 1½-3 inches long and ½-1 inch wide. Flower — spring; inconspicuous, male and female flowers on separate plants. Fruit — September to January; berry-like drupe, ¼-1/3 inch diameter; profuse, in clusters on upright stems.
Texture	Medium.
Color	Foliage — deep green. Flower — white. Fruit — brilliant red. Stems — black.
Culture	Sun to part shade. Soil — low to medium drainage; medium fertility; add organic matter; prefers acid pH. Moisture — high to medium. Pruning — tolerant. Pest Problems — none. Growth Rate — slow.
Notes	For shrub borders and wet soils; particularly attractive in groups in winter. May be trained as multi-trunk specimen.
Varieties	**Chrysocarpa** — yellow berries. **Jolly Red** — large red berries. **Red Sprite** — height 3-4 feet; compact growth habit; showy red berries. **Sparkleberry** — hybrid with *I. serrata*; height 10-12 feet; multi-stemmed with abundant bright red berries. **Winter Red** — height 8 feet; spread 10 feet; dark green foliage; fall, golden yellow. Large and abundant red berries.

Kolkwitzia (kolk-wit'zi-a)
  named for Richard Kolkwitz

amabilis (a-mab'i-lis)
  lovely

BEAUTYBUSH

Family Caprifoliaceae

Size	Height 6-7 feet; spread 6-8 feet.	Zones 6, 7, 8.
Form	Erect, vase-shaped, rather dense, broader than tall, branching to ground. Foliage — midspring to midfall; opposite, 2-3 inches long, ovate, shallowly toothed. Flower — early May; on short growth of current season; ½ inch long, in profuse clusters. Fruit — summer; dry capsule.	
Texture	Medium to fine.	
Color	Foliage — gray-green; fall, reddish. Flower — pink with yellow throat. Fruit — brown.	
Culture	Sun. Soil — tolerant; good drainage; medium fertility. Moisture — medium. Pruning — during first years pinch back to thicken growth. Pest Problems — none. Growth Rate — slow.	
Notes	Good mass when properly maintained, otherwise loose and open; useful in shrub borders. Transplants poorly, slow to re-establish.	
Variety	**Rosea (Pink Cloud)** — large and abundant pink flowers.	

Lonicera (lon-iss'er-ra)
honeysuckles

fragrantissima (fray-gran-tiss'i-ma)
very fragrant

WINTER HONEYSUCKLE

Family Caprifoliaceae

Size	Height 6-8 feet; spread 6-8 feet. Zones 6, 7, 8.
Form	Globe-shaped with arching branches; medium to heavy density. Foliage — opposite, simple, entire, 1-2 inches long, thick, leathery. Flower — January to early March; ½ inch long, bell-shaped, fragrant. Fruit — summer; small berry, inconspicuous.
Texture	Medium.
Color	Foliage — blue-green. Flower — creamy white. Fruit — red.
Culture	Sun or shade. Soil — medium drainage; medium fertility. Moisture — medium. Pruning — cut oldest branches to ground every 2 or 3 years for density and shape. Pest Problems — none. Growth Rate — rapid.
Notes	Very good for light screening and background. Flowers extremely fragrant. Easily transplanted.

Magnolia (mag-no'li-a)
   named for Pierre Magnol

stellata (stell-lay'ta)
   starlike

STAR MAGNOLIA

Family Magnoliaceae

Size	Height 10-12 feet; spread 8-10 feet. Zones 6, 7, 8.
Form	Broad and rounded mass becoming treelike with age. Foliage — late spring to early fall; alternate, simple, entire, leathery, 2-4 inches long. Flower — March before leaves appear; 3 inch diameter, fragrant. Fruit — autumn, not very persistant; 2 inches long, podlike, colorful. Bark — smooth with buds and branches densely hairy.
Texture	Coarse.
Color	Foliage — deep green; fall, bronze. Flower — white. Fruit — rosy-red.
Culture	Sun; cannot compete with tree roots and will not tolerate shade. Soil — good drainage; high fertility. Moisture — high. Pruning — not tolerant. Pest Problems — scale. Growth Rate — slow.
Notes	Very handsome specimen shrub for lawns and gardens; best with darker background to set off bloom. Blooms may be killed by frost. Difficult to transplant; move only when in active growth. Water through summer after moving.
Varieties	**Centennial** — open flower of 5 inch diameter, petals pink tinged on outside. **rosea** — pink flower buds, flower 4 inch diameter, pale pink fading to white. Pink Star Magnolia. **Royal Star** — fragrant pure white flowers; bronze fall foliage. **Waterlily** — upright habit of growth; fragrant pink flowers.

Malus (may'lus)
  ancient Latin
  name for apple

sargentii (sar-jent'ee-eye)
  named for C.S. Sargent,
  first director of
  Arnold Arboretum

SARGENT CRAB APPLE

Family Rosaceae

Size	Height 6-8 feet; spread 8-10 feet. Zones 6, 7.
Form	Irregularly rounded. Foliage — alternate, dense, 2-3 inches long. Flower — April and May with new leaves; ½-1 inch wide in clusters of 5 or 6. Fruit — fall; clusters of berrylike apples ½ inch diameter.
Texture	Medium.
Color	Foliage — dark green; fall, yellow-orange. Flower — white. Fruit — dark red.
Culture	Sun. Soil — tolerant in cool areas. Moisture — medium to low. Pruning — remove all understock sprouts. Pest Problems — fire blight, scab and borers. Growth Rate — moderate to slow.
Notes	Best flowering on mature plants. For large areas as specimen or border.
Varieties	**rosea** — red flower buds, flowers pink fading to white, 1½ inch diameter. **Roseglow** — height 6-8 feet with dense branching; fragrant white flowers, small dark red fruit.

Philadelphus (fil-a-del'fus)
  Greek name,
  deciduous shrubs

coronarius (kor-o-na'ri-us)
  crown or garland

SWEET MOCKORANGE

Family Saxifragraceae

Size	Height 10-12 feet; spread 10-12 feet. Zones 6, 7, 8.
Form	Dense, upright, older branches arching to ground; vigorous growth; extensive root system. Foliage — opposite, ovate, 1½-4 inches long and ¾-2 inches wide. Flower — May, June; 1-1½ inches wide in 5-7 flowered racemes, very fragrant. Fruit — ⅛-¼ inch, round.
Texture	Coarse.
Color	Foliage — medium green. Flower — cream-white. Fruit — green to black. Bark — orange-brown, peeling.
Culture	Sun or part shade. Soil — very tolerant; good drainage; medium fertility. Moisture — medium to high. Pruning — thin and shape; remove old wood. Pest Problems — none. Growth Rate — rapid.
Notes	Grown for exceptionally fragrant flowers; useful as filler in large shrub borders and woodland. Will thrive in most difficult situations; combines well with needleleaf evergreens.
Varieties	**Duplex** — dwarf form. **Variegatus** — height 5 feet; leaves with white and cream markings; very fragrant white flowers.

Poncirus (pon-si'rus)
  from French name of
  kind of citron

trifoliata (tri-fo-lee-ah'ta)
  with three leaves (leaflets)
  from China

HARDY ORANGE

Family Rutaceae

Size	Height 10-15 feet; spread 8-12 feet. Zones 6, 7, 8, 9.
Form	Irregular and rounded mound, dense, low branching; stems with heavy thorns 4 inches long. Foliage — alternate, 3 oval leaflets each 2 inches long. Flower — April, before leaves; 2 inches diameter, fragrant. Fruit — September; modified berry 1-3 inches diameter.
Texture	Medium.
Color	Foliage — glossy dark green; fall, yellow. Flower — white. Fruit — yellow-orange. Stems — bright green.
Culture	Sun. Soil — good drainage; medium fertility; prefers acid pH. Moisture — medium. Pruning — very tolerant. Pest Problems — none. Growth Rate — slow to moderate.
Notes	Vigorous and ornamental in all seasons. Will grow in dry, infertile soils. Interesting as specimen or espalier; forms impenetrable barrier and hedge with vicious thorns. Best fruiting when planted in groups. Combines well with yew or dark green evergreen plants.
Variety	**Flying Dragon** — twisting stems and sharply curved thorns; white flowers.

Rhododendron (ro-do-den'dron)
  Greek for rose and tree

prunifolium (pru-ni-fo'li-um)
  with cherrylike leaves

PLUMLEAF AZALEA

Family Ericaceae

Size	Height 6-10 feet; spread 5-8 feet.	Zones 6, 7, 8, 9.

Size   Height 6-10 feet; spread 5-8 feet.   Zones 6, 7, 8, 9.

Form   Mounded. Foliage — alternate, 2-5 inches long; elliptic to oblong; smooth.
           Flower — July and August; ¾-1 inch long; funnel shape; prominent
           stamens 2 inches long; fragrant.

Texture   Medium.

Color   Foliage — green, pale beneath. Flower — apricot to red.

Culture   Sun or part shade. Soil — very good drainage; medium fertility with
           high acid organic matter. Moisture — medium to high. Pruning — none.
           Pest Problems — spider mites, lacebugs, and root rot. Growth Rate —
           moderate.

Notes   Well suited for naturalized areas. Most glabrous of all American azaleas.
           Lateness of flowering is valuable garden addition.

Spiraea (spy-ree'a)
Greek for wreath
or garland

prunifolia (pru-ni-fo'li-a)
with cherrylike leaves

'Plena' (plee'na)
double, usually
doubled flowered

BRIDALWREATH SPIREA

Family Rosaceae

Size	Height 5-7 feet; spread 3-5 feet. Zones 6, 7, 8.
Form	Upright and graceful with branch tips curving toward ground; medium density. Foliage — alternate, simple, ½-2 inches long, finely toothed. Flower — March; double, like small buttons, in sprays profuse enough to completely cover branches.
Texture	Medium.
Color	Foliage — green; fall, red or orange. Flower — white.
Culture	Sun or shade. Soil — medium drainage; medium fertility. Moisture — medium. Pruning — annual thinning of old canes and spindly growth to ground after flowering. Pest Problems — aphids. Growth Rate — rapid.
Notes	Valuable shrub for flowers, foliage and fall color; useful for all informal plantings; combines well with perennials and roses.

Spiraea (spy-ree'a)
　　Greek for wreath
　　or garland

x vanhouttei (van-hoot'ee-i)
　　named for
　　Louis Van Houtte

VANHOUTTE SPIREA

Family Rosaceae

Size	Height 5-7 feet; spread 4-6 feet.　　　　　　　　　　Zones 6, 7, 8.
Form	Upright semi-vase with long branches drooping toward ground; medium density. Foliage — alternate, simple, ¾-1¾ inches long. Flower — April; flat clusters ½ inch wide.
Texture	Medium.
Color	Foliage — blue-green. Flower — white.
Culture	Sun or shade. Soil — medium drainage; medium fertility. Moisture — medium. Pruning — annual thinning of old and weak canes to ground after flowering. Pest Problems — aphids. Growth Rate — rapid.
Notes	Dependable plant which is frequently maintained poorly. Probably most popular of all spireas. Valued for form and flowers; useful as specimen or mass, as natural hedge, or in shrub borders.

Syringa (sir-ring'a)
Greek for pipe, referring
to hollow stem

x persica (per'si-ka)
from Persia

PERSIAN LILAC

Family Oleaceae

Size	Height 6-8 feet; spread 7-9 feet. Zones 6, 7, 8.
Form	Globe-shaped; very dense to medium. Foliage — opposite, simple, heart-shaped, 2 inches long. Flower — mid-April; clusters about 3 inches wide, fragrant.
Texture	Medium.
Color	Foliage — medium green. Flower — lavender pink.
Culture	Sun or part shade. Soil — medium to good drainage; medium fertility; prefers alkaline soil. Moisture — medium. Pruning — annual thinning of old wood and weak sucker growth. Pest Problems — lilac borers, aphids, and mildew. Growth Rate — rapid.
Notes	Good foliage and twig growth for screening and background. Long lasting plant of high quality with minimum problems. Useful in Southeast where *S. vulgaris* is unsatisfactory.
Varieties	**Alba** — white flowers. **laciniata** — cut leaf form with lacy foliage and pale lavender flowers. Grows well in southern climates. Also listed as *S. laciniata*. **Rubra** — rose-red flowers.

Syringa (sir-ring'a)
Greek for pipe, referring
to hollow stem

vulgaris (vul-gar'is)
common

COMMON LILAC

Family Oleaceae

Size	Height 10-12 feet; spread 8-10 feet.	Zones 6, 7.

Form   Upright shrub or small tree with stiff, ascending spreading branches and irregular outline. Foliage — early spring to late fall; opposite, simple, entire, heart-shaped, 3-4 inches long. Flower — mid-April; panicles about 7 inches long, fragrant. Fruit — summer, persisting through winter; capsule ⅝ inch long.

Texture   Medium to coarse.

Color   Foliage — deep green. Flower — white, pink, and purplish-blue. Fruit — brown.

Culture   Sun. Soil — good drainage; medium fertility; prefers alkaline soil. Moisture — medium. Pruning — remove suckers and faded flowers. Pest Problems — mildew, scale, aphids, and borers. Growth Rate — rapid.

Notes   Good foliage mass, valued for flowers; useful as specimen or mass and for clipped or unclipped hedges. Many varieties available; buy hybrids on their own roots.

Varieties   **alba** — white flowers; taller, more upright habit of growth. **Anne Tighe** — double purple flowers. **Belle de Nancy** — double pink flowers. **Cavour** — single violet flowers. **Christophe Colomb** — single lilac flowers. **Ellen Willmott** — double white flowers. **Leon Gambetta** — double lilac flowers. **Lucie Baltet** — single pink flowers. **Ludwig Spaeth** — single purple flowers. **Mme. Lemoine** — abundant double white flowers. **Mont Blanc** — single white flowers. **Rochester** — dwarf flowers. Excellent for containers. **Violetta** — double violet flowers.

Tamarix (tam'a-ricks)
from Tamaris

ramosissima (ram-o-sis'i-ma)

SALTCEDAR

Family Tamaricaceae

Size	Height 10-12 feet; spread 9-11 feet. Zones 6, 7, 8, 9.

Size
Height 10-12 feet; spread 9-11 feet.   Zones 6, 7, 8, 9.

Form
Broad-spreading, sparse, airy in appearance, sending out slender branches spreading flat and drooping at tips. Foliage — midspring to late fall; tiny, triangular, scalelike. Flower — early spring; dense, terminal racemes 2 inches long. Fruit — fall; inconspicuous.

Texture
Very fine.

Color
Foliage — dull blue-green. Flower — pink.

Culture
Sun. Soil — medium to good drainage; low to medium fertility in sandy loam. Moisture — high. Pruning — very tolerant. Pest Problems — none. Growth Rate — moderate.

Notes
Salt resistant. Valued for fine and airy texture, pronounced texture accent; useful near sea and mingled in shrub borders; requires facer shrubs. Short lived.

Varieties
Cheyenne Red — deep pink flowers. **Summer Glow** — blooms on new wood in July; deep pink flowers.

Viburnum (vy-bur'num)
classical Latin name
of wayfaring tree

x burkwoodii (berk'wood-eye)
named for A. Burkwood,
British nurseryman

BURKWOOD VIBURNUM

Family Caprifoliaceae

Size	Height 6-8 feet; spread 5-7 feet.	Zones 6, 7, 8.
Form	Open; irregular to round with age. Foliage — semi-evergreen in warm areas; opposite, 2-3 inches long; brown veins. Flower — spring with new leaves; ½ inch wide in clusters 3 inches wide, fragrant. Fruit — early fall; clusters of round berries, inconspicuous.	
Texture	Medium.	
Color	Foliage — lustrous dark green; fall, red. Flower — pinkish-white. Fruit — black.	
Culture	Sun or part shade. Soil — good drainage; high to medium fertility. Moisture — high to medium. Pruning — none. Pest Problems — bacterial leaf spot and mildew. Growth Rate — moderate to rapid.	
Notes	For flowering shrub borders, background, and naturalizing in woodlands. May be espaliered on fence or wall. Hybrid of V. *carlesii* and V. *utile*.	
Varieties	**Anne Russell** — upright habit; early blooming, pink budded fragrant flowers. **Chenault** — early profuse flowering, flower buds pale rose opening white; fall foliage bronze. **Fullbrook** — large, sweet-scented, pink-budded flowers that open white. **Mohawk** — compact growth habit; clear clove fragrance, deep red budded flowers opening white. Glossy dark green leaves, orange-red in fall. Resistant to bacterial leaf spot and powdery mildew.	

Viburnum (vy-bur'num)
   classical Latin name of
   wayfaring tree

dilatatum (di-la-ta'tum)
   dilated, expanded

LINDEN VIBURNUM

Family Caprifoliaceae

Size	Height 6-9 feet; spread 6-8 feet. Zones 6, 7, 8.
Form	Dense and rounded. Foliage — opposite, 4½ inches wide. Flower — May; profuse flat clusters 5 inches in diameter. Fruit — fall; showy clusters of round berries.
Texture	Medium to coarse.
Color	Foliage — medium green, hairy on both sides; fall, russet-red. Flower — white. Fruit — scarlet-red.
Culture	Sun or part shade. Soil — good drainage; low to medium fertility. Moisture — high to medium. Pruning — none. Pest Problems — bacterial leaf spot and anthracnose. Growth Rate — moderate.
Notes	Best flowering and fruiting in open situations and planted in groups. For borders, screens, or specimen use.
Varieties	**Catskill** — dwarf compact growth habit; excellent fall color. **Erie** — dwarf rounded growth habit; prolific red fruit. **Iroquois** — dense growth habit; large leaves and abundant glossy scarlet fruit. **Xanthocarpum** — yellow fruit.

Viburnum (vy-bur'num)
   classical Latin name
   of wayfaring tree

x juddii (judd'i-eye)
   named for William H. Judd
   of Arnold Arboretum

JUDD VIBURNUM

Family Caprifoliaceae

Size	Height 8 feet; spread to 6 feet.	Zones 6, 7, 8.

Form	Spreading and rounded, rather dense. Foliage — opposite, 2 inches wide, toothed, deeply veined. Flower — early spring; loose clusters 3½ inches wide, slightly fragrant. Fruit — fall; berrylike.
Texture	Coarse.
Color	Foliage — deep green, downy beneath. Flower — white. Fruit — reddish-black.
Culture	Sun or part shade. Soil — good drainage; medium to high fertility. Moisture — high. Pruning — remove winterkilled parts. Pest Problems — none. Growth Rate — rapid.
Notes	Useful as background or in mixed shrub borders. Fragrance of flowers pleasing. Excellent specimen or accent. Fruit attracts birds. Hybrid between V. *carlesii* and V. *bitchuense*.

Viburnum (vy-bur'num)
   classical Latin name
   of wayfaring tree

macrocephalum (mak-ro-sef'a-lum)
   large-headed

'Sterile' (ster'il)
   not fertile

CHINESE SNOWBALL

Family Caprifoliaceae

Size	Height 10-12 feet; spread 10-12 feet. Zones 6, 7, 8, 9.
Form	Massive and rounded with dense branching. Foliage — opposite, oval and pointed, finely toothed, 2-4 inches long and 1-2½ inches wide. Often semi-evergreen. Flower — April, May; globose heads 6-10 inches diameter, sterile. Fruit — none.
Texture	Medium.
Color	Foliage — dark green with light green midvein. Flower — pale green turning pure white.
Culture	Sun or part shade. Soil — tolerant; good drainage; medium fertility. Moisture — medium to high. Pruning — very tolerant. Pest Problems — aphids and powdery mildew. Growth Rate — moderate.
Notes	Vigorous and beautiful in protected locations; combines well with other spring-flowering plants in large scale borders. Long season of interest. May be espaliered or trained as multi-stemmed specimen.

Viburnum (vy-bur'num)
classical Latin name
of wayfaring tree

opulus (op'ew-lus)
Latin name for
kind of maple

'Roseum' (ro'ze-um)
rose-colored

EUROPEAN SNOWBALL

Family Caprifoliaceae

Size	Height 8-12 feet; spread 10-15 feet.	Zones 6, 7, 8.
Form	Upright, multi-stemmed with arching and spreading branches. Foliage — opposite, 3-5 lobed, 2-4 inches long and wide, maplelike. Flower — May; profuse ball-shaped clusters, 2½-3 inches diameter, sterile, not fragrant. Fruit — none.	
Texture	Medium.	
Color	Foliage — glossy dark green; fall, crimson and orange. Flower — pale green turning white; summer, pink-beige.	
Culture	Sun or part shade. Soil — very tolerant; good drainage; medium fertility. Moisture — high. Pruning — very tolerant. Pest Problems — aphids and powdery mildew. Growth Rate — moderate.	
Notes	Lovely flower display for large scale shrub borders; excellent as specimen or screening in park areas.	
Variety	**V.o. Compactum** — height 4-6 feet; white lace-cap flowers; scarlet-rose fall foliage; abundant glowing red fruit.	

Viburnum (vy-bur'num)
　　classical Latin name
　　of wayfaring tree

plicatum (ply-kay'tum)
　　plaited or folded in plaits

tomentosum (toe-men-toe'sum)
　　densely covered with matted,
　　flat hairs

DOUBLEFILE VIBURNUM

Family Caprifoliaceae

Size	Height 8-10 feet; spread 8-10 feet.　　Zones 6,7,8.
Form	Strong and vigorous with broad-spreading, almost horizontal branches. Foliage — midspring to midfall; opposite, 3-4 inches long with marked veins. Flower — April, after leaves; 4 inches wide, flat-topped cymes held above branches with sterile flowers bordering cluster. Fruit — summer; small drupes.
Texture	Coarse.
Color	Foliage — deep green; fall, deep red. Flower — white. Fruit — red turning black.
Culture	Sun or part shade. Soil — tolerant; medium drainage; medium fertility. Moisture — medium to high. Pruning — when needed to renew growth. Pest Problems — none. Growth Rate — moderate.
Notes	Very handsome specimen or accent plant; useful in shrub borders. Beautiful horizontal branching habit displaying flowers and fruit well. Will not tolerate drought.
Varieties	**Lanarth** — compact habit of growth; large flowers. **Mariesii** — graceful horizontal branching; large flowers. **Pink Beauty** — pink flowers. **Roseum** — less vigorous flowers open white and turn deep pink. **Rowallane** — less vigorous; prolific fruit. **Shasta** — height 5-7 feet with horizontal branching to 12 feet. Large and abundant flower clusters. **Shoshoni** — seedling of 'Shasta'; dwarf form with cream-white flowers, red berries, maroon fall foliage. **Summer Stars** — height 6-8 feet with compact habit of growth. Blooms all summer.

Viburnum (vy-bur'num)
  classical Latin name of
  wayfaring tree

wrightii (rite'e-i)
  for proper name

WRIGHT VIBURNUM

Family Caprifoliaceae

Size	Height 6-9 feet; spread 5-8 feet.	Zones 6, 7, 8, 9.

Form	Rounded with upright branching. Foliage — broad-ovate and coarsely toothed, 4-6 inches long, leathery. Flower — May or June; cymes 4 inches diameter. Fruit — summer to fall; clusters of drupes 1/3 inch long.
Texture	Coarse.
Color	Foliage — dark green; fall, crimson-red. Flowers — white. Fruit — brilliant red.
Culture	Sun or part shade. Soil — good drainage; medium fertility. Moisture — medium to high. Pruning — none. Pest Problems — none. Growth Rate — moderate.
Notes	Beautiful fruit display as specimen or in mixed shrub borders.
Variety	**Hessei** — compact dwarf form; small flower cymes and bright red fruit.

Vitex (vy'tex)
  ancient Latin name

agnus-castus (ag'nus-cast'us)
  ancient classical name for
  chaste lamb

CHASTE-TREE

Family Verbenaceae

Size	Height 10-12 feet; spread 8-10 feet. Zones 6,7,8,9.
Form	Semi-globe, open and irregular if not cut back each year. Foliage — late spring; opposite, 5-parted, with leaflets 1-4 inches long. Flower — July; small spikes. Fruit — fall; ¼ inch thick dry berries, aromatic. Twigs — 4-angled.
Texture	Medium.
Color	Foliage — gray-green. Flower — pale violet. Fruit — blue-black.
Culture	Sun or part shade. Soil — very tolerant; medium to good drainage; medium fertility. Moisture — medium to low. Pruning — cut back to ground every year or every few years for compactness and general appearance. Pest Problems — none. Growth Rate — rapid.
Notes	Foliage has pungent, aromatic, sagelike odor. Handsome mass, particularly attractive in bloom, but difficult to blend with other shrubs. May be used as small tree if unpruned.
Varieties	**Alba** — white flowers. **Latifolia** — height 15-20 feet; vigorous and more hardy than species. **Rosea** — pink flowers.

Weigela (wy-gee'la)
    named for C.E. Weigel

florida (flo'ri-da)
    freely flowering

WEIGELA

Family

Caprifoliaceae

Size	Height 6-8 feet; spread 8-10 feet. Zones 6, 7, 8.
Form	Erect and spreading branches finally arching to ground. Foliage — midspring to midfall; opposite, 4 inches long. Flower — late April or early May; very showy, bell-shaped, profuse clusters of 3 to 5. Fruit — late summer; smooth capsules splitting in 2 halves.
Texture	Coarse.
Color	Foliage — medium green to deep green; fall, slightly yellow. Flower — pink. Fruit — tan-brown.
Culture	Sun. Soil — tolerant; medium drainage; medium fertility. Moisture — high. Pruning — remove old branches and winter-killed twigs. Pest Problems — none. Growth Rate — moderate.
Notes	Valued for handsome flowers; at other seasons rather coarse, does not blend well with other shrubs; best as specimen or accent in very large gardens.
Varieties	**alba** — white flowers. **Bristol Ruby** — upright growth habit; red flowers. Attracts hummingbirds. **Eva Supreme** — compact dwarf form 5 feet in height; vigorous grower with crimson flowers. **Java Red (Foliis Purpuriis)** — purple-green foliage; pink flowers; height 4 feet. **Mont Blanc** — vigorous grower with fragrant white flowers. **Pink Princess** — height 4-5 feet; bright pink flowers. **Vanicek** — rose-red flowers; very hardy. **Variegata** — leaves bordered with yellow; deep rose flowers; height 4-6 feet. **venusta** — 4-6 feet high; leaves small, rose-purple flowers. Very hardy.

SMALL TREES — EVERGREEN

Cupressus (ku-pres'us)
cypress

arizonica (ari-zon'i-ca)
of Arizona

ARIZONA CYPRESS

Family Cupressaceae

Size	Height 25-35 feet; spread 20-35 feet.	Zones 6, 7, 8, 9.
Form	Upright columnar form. Foliage — opposite, scalelike, flattened and pointed; 1/16 inch long; aromatic. Flower — staminate and pistillate flowers on same plant. Fruit — 1-2 inch round cone.	
Texture	Fine.	
Color	Foliage — gray-green to pale bluish-green. Fruit — brown to bluish-gray. Bark — dark red brown.	
Culture	Sun. Soil — good drainage; low to medium fertility. Moisture — low. Pruning — none. Pest Problems — bagworms. Growth Rate — moderate.	
Notes	Excellent in natural form for screening. Withstands excessive drought and poor soil. Select grafted trees for stronger root system.	
Varieties	**bonita** — compact conical form; blue-gray foliage. **Verhalenii** — foliage bright blue-green; soft and graceful form. **Watersii** — compact, narrow pyramidal habit of growth.	

Eriobotrya (ear-i-o-bot'ri-a)
Greek for woolly cluster,
in allusion to hairy
flower cluster

japonica (ja-pon'i-ka)
from Japan

LOQUAT

Family Rosaceae

Size	Height 10-20 feet; spread 8-12 feet. Zones 8,9.
Form	Dense rounded head on short slender trunk. Foliage — alternate, 5-10 inches long, glossy above, tomentose beneath. Flower — November; ½ inch diameter, fragrant. Fruit — ripening in April; 1½ inches long, pear-shaped, edible.
Texture	Coarse.
Color	Foliage — dark green above, rusty beneath. Flower — white. Fruit — yellow.
Culture	Sun or part shade. Soil — good drainage; medium fertility. Moisture — medium. Pruning — none. Pest Problems — usually none but can develop pear blight. Growth Rate — rapid.
Notes	Excellent specimen or accent plant, especially effective against archi-tectural background. May be used in shrub borders, planter boxes, or as screen. Adaptable to any size area. Interesting espaliered.
Varieties	**Champagne** — excellent fruit quality; for zone 9. **Coppertone** — hybrid; dense growth with copper colored new foliage; pale pink flowers. **Golden Nugget** — large, pear-shaped yellow fruit. **Variegata** — white variegated leaves.

Ilex (eye'lecks)
  hollies

x attenuata (a-ten-u-a'ta)
  slenderly tapering

HYBRID HOLLY

Family Aquifoliaceae

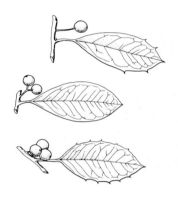

Size	Height 20-30 feet; spread 8-15 feet. Zones 6, 7, 8, 9.
Form	Upright, loosely pyramidal habit of growth. Foliage — alternate; obovate to lanceolate; 1½-4 inches long, ¾-1 inch wide; number of spines depends on variety. Flower — spring; inconspicuous. Fruit — fall and winter; clusters of berries ¼ inch diameter.
Texture	Fine to medium.
Color	Foliage — medium green. Fruit — red. Bark — light gray.
Culture	Sun to part shade. Soil — well-drained; medium to high fertility. Moisture — medium to high. Pruning — shape and balance. Pest Problems — none. Growth Rate — rapid.
Notes	Excellent as specimen, evergreen tall screen, or in groups. Good for background shrub or small tree.
Varieties	**East Palatka** — female plant with dark red berries. Glossy leaves with few spines. Adapted to moist, protected situations. **Hume 2** — small red berries. Glossy green leaves almost spineless. **Savannah** — female plant with red berries; foliage light green. Requires heavy fertilization for good leaf color. Leaf similar to *I. opaca*.

Ilex (eye'lecks)
hollies

x attenuata (a-ten-u-a'ta)
slenderly tapering

'Fosteri'
after E.E. Foster of
Bessemer, Alabama

FOSTER HYBRID HOLLY

Family Aquifoliaceae

Size	Height 20-30 feet; spread 7-10 feet. Zones 6, 7, 8, 9.
Form	Compact to loose pyramidal form; upright. Foliage — alternate, 1½-2½ inches long, ¾ inch wide, spiny pointed with 1 to 4 spines on each side. Flower — spring; inconspicuous. Fruit — fall and winter; profuse clusters of berries ¼ inch across.
Texture	Medium to fine.
Color	Foliage — glossy dark green. Flower — white. Fruit — bright red. Bark — light gray.
Culture	Sun to part shade. Soil — well-drained; medium to high fertility. Moisture — medium to high. Pruning — shape and balance. Pest Problems — none. Growth Rate — rapid.
Notes	Excellent as specimen and for border or groups. Good for narrow spaces. Heavy fruit production. Tolerates city conditions. May be grown in containers. Most popular form is Foster #2, very heavily fruiting.

Ilex (eye'lecks)
   hollies

cassine (ka-seen')
   from Timucua Indians

DAHOON

Family Aquifoliaceae

Size	Height 20-30 feet; spread 10-15 feet.	Zones 7, 8, 9.
Form	Large shrub or small tree, usually single trunked; rounded with dense branching. Foliage — alternate, 1½-4 inches long, entire or with slight serrations. Flower — inconspicuous. Fruit — fall and winter; ¼ inch berries in clusters.	
Texture	Fine.	
Color	Foliage — green to yellow-green; fall, purple-green. Fruit — red.	
Culture	Sun or part shade. Soil — tolerant; prefers sandy loam. Moisture — medium to high. Pruning — none. Pest Problems — none. Growth Rate — medium.	
Notes	Remains somewhat shrubby in colder areas. Native to swampy locations, good for naturalizing in these areas. Interesting gray bark, evergreen foliage, and attractive fruit.	
Varieties	**Angustifolia** — Alabama Dahoon; narrow, linear leaves; much improved selection. **Lowii** — yellow berries and dark green foliage.	

Ilex (eye'lecks)
  hollies

cassine (ka-seen')
  from Timucua Indians

myrtifolia (mert-i-fo'li-a)
  leaves like myrtle

MYRTLE-LEAVED HOLLY

Family Aquifoliaceae

Size	Height 20 feet; spread 7-9 feet. Zones 8,9.
Form	Narrow and rounded with open branches. Foliage — alternate, entire, 1-2 inches long, oblong to linear, prominent midrib. Flower — spring, on current season's wood; inconspicuous. Fruit — fall and winter; berry-like drupe, ⅛ inch diameter.
Texture	Fine.
Color	Foliage — dark green above, pale beneath. Flower — white. Fruit — red, rarely yellow.
Culture	Part shade. Soil — good drainage; medium to high fertility. Moisture — high. Pruning — none. Pest Problems — leaf miner. Growth Rate — moderate.
Notes	Grown for attractive habit, foliage, and berries. Excellent for tall screens or borders. Smaller leaves and fruit than *I. cassine*.
Variety	**Lowii** — small yellow berries; dark green foliage.

Ilex (eye'lecks)
   hollies

x 'Nellie R. Stevens'
   after N.R. Stevens,
   Oxford, Maryland

NELLIE STEVENS HOLLY

Family Aquifoliaceae

Size	Height 15-25 feet; spread 10-15 feet.	Zones 6, 7, 8, 9.
Form	Upright and pyramidal, becoming dense and rounded with age. Foliage — alternate, slightly bullate, 1-3 terminal spines. Flower — inconspicuous, male and female flowers on separate plants. Fruit — fall and winter; berrylike, ¼ inch diameter; heavily fruiting.	
Texture	Medium.	
Color	Foliage — glossy dark green. Fruit — bright red.	
Culture	Sun to part shade. Soil — good drainage; medium fertility. Moisture — medium. Pruning — tolerant. Pest Problems — scale. Growth Rate — rapid.	
Notes	Excellent as specimen or in groups, and in foundation plantings. Good screening and background for smaller shrubs. May be pollinated by male *I. cornuta*. Vigorous and drought resistant.	

Ilex (eye'lecks)
  hollies

opaca (o-pay'ka)
  opaque or pale

AMERICAN HOLLY

Family Aquifoliaceae

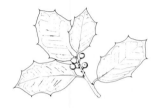

Size	Height 15-30 feet; spread 10-20 feet. Zones 6, 7, 8, 9.
Form	Upright and conical with horizontal branches or open in poor growing conditions; medium density. Foliage — alternate, 2-4 inches long, 1-2 inches wide, stiff and leathery, not lustrous, margins usually spiny-toothed. Flower — spring; inconspicuous, male and female flowers on separate plants. Fruit — fall and winter; berrylike, ¼ inch diameter; both male and female plants must be present for fruit.
Texture	Medium to slightly coarse.
Color	Foliage — dark green, light green beneath. Flower — white. Fruit — red. Bark — gray, smooth.
Culture	Sun to part shade. Soil — good drainage; medium fertility. Moisture — medium to high. Pruning — balance and retain central leader. Pest Problems — leaf miner. Growth Rate — slow.
Notes	Foliage sometimes disfigured by winter sun. Difficult to transplant from wild. Best employed as specimen plant or in clumps as screen and border material. Fruit production best in full sun. Allow lower limbs to branch to ground naturally. Interesting topiary. Will not tolerate direct salt spray.
Varieties	**Carolina #2** — dark green leaves; abundant fruit. **Croonenburg** — pyramidal form, abundant fruit. **George E. Hart** — narrow conical growth habit with small dark green leaves. **Greenleaf** — softer in form than 'Croonenburg', fast-growing, responds well to shearing. **Howard** — compact habit; leaves dense, glossy green with few spines. **Jersey Knight** — very hardy; excellent foliage. Male. **Jersey Princess** — shining dark green leaves, excellent form. Female. **Rotunda** — upright growth habit; leaves smooth, entire, dark glossy green. Profuse fruiting.

Osmanthus (oz-man'thus)
Greek for fragrance
and flower

americanus (a-me-ri-cay'nus)
from North or South America

DEVILWOOD

Family Oleaceae

Size	Height 15-20 feet; spread 10-15 feet. Zones 6, 7, 8, 9.
Form	Irregularly rounded with open, thin branching. Foliage — opposite, entire, oblong-lanceolate, 2-6 inches long and 1-2½ inches wide. Flower — early spring; inconspicuous, fragrant. Fruit — fall; drupe ½ inch diameter.
Texture	Coarse.
Color	Foliage — glossy olive green. Fruit — dark purple-blue. Bark — gray-brown.
Culture	Sun to part shade. Soil — good drainage; medium to high fertility. Moisture — high. Pruning — none. Pest Problems — none. Growth Rate — moderate to rapid.
Notes	Interesting low maintenance tree for urban or natural areas. Useful as hedge or screen and in mixed shrub borders. Easily transplanted. May be trained as multi-trunk specimen.

Phyllostachys (fil-o-sta'kis)
 from Greek meaning
 leaf and spike

aureosulcata (aw-ree-o-sul-ca'ta)
 golden

YELLOW-GROOVE BAMBOO

Family Gramineae

Size	Height 20-30 feet; spread indeterminate. **Zones 7, 8, 9.**
Form	Dense upright canes (culms), 1-2 inches in diameter with canopy of foliage. Foliage — alternate; 4-6 inches long, ¾ inch wide, flat, glabrous; 3-5 leaves on each small branch.
Texture	Medium.
Color	Foliage — medium green. Stems — olive green.
Culture	Sun or shade. Soil — tolerant; medium fertility with organic matter added. Moisture — medium to high. Pruning — none. Pest Problems — none. Growth Rate — rapid.
Notes	Hardiest of all bamboos. Beautiful canes (culms) very effective for vertical line in design. Good for narrow spaces. Requires confinement of roots. Shoots in early spring are edible. Used for screens, hedges and groves.

Pinus (py'nus)
  old Latin
  name for pine

nigra (ny'gra)
  black

AUSTRIAN PINE

Family Pinaceae

Size	Height 20-40 feet; spread 12-20 feet.	Zones 6, 7, 8.

Size   Height 20-40 feet; spread 12-20 feet.   Zones 6, 7, 8.

Form   Conical, semi-round top; medium density. Foliage — 2 needles per
         bundle, 3-6 inches long. Fruit — cones 2-4 inches long.

Texture Medium.

Color   Foliage — medium green. Fruit — greenish-brown.

Culture Sun. Soil — good drainage; medium fertility. Moisture — medium.
         Pruning — maintain central leader and general balance. Pest
         Problems — pine-tip moth and pine needle blight. Growth Rate —
         moderate.

Notes   Picturesque with age. Easily transplanted. Use as texture contrast in
         shrub borders or as screen when spaced 12-15 feet apart. Fairly tolerant
         of seashore conditions.

Varieties **Arnold Sentinel** — height 18 feet; spread 5-6 feet; dense upright form.
         Hornibrookiana — dwarf and compact shrub. Height less than 2 feet, needles 2½
         inches long. **maritima** — horizontal branches with slender needles 5-6 inches
         long and slender. Excellent tree for coastal areas. Corsican Pine. **Pyramidalis** —
         narrow ascending branches.

Pinus (py'nus)
old Latin name
for pine

virginiana (vir-gin-i-a'na)
from Virginia

VIRGINIA PINE

Family Pinaceae

Size	Height 20-40 feet; spread 10-30 feet.　　　　　　　Zones 6, 7, 8.
Form	Irregular and open with sparse branching; wide flat top with age. Retains lower branches. Foliage — twisted soft needles 1¼-3 inches long, 2 in bundle. Fruit — sharp cones 1½-2½ inches long, in pairs. Bark — thin, smooth.
Texture	Medium.
Color	Foliage — dark green; winter, dull yellow-green. Fruit — dark brown. Bark — reddish gray to brown.
Culture	Sun. Soil — very tolerant; well-drained; medium fertility. Moisture — medium. Pruning — none. Pest Problems — pine beetles. Growth Rate — slow.
Notes	Will grow on windswept, dry, open sites. Good cover for difficult areas; use as mass screen or windbreak. Interesting growth habit with gnarled branches.

Prunus (proo'nus)
    classical Latin
    name of plum

caroliniana (ka-ro-lin-i-a'na)
    from Carolinas

CAROLINA CHERRY-LAUREL

Family Rosaceae

Size	Height 20-30 feet; spread 15-20 feet.	Zones 7, 8, 9.
Form	Dense rounded head with single trunk or rounded and shrubby. Foliage — alternate, 2-4 inches long. Flower — March to April; short racemes 2-5 inches long, fragrant. Fruit — fall; ½ inch long.	
Texture	Medium.	
Color	Foliage — glossy dark green. Flower — white. Fruit — black.	
Culture	Sun or part shade. Soil — well-drained; medium fertility. Moisture — medium. Pruning — tolerant. Pest Problems — none. Growth Rate — rapid.	
Notes	Excellent in natural form; may be sheared for hedges or topiary work. Grown primarily for excellent foliage. Forms good windbreak. Use as specimen, screen, or border. Difficult to transplant in large sizes. Not cold hardy in mountain areas.	
Variety	**Compacta (Bright 'n Tight)** — dense, compact habit of growth. Leaf margins smooth.	

Quercus (kwer'kus)
classical Latin
name for oak

acuta (a-cu'ta)
with acute leaves

JAPANESE EVERGREEN OAK

Family Fagaceae

Size	Height 20-30 feet; spread 15-20 feet. Zones 7, 8, 9.
Form	Oval to rounded with low branching, often multi-trunked. Foliage — leathery; oblong to oval with blunt point and rounded base, margins entire and wavy, 2½-5½ inches long. Flower — inconspicuous. Fruit — acorn, cup encloses ¼ of acorn.
Texture	Coarse.
Color	Foliage — glossy dark olive-green. Fruit — brown. Bark — smooth gray.
Culture	Sun or part shade. Soil — good drainage; medium to high fertility; prefers acid pH. Moisture — medium. Pruning — none. Pest Problems — none. Growth Rate — moderate to slow.
Notes	Refined and handsome as lawn specimen or screen. Tolerates urban conditions; casts dense shade.

Quercus (kwer'kus)
  classical Latin
  name for oak

glauca (gla'ka)
  with white or gray bloom

RING-CUPPED OAK

Family Fagaceae

Size	Height 20-40 feet; spread 10-20 feet. Zones 7, 8, 9.
Form	Rounded with low branching to ground; multiple trunks. Foliage — alternate, 3-5 inches long, toothed at upper end. Flower — inconspicuous. Fruit — small acorn, cup encloses 1/3 of acorn, pubescent.
Texture	Coarse.
Color	Foliage — glossy olive-green with grayish cast on underside. Bark — smooth, gray.
Culture	Sun. Soil — good drainage; medium to high fertility. Moisture — medium. Pruning — shape. Pest Problems — none. Growth Rate — moderate.
Notes	Specimen or screening material with heavy low branching and elegant foliage.

Sabal (say'bal)

palmetto (pal-met'to)
little palm

PALMETTO

Family Palmaceae

Size	Height 20-30 feet; spread 10-15 feet. Zones 8, 9.
Form	Straight, single trunk with compact crown, upper portion of trunk covered with persistant leaf bases. Foliage — to 5-6 feet long and 4-7 feet across deeply cut, palmate. Flower — spring; 1/3 inch diameter in drooping clusters 2-2½ feet long, fragrant. Fruit — fall; 1/3 inch diameter.
Texture	Medium.
Color	Foliage — lustrous green. Flower — white. Fruit — black.
Culture	Sun or shade. Soil — very tolerant; medium drainage; medium fertility. Moisture — high. Pruning — none. Pest Problems — palmetto weevil and palm leaf skeletonizer. Growth Rate — moderate.
Notes	Excellent as street tree, specimen, patio, or terrace tree. Creates interesting shadow patterns against walls. Very tolerant of salt, recommended for seaside plantings. Easy to transplant in June and July. Not hardy in Piedmont or mountain areas.

Trachycarpus (trayk-i-karp'us)
from Greek for rough or
harsh and for fruit

fortunei (for-too'nee-i)
named for Robert Fortune

WINDMILL PALM

Family Palmaceae

Size	Height 15-35 feet; spread 10-15 feet.	Zones 8, 9.

Form   Trunk solitary and post-like; covered with black hair-like fiber. Foliage — fan-shaped, 2-3 feet wide. Flower — spring; small, in large panicles to 2 feet long.

Texture   Coarse.

Color   Foliage — medium to dull green. Flower — yellow.

Culture   Part shade with wind protection. Soil — good drainage; medium fertility with organic matter added. Moisture — high when young. Pruning — remove dead leaves. Pest Problems — scale. Growth Rate — rapid.

Notes   Cold tender but will not tolerate extreme heat. Frequently used in containers and as street tree. Transplant in spring or summer when roots are active. Excellent trunk effect; strong accent plant.

SMALL TREES — DECIDUOUS

Acer (a'sir)
  ancient Latin name
  of maple

buergeranum (ber-jar-a'num)

TRIDENT MAPLE

Family Aceraceae

Size	Height 25-35 feet; spread 20-30 feet.	Zones 6, 7, 8, 9.

Form
Upright to oval-rounded. Foliage — opposite, simple, 3 shallow lobes, irregularly toothed, 2¼-4 inches long and 1½-3 inches wide. Flower — May; inconspicuous. Fruit — samaras ¾-1 inch long.

Texture
Medium.

Color
Foliage — deep shiny green above, glaucous beneath; fall, red to orange. Flower — greenish-yellow. Fruit — brown-red. Bark — smooth gray-brown, orange-brown with age.

Culture
Sun. Soil — medium drainage; medium fertility. Moisture — tolerant. Pruning — shape. Pest Problems — none serious. Growth Rate — moderate.

Notes
Attractive urban trees with good foliage, form and fall color. Good structural strength. Exfoliating bark. May be used as patio, lawn or street tree. Tolerant of wind, drought, salt, air pollution and soil compaction. Dwarfs well in container culture.

Varieties
Iwao kaede — leaves slightly larger than species. New foliage dark green-red to bright red, later becoming shiny dark green with leathery texture. **Jako kaede** — dwarf shrubby form. Musk-scented deep green leaves. **Kyu den** — dwarf form with dense foliage, very shiny deep green above and glaucous beneath. **Mino yatsubusa** — dwarf, shrub-like habit of growth. Leaves three-lobed with center lobes long and narrow. Shiny green foliage color.

Acer (a'sir)
    ancient Latin name
    of maple

ginnala (gin-nah'la)
    Asiatic vernacular name

AMUR MAPLE

Family Aceraceae

Size	Height 15-20 feet; spread 18-20 feet.	Zones 6, 7, 8.
Form	Multi-stemmed with rounded form and dense branching. Foliage — opposite, simple, 3 inches long and 2½ inches wide, doubly serrate, 3-lobed. Flower — fragrant small panicles in April to May. Fruit — samaras 1 inch long, September and October.	
Texture	Medium.	
Color	Foliage — dark green above, light green beneath; fall, scarlet. Flower — white-yellow. Fruit — red in summer. Bark — gray-brown.	
Culture	Sun or part shade. Soil — well-drained; medium fertility. Moisture — high. Pruning — shape and thin. Pest Problems — leaf spot. Growth Rate — moderate.	
Notes	Good for massing or specimen use. Tolerant of heavy pruning and may be used as hedge. Needs minimum maintenance; easy to transplant. Excellent in containers.	
Varieties	**Compactum** — height 5-6 feet; foliage dark green turning red-purple in fall. **Durand Dwarf** — height 3-4 feet; dwarf shrubby form; foliage light green. **semenowii** — height 10-15 feet; foliage smaller than species with deeper cut lobes, dark green turning red-purple in fall. Good screening material.	

Acer (a'sir)
    ancient Latin name
    of maple

griseum (gris'ee-um)
    gray

PAPERBARK MAPLE

Family Aceraceae

Size	Height 20-30 feet; spread 15-25 feet.	Zones 6, 7, 8.

Form   Upright oval branching with rather narrow domed head. Foliage —
          opposite, trifoliate with each leaflet 1½-3 inches long. Flower —
          inconspicuous. Fruit — samara, 1¼ inches long, pubescent. Bark — thin
          papery flakes, exfoliating.

Texture   Medium.

Color   Foliage — soft green above, silvery beneath; fall, bright scarlet and
          orange. Flower — greenish. Fruit — greenish-brown. Bark — cinnamon-
          brown, new bark orange-red.

Culture   Sun. Soil — prefers well-drained loam soil but tolerant of clay soil.
          Moisture — high. Pruning — shape. Pest Problems — none. Growth
          Rate — slow.

Notes   Bark creates interest throughout year; excellent accent tree, especially
          beautiful in winter. Long-lasting fall color; ideal for small gardens and
          patios. May be trained as multi-trunk specimen.

Acer (a'sir)
   ancient Latin name
   of maple

palmatum (pal-may'tum)
   with leaflets or with
   lobes or veins of leaf
   radiating from one point

JAPANESE MAPLE

Family Aceraceae

Size	Height 15-20 feet; spread 10-15 feet. Zones 6,7,8.
Form	Low and round-topped with open, irregular crown, and ascending, spreading branches. Foliage — opposite, simple, palmately lobed, 2-4 inches across. Flower — March; erect clusters. Fruit — spring; samara, 1 inch long, 2-winged.
Texture	Medium.
Color	Foliage — green to red; fall, scarlet. Flower — purple-red. Fruit — red.
Culture	Part shade. Soil — good drainage; high fertility. Moisture — medium. Pruning — shape. Pest Problems — maple insects and diseases. Growth Rate — slow.
Notes	Beautiful tree for small gardens and terraces. Refined in character. Many varieties useful as specimens or accent plants in borders and rock gardens. Difficult to transplant.
Varieties	**Atropurpureum** — dark red leaves throughout growing season; small 5-lobed leaf. Excellent strong growth. **Bloodgood** — red leaf color throughout growing season; superior cultivar. **Burgundy Lace** — finely divided red-purple leaves; slow grower. **Osakazuki** — height 6 feet; green foliage; fall color orange and scarlet. **Sango Kaku** — light green foliage, turns golden apricot in fall; red young stems throughout winter. Erect in growth habit. **Scolopendrifolium** — green foliage cut to center, leaflets narrow. **Senkaki** — coral-pink stems and light green leaves. **Yezo-Nishiki** — blood-red leaves.

Acer (a'sir)
    ancient Latin
    of maple

palmatum (pal-may'tum)
    with leaflets or
    with lobes or veins
    of leaf radiating
    from one point

dissectum (dis-sek'tum)
    finely cut

LACELEAF
JAPANESE
MAPLE

Family
Aceraceae

Size	Height 4-6 feet; spread 8-10 feet.	Zones 6, 7, 8.
Form	Rounded with graceful horizontal to pendulous branches, sculptural in aspect. Foliage — opposite, simple, palmately lobed with 7-11 lobes deeply cut and finely toothed, 2-4 inches long. Fruit — spring; samara.	
Texture	Fine to medium.	
Color	Foliage — light bright green; fall, yellow to crimson.	
Culture	Sun to part shade. Soil — good drainage essential; high fertility with high organic content. Moisture — medium. Pruning — shape. Pest Problems — maple insects and diseases. Growth Rate — very slow.	
Notes	Striking in planter boxes, rock gardens or as accent plant; looks best with contemporary architecture. Protect from wind.	
Varieties	**Atropurpureum** — mounded form with lovely twisted branching pattern; height 5-8 feet. Purple-red lacy foliage turning orange in fall. **Red Filigree Lace** — pendulous growth habit; foliage doubly dissected, purple-red turning to crimson in autumn. **Seiryu** — upright growth habit; height 10-12 feet. Bright green foliage; fall, golden yellow. Multi-branched; vigorous. Grows well in restricted spaces. **Viride** — bright green leaves; fall, yellow.	

Acer (a'sir)
    ancient Latin name
    of maple

tegmentosum (teg-men-to'sum)

MANCHUSTRIPED MAPLE

Family Aceraceae

Size	Height 25-30 feet; spread 20-25 feet.	Zones 6, 7.

Form   Oval to rounded head with short, thin trunk; branches begin close to ground. Foliage — opposite, simple, 3-5 lobes; 4-6 inches long and wide. Flower — pendulous racemes 3 inches long. Fruit — May; samaras 1¼ inches long.

Texture   Medium to coarse.

Color   Foliage — pale green; fall, yellow. Flower — yellow-green. Bark — gray-green with long vertical white stripes.

Culture   Part shade. Soil — well-drained; medium fertility. Moisture — high. Pruning — remove lower side-branches when young to show bark pattern. Pest Problems — maple insects and diseases. Growth Rate — slow.

Notes   Specimen for small gardens and naturalized areas; bark pattern interesting year-round. Best in cool, shady sites.

Aesculus (es'ku-lus)
    oak

glabra (glay'bra)
    smooth

OHIO BUCKEYE

Family Hippocastanaceae

Size	Height 20-35 feet; spread 20-35 feet.	Zones 6, 7.
Form	Oval to rounded crown with low branching and short trunk. Foliage — opposite, palmately compound with 5 leaflets; 4-6 inches long. Flower — May; erect panicles 6 inches long. Fruit — late summer; prickly capsules 1-2 inches long. Bark — corky and furrowed.	
Texture	Coarse.	
Color	Foliage — bright green to yellow-green; fall, bright orange. Flower — yellow-green. Fruit — light brown. Bark — gray-brown.	
Culture	Sun. Soil — well-drained; medium fertility. Moisture — high. Pruning — none. Pest Problems — leaf blotch, powdery mildew, and leaf scorch. Growth Rate — moderate to slow.	
Notes	Use as filler in natural areas and parks or as small shade tree. Not suitable as street tree; will not tolerate heat or drought. Valued for autumn color.	
Variety	**Pyramidalis** — upright habit of growth.	

Albizia (al-bizz'ee-a)
    named for Albizzi,
    Italian naturalist

julibrissin (jew-lee-bris'in)
    Persian vernacular
    for silk tree

MIMOSA

Family

Fabaceae

Size	Height 20-30 feet; spread 25-30 feet. Zones 6, 7, 8, 9.
Form	Spreading, low, and fairly open. Foliage — alternate, twice compound, 12-18 inches long. Flower — June and July; silky pompoms 2 inches in diameter, fragrant. Fruit — late summer and fall; flattened pods 4-6 inches long.
Texture	Fine.
Color	Foliage — gray-green. Flower — rose-red to pink. Fruit — brown. Bark — light gray.
Culture	Sun. Soil — medium to good drainage; medium fertility. Moisture — medium. Pruning — train young trees to prevent weak branch formation. Pest Problems — mimosa wilt disease and webworms. Growth Rate — rapid.
Notes	Comparatively short life, breaks easily. Low branching habit creates circulation problems for some locations. Interesting small temporary shade tree or specimen. Germinates freely from seed. Difficult to transplant large sizes.
Varieties	**Charlotte** — wilt-resistant. **Ernest Wilson (Rosea)** — flower bright pink; hardier than species. Height 10-15 feet. **Rubra** — deep pink flowers. **Tryon** — wilt-resistant. **Union** — wilt-resistant.

Amelanchier (am-e-lank'i-er)

arborea (ar-bo're-a)
   treelike, woody

SERVICEBERRY

Family Rosaceae

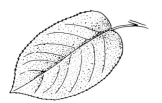

Size	Height 10-20 feet; spread 8-15. Zones 6, 7, 8, 9.
Form	Upright, irregular, and graceful; medium density. May be multi-trunked. Foliage — alternate, simple, toothed, base usually rounded, 2-3 inches long. Flower — spring; racemes 2-3 inches long. Fruit — June; berrylike, edible.
Texture	Medium.
Color	Foliage — medium green, gray in early spring; fall, red to yellow. Flower — pink, becoming white. Fruit — dark red. Bark — light gray.
Culture	Sun or part shade. Soil — very tolerant; medium drainage; medium fertility. Moisture — medium. Pruning — thin side branches for shape. Pest Problems — leaf defoliators, scale, borer, and fire blight. Growth Rate — moderate.
Notes	Blooms just before dogwood. Attractive with background of loblolly pines or planted along edge of wild areas. Native to mountains of Southeast. May be trained as multi-trunk specimen.
Varieties	**Prince William** — multiple stems; blue fruit. **Robin Hill Pink** — pink flowers; best in cool, moist sites.

Betula (bet'you-la)
classical name
of birch

nigra (ny'gra)
black

RIVER BIRCH

Family Betulaceae

Size	Height 20-40 feet; spread 16-20 feet. Zones 6, 7, 8, 9.
Form	Upright and open with thin and slightly drooping twigs. Foliage — alternate, simple, double toothed, 1½-3 inches long. Flower — inconspicuous hanging catkins. Fruit — late spring; samara ¼ inch long. Bark — exfoliating, papery.
Texture	Fine to medium.
Color	Foliage — medium green, whitish beneath; fall, rich yellow. Fruit — brown. Bark — reddish brown.
Culture	Part shade. Soil — medium drainage; medium to high fertility. Moisture — high. Pruning — not tolerant. Pest Problems — none. Growth Rate — moderate.
Notes	Frequently seen along creeks and streams in southeast. Grows well on high or low ground. Adaptable to multiple trunk. Graceful branching habit; interesting informal tree for lawns or gardens. Select specimens with thin trunks and low arching branches for best effect.
Variety	**Heritage** — hardy and vigorous form with rich dark green leaves and whitish bark.

Betula (bet'you-la)
classical name
of birch

pendula (pen'dew-la)
pendulous, hanging

EUROPEAN WHITE BIRCH

Family Betulaceae

Size	Height 20-40 feet; spread 8-16 feet.	Zones 6, 7.

Form   Slender, rounded, and graceful; pendulous in age with fine and hazy winter effect. Foliage — alternate, simple, double toothed, 1½-3 inches long. Flower — early spring; catkins. Fruit — small samara. Bark — peeling.

Texture   Fine.

Color   Foliage — light green. Flower — pale yellow. Bark — chalky white to creamy white.

Culture   Sun. Soil — medium drainage; medium fertility. Moisture — high. Pruning — not very tolerant; remove dead wood and broken branches. Pest Problems — bronze birch borer; sometimes host of fungus disease of Larch. Growth Rate — fairly rapid.

Notes   Difficult to transplant and short lived. Unrivaled in lightness, grace and elegance; light accent, useful as specimen. Multiple trunk forms usually available. Good in mountains and upper southeast.

Varieties   **Dalecarlica** — leaves deeply lobed, branches pendulous. Very popular. **Fastigiata** — dense and columnar with erect branches. Excellent for narrow spaces. **Gracilis** — finely dissected leaves; pendulous branches. **Purpurea** — dark purple-red leaves becoming green in summer. **Youngii** — slender, drooping branches forming mushroom-shaped head; height 10-18 feet. Requires training for best form.

Betula (bet'you-la)
   classic name
   of birch

platyphylla (plat-i-fil'la)

japonica (ja-pon'i-ka)
   from Japan

JAPANESE WHITE BIRCH

Family Betulaceae

Size	Height 25-30 feet; spread 10-15 feet.　　　　Zones 6, 7, 8.
Form	Slender and pyramidal with central leader. Foliage — alternate, simple, 1½-3 inches long; shaped like arrowhead. Flower — inconspicuous catkins. Fruit — small samara.
Texture	Fine.
Color	Foliage — glossy dark green; fall, yellow. Bark — white.
Culture	Sun. Soil — good drainage; medium fertility. Moisture — medium. Pruning — none. Pest Problems — bronze birch borer. Growth Rate — moderate.
Notes	Graceful and attractive specimen or lawn tree for cool areas.
Varieties	**B.p. szechuanica** — silver-white bark peeling in thin strips; red-brown stems and blue-green leaves. Open and spreading habit of growth. **Whitespire** — glossy dark green foliage; fall, clear golden yellow. Narrow pyramidal form; height 30 feet. Heat tolerant and borer resistant. Beautiful as specimen.

Carpinus (kar-py'nus)
    ancient name
    of hornbeam

caroliniana (ka-ro-lin-i-a'na)
    from Carolinas

AMERICAN HORNBEAM

Family Betulaceae

Size	Height 20-30 feet; spread 15-20 feet.	Zones 6, 7, 8, 9.

Form	Refined in character; light and informal growth with horizontal branching. Foliage — alternate, simple, double toothed, 2-4 inches long, parallel venation. Flower — spring; hanging catkins. Fruit — summer; small winged nut. Bark — smoothly ridged or knotted.
Texture	Fine.
Color	Foliage — dull green; fall, reddish. Flower — green. Fruit — black. Bark — gray.
Culture	Sun or shade. Soil — tolerant; medium drainage; medium fertility. Moisture — medium. Pruning — tolerant. Pest Problems — none. Growth Rate — very slow.
Notes	Good street or shade tree with refined character; also for hedges, game-cover, and natural areas. Trunk interesting for sculptural appearance. Transplant while young. May be trained as multi-trunk specimen.

Cercis (sir'sis)
   ancient Greek name

canadensis (kan-a-den'sis)
   from Canada

EASTERN REDBUD

Family Fabaceae

Size	Height 20-30 feet; spread 12-25 feet. Zones 6, 7, 8, 9.
Form	Dense and round in sun, loose and open in shade. Foliage — alternate, heart-shaped to 5 inches long, 3-5 inches wide. Flower — March and April before leaves appear; small and pealike, in clusters nearly covering bare branches. Fruit — late summer and fall; long, flattened pods.
Texture	Medium to coarse.
Color	Foliage — dark green; fall, yellow. Flower — lavender-pink. Fruit — green turning brown.
Culture	Sun or part shade. Soil — good drainage; medium fertility. Moisture — medium. Pruning — encourage low branching; multiple trunk desirable. Pest Problems — leaf rollers, aphids, spider mites, and leaf diseases. Growth Rate — slow to moderate.
Notes	Good foliage and very beautiful in blossom; interesting specimen or filler. Very drought resistant. Fruit sometimes unsightly when mature. Difficult to transplant when large or from woodlands.
Varieties	**alba** — white flowers. Outstanding specimen tree. **Flame** — large semi-double pink flowers; upright growth habit. **Forest Pansy** — dark purple leaves becoming dark green in June; rose-purple flowers. Very hardy. **Oklahoma** — glossy foliage; purple flowers. **Pinkbud** — bright pure pink flowers. **Royal** — abundant white flowers; outstanding specimen tree. **Texensis** — rose-pink flowers; grows well in dry soils. **Wither's Pink Charm** — flowers soft pale pink.

Cornus (kor'nus)
Latin horn, from
toughness of wood

florida (flo'ri-da)
freely flowering

FLOWERING DOGWOOD

Family Cornaceae

Size	Height 15-30 feet; spread 15-20 feet. Zones 6, 7, 8, 9.
Form	Semi-round top with horizontal branching; dense to fairly open; single or multi-trunked. Foliage — opposite, simple, entire or somewhat wavy, 3-6 inches long. Flower — mid-April; small compact heads surrounded by 4 petal-like bracts. Fruit — fall; ovoid, in clusters. Bark — scalelike.
Texture	Medium.
Color	Foliage — medium green; fall, scarlet. Flower — white. Fruit — red.
Culture	Part shade. Soil — good drainage; medium fertility. Moisture — medium. Pruning — remove half of top if transplanting bare-root. Pest Problems — dogwood borers under bark and anthracnose on foliage; dogwood canker. Growth Rate — moderate.
Notes	Interesting horizontal branch structure. Use in group plantings or as accent in borders and margins of woods and undergrowth. Most popular of flowering trees with year-round interest. Develops thinner and more graceful habit in part shade rather than full sun.
Varieties	**Barton** — large white flowers, blooms at early age. **Cherokee Chief** — ruby-red flowers; branches uniformly, ideal specimen. **Cherokee Princess** — early white flowers; upright habit of growth. **Cloud Nine** — slow grower with white flowers; spreading branches. Blooms at early age. **Fastigiate** — upright branching habit when young. **Fragrant Cloud** — abundant white flowers with slight fragrance. **Gigantea** — flower 6 inches in diameter. **Nana (Pygmaea)** — height 5-6 feet; dark green foliage. **plena** — double flowers. **Purple Glory** — dark purple leaves; dark red flowers. **Rubra** — soft pink or rose flowers. **White Cloud** — profusion of creamy-white flowers. **Xanthocarpa** — yellow fruit.

Cornus (kor'nus)
Latin horn, from
toughness of wood

kousa (kou'suh)
Japanese vernacular
name

KOUSA DOGWOOD

Family Cornaceae

Size	Height 10-15 feet; spread 10 feet. Zones 6, 7, 8.
Form	Large shrub or small tree; single or multi-stem with horizontal branching. Foliage — opposite, dense, 4 inches long. Flower — early May; inconspicuous, surrounded by large pointed bracts 1½-2 inches long. Fruit — late summer; raspberry-like, ½-1 inch diameter.
Texture	Medium.
Color	Foliage — lustrous green; fall, scarlet. Flower — white. Fruit — pinkish-red.
Culture	Sun or part shade. Soil — good drainage; medium fertility. Moisture — medium. Pruning — shape. Pest Problems — borers. Growth Rate — moderate.
Notes	Blooms after leaves appear. Useful as specimen or accent in background; excellent border or hedge for large areas. Attractive against large evergreens. Resistant to dogwood canker.
Varieties	**chinensis** — Chinese Dogwood. Bracts slightly longer (2-3½ inches) than species; scarlet autumn leaf coloring. **Gold Star** — variegated leaves and bracts. **Kessoni** — blooms later than *chinensis*. **Lustgarten Weeping** — pendulous branches. **Milky Way** — profusely flowering cultivar of *C. kousa chinensis*. **Rosabella** — bright pink bracts; slow-growing. **Summer Stars** — long flowering period, dark green foliage changing to maroon in fall.

Cornus (kor'nus)
Latin horn, from
toughness of wood

mas (mahs)
male, robust

CORNELIAN-CHERRY DOGWOOD

Family Cornaceae

Size	Height 20-25 feet; spread 15-20 feet. Zones 6, 7, 8.
Form	Oval head with lower branches spreading widely. Foliage — opposite, simple, 3-4 inches long, ovate to elliptic. Flower — very early spring, appearing before leaves; minute and very abundant, covering twigs. Fruit — spring to summer; oval drupe, ⅝ inch long.
Texture	Medium.
Color	Foliage — lustrous bright green; fall, reddish-green. Flower — bright yellow-green. Fruit — shiny dark scarlet. Bark — dark brown.
Culture	Sun to part shade. Soil — tolerant; good drainage; high fertility. Moisture — medium. Pruning — tolerant. Pest Problems — none. Growth Rate — moderate.
Notes	Remove lower branches to create small tree or patio specimen. Good screen or windbreak in natural areas. Combines well with evergreens; withstands city conditions.
Varieties	**Aureo-elegantissima** — leaves variegated with cream-white and pink tinged. **Golden Glory** — more flowers than species; upright growth habit.

Cotinus (ko-ty'nus)
  ancient Greek name
  for tree with red wood

coggyria (ko-gig'ree-uh)
  ancient Greek name

SMOKETREE

Family

Anacardiaceae

Size	Height 10-15 feet; spread 8-14 feet. Zones 6, 7, 8.
Form	Shrub or small tree; open and irregular. Foliage — alternate, 3 inches long, oval. Flower — June and July; inconspicuous clusters. Fruit — August and September; 7-10 panicles on female plants; stalks of fruiting panicles create smoky effect.
Texture	Medium.
Color	Foliage — reddish turning green; fall, red, orange, or yellow. Flower — greenish-yellow. Fruit — light pink to gray.
Culture	Sun. Soil — good drainage; low fertility. Moisture — low when established. Pruning — remove dead branches. Pest Problems — nematodes and verticillium wilt. Growth Rate — moderate to rapid in sandy soils.
Notes	Maintain high moisture until well established. Interesting specimen or border plant for cooler areas.
Varieties	**Daydream** — large purple-pink fruiting panicles. **Flame** — orange-red fall color; pink panicles. **Nordine** — purple-red foliage in summer; fall color yellow-orange; panicles of ruby red. Very hardy. **Pendulus** — branches drooping. **Purpureus** — purplish leaves and purple-pink fruiting panicles. **Velvet Cloak** — dark purple foliage in summer; fall color bright maroon.

Crataegus (kra-tee'gus)
　　Greek meaning strength,
　　referring to hard wood

phaenopyrum (fe-no-pi'rum)

WASHINGTON HAWTHORN

Family Rosaceae

Size	Height 25-30 feet; spread 20-25 feet. Zones 6, 7, 8.
Form	Dense, compact, upright with rounded broad head; slender horizontal thorny branches. Foliage — alternate, simple, triangular-ovate, doubly toothed, 1-3 inches long with 3-5 lobes. Flower — late spring; abundant terminal corymbs. Fruit — late summer; pendulous clusters of berries, ¼ inch diameter, persisting through winter.
Texture	Medium to fine.
Color	Foliage — glossy deep green; fall, orange to scarlet. Flower — white. Fruit — glossy bright red. Bark — brown-gray.
Culture	Sun. Soil — tolerant; medium drainage; medium fertility. Moisture — medium. Pruning — very tolerant. Pest Problems — fire blight and cedar-apple rust. Growth Rate — rapid when young.
Notes	Especially attractive in winter; use as specimen, dense barrier hedge or deciduous screen. Excellent in large shrub borders and highway plantings.
Variety	**Fastigiata** — columnar habit of growth; small fruit.

Elaeagnus (eel-ee-ag'nus)
from Greek for olive
and chaste tree

angustifolius (an-gus-tee-fo'li-us)
narrow-leaved

RUSSIAN-OLIVE

Family Elaeagnaceae

Size	Height 15-20 feet; spread 20-30 feet. Zones 6, 7, 8.
Form	Wide-spreading and open. Foliage — late spring to late fall; alternate, simple, entire, 2-3½ inches long. Flower — late spring; inconspicuous, fragrant. Fruit — summer to late fall; ½ inch long, egg-shaped.
Texture	Fine.
Color	Foliage — silver-gray. Flower — yellow. Fruit — yellow with silvery scales.
Culture	Sun. Soil — tolerant; medium drainage; medium fertility. Moisture — low to medium. Pruning — maintain desired shape and remove dead twigs. Pest Problems — none. Growth Rate — rapid.
Notes	Withstands severe exposures. Of value for rapid growth. Use as accent, hedge, or light-toned mass against evergreen background. Rather short lived. Grows well in coastal areas.

Firmiana (fir-mi-a'na)
   Phoenix tree

simplex (sim'pleks)
   simple, unbranched

CHINESE PARASOL TREE

Family Sterculiaceae

Size	Height 30-40 feet; spread 25-30 feet. Zones 7, 8, 9.
Form	Upright with round head. Foliage — alternate, simple, palmately lobed, 8-12 inches long and wide. Flower — June; terminal panicles 10-20 inches long. Fruit — carpels splitting to show pea-sized seeds.
Texture	Coarse.
Color	Foliage — rich green; fall, bright yellow. Flower — lemon-yellow. Fruit — light brown. Bark — smooth gray-green.
Culture	Sun. Soil — medium drainage; medium fertility. Moisture — medium. Pruning — none. Pest Problems — none. Growth Rate — rapid.
Notes	Interesting in all seasons as specimen or shade and street tree. Tropical in appearance; casts dense shade.
Variety	**Variegata** — leaves mottled with white.

Franklinia (frank-lin'i-a)
named for Benjamin Franklin

alatamaha (al-tah-ma'ha)
named for Alatamaha River,
Georgia

FRANKLINIA

Family Theaceae

Size	Height 20-30 feet; spread 15-18 feet. Zones 6, 7, 8, 9.
Form	Pyramidal with spreading branches; large shrub or small tree. Foliage — midspring to midfall; alternate, simple, finely toothed, 5-7 inches long, lustrous above, pubescent beneath. Flower — September to October; 3 inch diameter, clustered buds developing singly, each lasting several days, cup-shaped, fragrant.
Texture	Coarse.
Color	Foliage — glossy green; fall, brilliant red or orange. Flower — white with yellow stamens.
Culture	Sun. Soil — medium drainage; high fertility. Moisture — medium to high. Pruning — shape and clean. Pest Problems — none. Growth Rate — moderate to slow.
Notes	Valued for showy, fragrant late summer flowers and colorful autumn foliage. Use as accent, specimen, or filler in shrub borders. Difficult to transplant successfully.

Halesia (hal-ee'si-a)
  silverbell

carolina (ka-ro-lin'a)
  from Carolina

CAROLINA SILVERBELL

Family Styracaceae

Size	Height 20-40 feet; spread 20 feet. Zones 6, 7, 8.
Form	Rounded, open, irregular. Foliage — alternate, 2-5 inches long. Flower — mid-April; bell-shaped, pendulous, ½-¾ inches long, 2-5 in cluster. Fruit — fall; dry winged pods 1-2 inches long. Bark — scales large and loose.
Texture	Medium to coarse.
Color	Foliage — light green; fall, yellow. Flower — white. Fruit — translucent yellow, turning brown. Bark — gray to brown.
Culture	Part shade or shade. Soil — good drainage; medium to low fertility. Moisture — medium. Pruning — none. Pest Problems — none. Growth Rate — slow to moderate.
Notes	Attractive multi-stem small tree. Interesting effect with night lighting against evergreen background. Useful in borders and along paths or streets where flowers can be seen. Excellent as naturalizing material.
Varieties	**Meehanii** — numerous small white flowers; rounded shrub-like habit of growth to 12 feet height. **rosea** — pale pink flowers.

Hamamelis (ham-am-ee'lis)
Greek for together and apple;
flowers and fruit
appear together

mollis (mol'lis)
soft

CHINESE WITCH-HAZEL

Family Hamamelidaceae

Size	Height 15-20 feet; spread 8-10 feet. Zones 6, 7.
Form	Graceful and broadly spreading. Young twigs and buds pubescent. Foliage — alternate, 4-7 inches long. Flower — February to March; 1½ inches wide with 4 ribbonlike petals, very fragrant. Fruit — dry capsule.
Texture	Coarse.
Color	Foliage — medium green; fall, bright yellow. Flower — bright yellow. Fruit — brown with black seeds.
Culture	Sun or part shade. Soil — medium drainage; medium fertility with humus added. Moisture — medium to high. Pruning — train to tree form if desired. Pest Problems — none. Growth Rate — slow to moderate.
Notes	Valued for very early spring flowering and beautiful autumn coloring. For specimen use or naturalizing.
Varieties	**Arnold Promise** — hybrid between *H. mollis* and *H. japonica*. **Diana** — hybrid with *H. japonica*. Bright copper-red flowers and red-orange fall foliage. **Goldcrest** — large golden flowers with sweet fragrance, late-blooming. **Pallida** — conspicuous lemon-yellow flowers; lustrous foliage. **Primavera** — hybrid with *H. japonica*; vigorous form, abundant canary-yellow flowers. Orange-red fall foliage.

Koelreuteria (kel-roo-teer'i-a)
named for
Joseph G. Koelreuter

bipinnata (bi-pin-a'ta)
twice pinnate

CHINESE FLAME TREE

Family Sapindaceae

Size	Height 20-30 feet; spread 15-20 feet.	Zones 7, 8, 9.
Form	Irregular with spreading crown. Foliage — alternate, bipinnately compound, 18 inches long with 7-12 ovate to oblong leaflets 4-5 inches long. Flower — early summer; showy terminal panicles. Fruit — late summer to fall; capsules 2½ inches long, conspicuous and showy.	
Texture	Medium.	
Color	Foliage — dark green. Flower — yellow. Fruit — rose-pink. Bark — light brown.	
Culture	Sun. Soil — very tolerant; good drainage; medium fertility. Moisture — medium. Pruning — none. Pest Problems — none. Growth Rate — moderate to rapid.	
Notes	Excellent as lawn or street tree or as specimen where space is limited. May be trained as multi-trunk form; gives textural interest all seasons.	

Koelreuteria (kel-roo-teer'i-a)
named for
Joseph G. Koelreuter

paniculata (pan-ick-kew-lay'ta)
compound raceme

GOLDEN-RAIN-TREE

Family Sapindaceae

Size	Height 20-30 feet; spread 15-20 feet. Zones 6, 7, 8, 9.
Form	Upright, irregular; medium to open density. Foliage -- alternate, single or double pinnately compound, 9-14 inches long. Flower — June; pyramidal clusters 1-1½ feet long. Fruit — midsummer to fall; clusters of 2 inch papery pods.
Texture	Medium.
Color	Foliage — dark green. Flower — yellow. Fruit — light brown.
Culture	Sun or part shade. Soil — good drainage essential; medium fertility. Moisture — medium. Pruning — remove weak limbs. Pest Problems — none. Growth Rate — moderate to rapid.
Notes	Foliage similar to chinaberry. Valuable for flower and showy seed pods. Best used in groups; withstands city conditons. Short lived. May be trained as multi-trunk specimen.
Varieties	**Fastigiata** — columnar habit of growth; 4-7 feet wide. Sparse flowering. **September** — golden flowers in August and September. Height 30-40 feet. Pink-bronze fruit capsules.

Laburnum (la-bur'num)
   ancient Latin name

anagyroides (a-na-ju-roy'deez)
   bearing recurved pods

GOLDEN-CHAIN

Family Fabaceae

Size	Height 20-30 feet; spread 10-15 feet.	Zones 6, 7.
Form	Stiff and upright; multi-trunked; sparsely branched with erect or ascending branches. Foliage — alternate, compound with leaflets 1½-2½ inches long, cloverlike and silky pubescent when young. Flower — May after leaves appear; pendulous clusters to 12 inches long, pealike, profuse. Fruit — mid-summer; long persistant; pods 12 inches long; seeds very poisonous.	
Texture	Fine.	
Color	Foliage — bright green. Flower — bright yellow. Fruit — green turning black.	
Culture	Sun. Soil — well-drained; medium fertility. Moisture — medium. Pruning — shape. Pest Problems — mildew. Growth Rate — slow.	
Notes	Exotic; occasionally useful as specimen or in masses. Adapted for planting on rocky slopes. Foliage often harmed by frost; rather short-lived. Needs protection from winds and drought.	
Variety	**Pendulum** — hybrid with *L. alpinum*; graceful weeping form.	

Lagerstroemia (lay-ger-stree'mi-a)
named for Magnus
von Lagerstroem

indica (in'di-ka)
from India

CRAPE-MYRTLE

Family Lythraceae

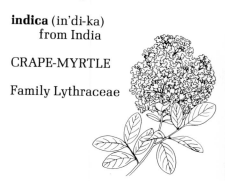

Size	Height 15-25 feet; spread 5-15 feet. Zones 6, 7, 8, 9.
Form	Upright and open or rounded; multiple trunk with dense branching. Foliage — emerging in late spring; opposite, 1-2 inches long. Flower — July and August; dense clusters 4-9 inches long on new wood.
Texture	Medium.
Color	Foliage — medium green; fall, yellow, red, or rust-red. Flower — white, pink, red, or lavender. Bark — pale gray-brown, shredding to reveal lighter underbark.
Culture	Sun. Soil — medium to good drainage; medium to high fertility. Moisture — medium to high. Pruning — lightly for shape. Pest Problems — mildew when grown in shade. Growth Rate — moderate.
Notes	Decorative and effective throughout year as specimen or multi-trunked small tree. Not screening material; use with evergreen background. May be pruned annually to ground to maintain shrub size. Difficult to transplant large sizes.
Varieties	**Acoma** — height 4-6 feet; pendulous branches with white flowers. Mildew resistant foliage. **Cherokee** — height 10-12 feet; mildew resistant dark green foliage and bright red flowers. **Hopi** — height 7-9 feet; pink flowers and mildew resistant foliage; very cold hardy. **Muskogee** — height 18-20 feet; glossy green mildew resistant foliage and lavender flowers. **Natchez** — height 18-20 feet; glossy green mildew resistant foliage; pure white flowers. Distinctive bark throughout year. **Near East** — exquisite pale-pink flowers. Height 18-20 feet. **Pecos** — medium pink flowers July to September. Semi-dwarf growth habit. Maroon fall foliage. Mildew resistant. **Potomac** — height 18-20 feet, upright growth. Dark green mildew resistant foliage and clear pink flowers. **Powhaten** — height 14-16 feet; medium purple flowers; moderate mildew resistance. **Tuskegee** — horizontal growth habit; dark pink flowers. Mildew resistant. **William Toovey** — watermelon pink flowers; shiny green foliage. Height 12-15 feet; moderate mildew resistance. **Zuni** — semi-dwarf growth habit; lavender flowers. Mildew resistant.

Magnolia (mag-no'li-a)
   named for Pierre Magnol

macrophylla (mak-ro-fil'a)
   large-leaved

BIGLEAF MAGNOLIA

Family Magnoliaceae

Size	Height 30-40 feet; spread 20-25 feet. Zones 6, 7, 8.
Form	Open, ascendant habit with round head. Foliage — alternate, simple, oblong-obovate, 12 to 30 inches long, 7-12 inches across. Flower — June; 10-12 inches across with 6 petals. Fruit — egg-shaped, 3 inches long.
Texture	Coarse.
Color	Foliage — bright green above, silver-gray beneath. Flower — cream-white. Fruit — rose to brown.
Culture	Sun to part shade. Soil — good drainage; medium fertility. Moisture — high. Pruning — none. Pest Problems — none. Growth Rate — slow.
Notes	Native plant of use as specimen and in large parks and natural areas. Looks best with dark evergreen background; combines well with dogwoods.
Varieties	**Palmberg** — very large flowers. **Purple Spotted** — flowers with purple markings in center.

Magnolia (mag-no'li-a)
named for Pierre Magnol

x soulangiana (su-lan'gee-ana)
named for C. Soulange-Bodin

SAUCER MAGNOLIA

Family Magnoliaceae

Size	Height 15-25 feet; spread 15-25 feet. Zones 6, 7, 8, 9.
Form	Upright and irregular with open branching. Foliage — alternate, simple, entire, 4-6 inches long. Flower — March before leaves appear; cup-shaped, 6 inch diameter.
Texture	Medium to coarse.
Color	Foliage — medium green. Flower — purple to white. Bark — gray-brown.
Culture	Sun or part shade. Soil — medium to good drainage; medium to high fertility. Moisture — medium to high. Pruning — none. Pest Problems — scale. Growth Rate — moderate.
Notes	Best suited to city gardens; espaliers well in limited areas. Often begins blooming when very young. Select late-blooming varieties to avoid damage from late freezes.
Varieties	**Alba Superba** — compact growth habit; white flowers. **Alexandrina** — flowers large, light pink outside, white inside. **Brozzoni** — white flowers, 10 inch diameter; late-flowering. **Burgundy** — large deep red-purple flowers; early flowering. **Lennei** — flowers large, saucer-shaped, petals deep purple on outside and white on inside; late-blooming. **Lennei Alba** — pure white flowers. **Speciosa** — pale pink-white flowers; late-blooming. **Susan** — blooms in spring and again in summer, dark pink-purple flowers. **Verbanica** — late-flowering, rose to white petals.

Magnolia (mag-no'li-a)
   named for Pierre Magnol

tripetala (tri-pe'ta-la)
   with three petals

UMBRELLA MAGNOLIA

Family Magnoliaceae

		Zones 6, 7, 8.
Size	Height 20-30 feet; spread 20-25 feet.	
Form	Open habit of growth with leaves clustered at ends of branches creating umbrella effect. Foliage — alternate, simple, oblong-ovate, 10-24 inches long and 6-10 inches wide. Flower — May; 6-10 inches across. Fruit — September; cone-shaped, 4 inches long.	
Texture	Coarse.	
Color	Foliage — dark green above, pale green beneath. Flower — cream-white. Fruit — rose-red.	
Culture	Sun to part shade. Soil — tolerant; medium drainage; medium fertility. Moisture — medium. Pruning — none. Pest Problems — none. Growth Rate — rapid.	
Notes	Native plant; use in parks and natural areas. Interesting as specimen. Exotic and tropical in effect.	
Varieties	**Bloomfield** — very large cream-white flowers. **Woodlawn** — showy large fruit.	

Malus (may'lus)
   ancient Latin name
   of apple

domestica (doe-mest'i-ca)
   domesticated

APPLE

Family Rosaceae

Size	Height 25-40 feet; spread 25-40 feet.　　　　Zones 6, 7, 8.
Form	Spreading to semi-round top, compact. Foliage — alternate, 2-4 inches long. Flower — spring; clusters borne on spurs. Fruit — late summer; pome.
Texture	Medium.
Color	Foliage — dark green. Flower — pinkish-white. Fruit — yellow to red.
Culture	Sun. Soil — medium to good drainage; medium fertility. Moisture — medium. Pruning — train for strength of branches. Pest Problems — scale, fruit worms, cedar apple rust, scab, blotch, and fire blight. Growth Rate — moderate.
Notes	Develops rugged, sculptural form with careful pruning. Size between 8-15 feet controlled by use of dwarfing rootstocks; cross-pollination required for good fruiting in some varieties. Follow regular spray schedule.
Varieties	**Arkansas Black** — red fruit; cross-pollination necessary. **Golden Delicious** — yellow apples; self-fruitful. **Red Delicious** — cross-pollination necessary. **Red Rome** — very late ripening; self-fruitful.

Malus (may'lus)
ancient Latin name
of apple

hybrida (hy'brid-a)
hybrid

FLOWERING CRAB APPLE

Family Rosaceae

Size	Height 15-25 feet; spread 10-20 feet.	Zones 6, 7, 8.
Form	Round to spreading crown with irregular or horizontal branching. Foliage — alternate, 1-3 inches long. Flower — April; 1-2 inches wide in clusters. Fruit — midsummer; ¼-1½ inch diameter.	
Texture	Medium.	
Color	Foliage — medium green. Flower — white to rose. Fruit — red or yellow.	
Culture	Sun. Soil — medium drainage; medium fertility. Moisture — medium. Pruning — develop central trunk. Pest Problems — leaf defoliators, borers, scale, fire blight, powdery mildew, and rust. Growth Rate — moderate.	
Notes	More susceptible to fire blight when forced by too much fertilizer or heavy pruning. Many fine species available for specimen use and massing, such as *M. floribunda, M. arnoldiana, M. sargentii,* and *M. toringoides.*	
Varieties	**Callaway** — pink buds open to large white flowers; 1 inch bright red fruit. Good disease resistance. **Dolgo** — fragrant white flowers; large red-purple fruit. **Donald Wyman** — pink buds, white flowers; ½ inch bright red fruit. Susceptible to mildew. **Harvest Gold** — single white flowers; yellow fruit persists until December; upright growth habit. Excellent disease resistance. **Katherine** — large double white flowers; yellow fruit with red blush. Good disease resistance. **Pink Spires** — pale lavender flowers; persistant red-purple fruit. **Red Jade** — weeping habit; white flowers; cherry-red fruit. **Red Jewel** — single white flowers; bright red fruit persists into December. **Selkirk** — rose-red flowers; shiny red-purple fruit. Upright growth habit. **White Angel** — single white flowers; abundant glossy red fruit. **Zumi** — large white flowers, fragrant. Bright red fruit persists into December. Fall foliage golden-orange.	

Morus (mo'rus)
  mulberry

alba (al'ba)
  white

WHITE MULBERRY

Family Moraceae

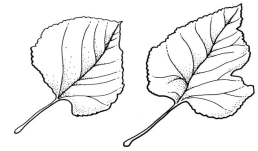

Size	Height 30-35 feet; spread 25-30 feet. Zones 6, 7, 8, 9.
Form	Dense and broad-spreading with round top, often multi-trunked. Foliage — alternate, simple, undivided or irregularly lobed, 2-7 inches long, 2-6 inches wide. Flower — April; small pendulous catkins, inconspicuous. Fruit — June to July; fleshy drupes ½-1 inch long. Bark — rough.
Texture	Coarse.
Color	Foliage — glossy bright green. Flower — greenish-white. Fruit — white, pink, and dark purple. Bark — gray.
Culture	Sun to part shade. Soil — very tolerant; adapts easily to most soil conditions. Moisture — medium. Pruning — very tolerant. Pest Problems — mildew and scale. Growth Rate — rapid.
Notes	Will grow rapidly in poorest soils and at seashore. Withstands drought and worst city conditions; gives quick shade where nothing else will grow. Select fruitless varieties for street and patio planting. Fruiting varieties suitable only for natural areas or to attract birds.
Varieties	**Beautiful Day** — large white fruit. **Kingan** — leathery foliage; fruitless. **Pyramidalis** — upright conical habit of growth. **Rupp's** — large fruit 1¾ inches long. **Stribling** — fall foliage bright yellow; fruitless.

Morus (mo'rus)
  mulberry

alba (al'ba)
  white

'Pendula' (pen'dew-la)
  pendulous, hanging

WEEPING WHITE MULBERRY

Family Moraceae

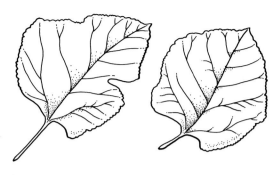

Size	Height 25-30 feet; spread 20-25 feet.	Zones 6, 7, 8, 9.

Form   Twisted, gnarled growth habit with slender pendulous branches sweeping ground. Foliage — alternate, simple, undivided, or irregularly lobed, 2-6 inches long, 2-5 inches wide. Flower — inconspicuous. Fruit — drupes ½-1 inches long.

Texture   Coarse.

Color   Foliage — glossy bright green. Fruit — white, pink and dark purple.

Culture   Sun to part shade. Soil — very tolerant. Moisture — medium. Pruning — very tolerant; maintain shape. Pest Problems — mildew and scale. Growth Rate — rapid.

Notes   Interesting as accent plant in all seasons; useful contrast in large scale ground-cover plantings. Dense weeping branches hide fruit litter. Withstands worst soil conditions; easily transplanted, grows rapidly.

Varieties   **M.a. Chaparral** — weeping growth habit; fruitless. **M.a. Urbana** — weeping habit; fruitless.

Oxydendrum (ok-si-den'drum)
Greek for sour tree, from
acid taste of foliage

arboreum (ar-bore'ee-um)
treelike

SOURWOOD

Family Ericaceae

Size	Height 20-30 feet; spread 10-15 feet. Zones 6, 7, 8, 9.
Form	Erect with slender trunk and slender upright branches, oval to cylindrical crown. Foliage — alternate, simple, toothed, to 8 inches long. Flower — summer; terminal clusters of one-sided racemes, spreading and curving out and up. Fruit — late fall, persisting; ovoid-pyramidal capsules.
Texture	Coarse.
Color	Foliage — shiny green; fall, brilliant red. Flower — white. Fruit — gray. Bark — reddish gray, branchlets brown or reddish.
Culture	Sun or shade. Soil — medium drainage; medium fertility; prefers acid soil. Moisture — medium to low. Pruning — trim for shape. Pest Problems — fall webworm. Growth Rate — slow.
Notes	Slender and handsome; valued for summer flowering and for brilliant fall coloring; useful in borders and as undercover in woodland. Best effect when planted in groups. Easy to transplant when young. May be trained as multi-trunk specimen.

Pistacia (pis-ta'shi-a)
from Greek pistake,
pistachio nut

chinensis (chi-nen'sis)
from China

PISTACHIO

Family Anacardiaceae

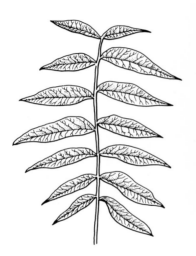

Size	Height 25-40 feet; spread 25-35 feet. Zones 6, 7, 8, 9.
Form	Oval and rounded with light, open branching. Foliage — pinnately compound with 10-12 leaflets 2-4 inches long and ¾ inch wide. Flower — April; dioecious, male racemes 2-3 inches long, female panicles 7-9 inches long. Fruit — October; clusters of drupes ½-1 inch diameter. Bark — furrowed, scaly.
Texture	Medium to fine.
Color	Foliage — lustrous dark green; fall, brilliant orange-red. Fruit — red to purple. Bark — gray, inner layers salmon-red.
Culture	Sun. Soil — tolerant; good drainage; medium fertility. Moisture — high to medium. Pruning — tolerant; maintain shape. Pest Problems — none. Growth Rate — moderate to rapid.
Notes	Outstanding as park, street, or lawn tree; excellent fall foliage color. Adaptable to most soil conditions, drought resistant and easily transplanted.
Variety	**Keith Davey** — outstanding autumn color.

Prunus (proo'nus)
    classical Latin name
    of plum

cerasifera (ser-ra-sif'fer-ra)
    bearing cherries or
    cherrylike fruit

'Atropurpurea' (at-ro-per-pu're-a)
    dark purple

PISSARD PLUM

Family Rosaceae

Size	Height 15-20 feet; spread 10-15 feet. Zones 6, 7, 8.
Form	Smaller than domestic plum, twiggy and rounded, with ascending, spreading branches. Foliage — early spring to midfall; alternate, simple, 1½-2 inches long. Flower — spring with leaves; ¾ inch wide, often crowded on short twigs. Fruit — early summer; subglobose, 1 inch diameter, edible.
Texture	Medium.
Color	Foliage — reddish-purple. Flower — pinkish-white. Fruit — purple. Bark — dark gray.
Culture	Sun. Soil — medium drainage; medium fertility. Moisture — medium. Pruning — remove crossed branches. Pest Problems — fruit insects and diseases. Growth Rate — moderate to rapid.
Notes	Use as specimen or accent. Withstands hot, dry conditions. Ornamental varieties with colored foliage suitable for limited landscape use. Plant 2 feet apart for flowering hedge.
Variety	**P.c. Newport** — height 20-25 feet; purple-red foliage spring to fall. Remove crossing branches to maintain shape. Very hardy. May be trained as multi-trunk specimen. Combines well with pale yellow *Potentilla*.

Prunus (proo'nus)
    classical Latin name
    of plum

cerasus (ser'a-sus)
    name for cherry

SOUR CHERRY

Family Rosaceae

Size	Height 20-30 feet; spread 15-20 feet.	Zones 6, 7, 8.

Form   Rounded with open branching, light in effect. Foliage — alternate, simple, serrated, glabrous, 2-3½ inches long with petioles to 1 inch long. Flower — April, before leaves appear; single, ¾-1 inch wide in small clusters; self-fertile. Fruit — early summer; drupe ¾ inch diameter in small clusters, edible.

Texture   Medium.

Color   Foliage — light green. Flower — white. Fruit — shiny red to black. Bark — shiny black.

Culture   Sun or part shade. Soil — medium drainage; medium fertility. Moisture — medium. Pruning — remove weak and crossed branches. Pest Problems — usually none; occasionally caterpillars and virus diseases. Growth Rate — moderate.

Notes   Excellent form and pleasing natural appearance all seasons; flowers most effective against evergreen background. Tolerant of shaded situations in light woodlands or may be used as specimen or espaliered. Fruit attracts birds; avoid placing near drives, walks, and patios. Easily transplanted while young; lives 15-20 years.

Varieties   **austera** — dark red fruit. Morello Cherry. **Rhexii** — double white flowers; 1½ inches in diameter.

Prunus (proo'nus)
   classical Latin
   name of plum

persica (per'si-ka)
   from Persia

PEACH

Family Rosaceae

Size	Height 10-15 feet; spread 10-15 feet. Zones 6, 7, 8.
Form	Rounded or low and spreading when center opened by pruning. Medium density. Foliage — alternate, simple, toothed, slightly folded along midrib 3-6 inches long. Flower — early spring before leaves appear; single or double, 1-1½ inch diameter. Fruit — none on double-flowering types; summer; 1-3 inches in diameter on single flower types; drupe, indented on one side.
Texture	Medium.
Color	Foliage — shiny green. Flower — pink to rose. Fruit — yellow to pinkish-red.
Culture	Sun. Soil — good drainage; medium fertility. Moisture — medium. Pruning — annually to maintain shape and vigor. Pest Problems — complete spray program annually for control of scale, curculio, peach tree borer, leaf curl, brown rot, and scab. Growth Rate — rapid.
Notes	Nonfruiting or ornamental flowering peaches widely used for landscape purposes with no regular spray schedule required. Use as screen, border, or specimen where spectacular color display can be appreciated.
Varieties	**Alboplena** — height 20-25 feet; double white flowers. **Candor** — nonshowy flower; nonbrowning fruit. **Double White** — double white flowers. **Helen Borchers** — pink flower 2½ inch diameter. **Red Globe** — showy pink flowers; delicious large fruit. **Redhaven** — nonshowy flower; delicious fruit. **Weeping Double Pink** — double pink flowers; pendulous branches.

Prunus (proo'nus)
    classical Latin name
    of plum

serrulata (sir-roo-lay'ta)
    having minute, sawlike
    teeth

JAPANESE CHERRY

Family Rosaceae

Size	Height 15-25 feet; spread 15-20 feet.	Zones 6, 7,8,9.

Form   Upright with spreading branches. Foliage — alternate, simple, toothed, 2-4 inches long. Flower — April and May; single and double forms, ½-2½ inch diameter. Fruit — summer; ¼ inch diameter; no fruit on double-flowered varieties.

Texture   Medium.

Color   Foliage — medium green; fall, yellowish-orange. Flower — white to pink. Fruit — black.

Culture   Sun to part shade. Soil — very good drainage; medium fertility. Moisture — medium. Pruning — tolerant. Pest Problems — borers, scale, aphids, and various virus diseases. Growth Rate — moderate.

Notes   Outstanding for quick effect; usual life span 15-20 years. Select fragrant varieties if available.

Varieties   **Amanogawa** — fastigiate form; fragrant semi-double light pink flowers. **Botanzakura** — fragrant semi-double pale pink flowers. **Jo-nioi** — upright and spreading growth; fragrant single white flowers 1½ inch diameter. **Lannesiana** — fragrant pink flowers. **Paul Wohlert** — height 8-10 feet; semi-double deep pink flowers, early blooming. **Shirotae** — fragrant double white flowers 2½ inch diameter; semipendulous branching. **Shogetsu** — broad with flattened crown; double pale pink flowers 2 inch diameter.

Prunus (proo'nus)
classical Latin
name of plum

subhirtella (sub-hir-tell'a)
classical Latin
name of plum

pendula (pen'dew-la)
pendulous, hanging

WEEPING CHERRY

Family Rosaceae

Size	Height 15-30 feet; spread 10-15 feet. Zones 6, 7, 8.
Form	Forked trunk and drooping twiggy branches with slender, whiplike twigs, sometimes shrubby. Foliage — midspring to midfall; alternate, simple, 2-5 inches long. Flower — late March or early April; very numerous in clusters of 2-5, 1 inch wide, single. Fruit — summer; spherical drupes 1/3 inch diameter. Bark — smooth, lustrous, peeling in layers.
Texture	Medium to fine.
Color	Foliage — medium green. Flower — light pink. Fruit — black. Bark — red-brown.
Culture	Sun. Soil — medium drainage; medium fertility. Moisture — medium. Pruning — lightly for shape. Pest Problems — rot, borers, scale, and other insects. Growth Rate — moderate to rapid.
Notes	Valued for exquisite flowering effect. Graceful and airy. Excellent accent tree. Easily transplanted when young. Grafted on seedling stock of upright species. Not well adapted to Coastal Plains.
Varieties	**P.s. autumnalis** — semi-double soft pink flowers in spring and autumn; branches not pendulous. May be trained as multi-trunk specimen. **P.s. Yae-shidare-higan** — abundant long-lasting double pink flowers; pendulous branches. **Pink Cloud** — double pink flowers; pendulous branches. **Rubra** — deep rose flowers; pendulous branches. Looks best planted on steep bank. Height 10-15 feet; spread 18-20 feet.

Prunus (proo'nus)
  classical Latin name
  of plum

yedoensis (yed-o-en'sis)
  from district of Yeddo
  or Tokyo in Japan

YOSHINO CHERRY

Family Rosaceae

Size	Height 20-40 feet; spread 20-30 feet. Zones 6, 7, 8.
Form	Upright or pyramidal when young; broad, rounded, or flat-topped with age. Dense with foliage. Foliage — alternate, simple, toothed, 3-5 inches long. Flower — mid-March; single, 1-1½ inches diameter, slightly fragrant. Fruit — summer; ½ inch diameter.
Texture	Medium.
Color	Foliage — pale green; deep brownish-red when unfolding. Flower — white to pink. Fruit — purplish-black.
Culture	Sun. Soil — tolerant. Moisture — medium. Pruning — remove diseased wood and suckers from trunk. Pest Problems — borers. Growth Rate — rapid.
Notes	Excellent floral display in front of dense evergreens; flowers appear before leaves. Predominant species around Tidal Basin in Washington, D.C. Life span 15-20 years.
Varieties	**Akebono (Daybreak)** — double soft pink flowers. **Ivensii** — fragrant white flowers. Weeping growth habit; vigorous. **Perpendens (Shidare Yoshino)** — irregularly pendulous branches. **Pink Shell** — pink flowers becoming white. **Yoshino Pink Form** — pink flowers opening later than other varieties.

Punica (pew'nik-a)
  pomegranate

granatum (gra-na'tum)
  old substantive name

POMEGRANATE

Family Punicaceae

Size	Height 12-25 feet; spread 12-15 feet. Zones 7, 8, 9.
Form	Wide spreading, shrublike. Foliage — opposite, 1½-3 inches long. Flower — May to June; 5-7 wrinkled petals 1-2 inches wide in small clusters, single or double. Fruit — fall; berry 3-5 inch diameter, edible, tart.
Texture	Medium.
Color	Foliage — lustrous green to gray-green. Flower — scarlet-orange, white, yellow, and variegated. Fruit — yellow to red.
Culture	Sun. Soil — tolerant; good drainage; low to medium fertility. Moisture — medium. Pruning — for tree form remove water sprouts annually; thin out excessive growth. Pest Problems — none. Growth Rate — slow.
Notes	Use as specimen or as high hedge closely planted and pruned. Double-flowering varieties non-fruiting. Grows well in containers.
Varieties	**Alba-Plena (Multiplex)** — double white flowers; height 8 feet. **Chico** — height 6-8 feet; double orange-red flowers all summer. **Flore Pleno** — double red flowers. **Legrellei** — double orange-red flowers; no fruit. **nana** — dwarf form, 3 feet with scarlet orange flowers; and small inedible decorative fruit. May be used as unclipped hedge. **Wonderful** — scarlet flowers; large crimson fruit in fall.

Pyrus (py'rus)
    classical Latin
    name of pear tree

calleryana (kall-er-a'na)
    named for J.M.M. Callery

CALLERY PEAR

Family Rosaceae

Size	Height 20-40 feet; spread 20-30 feet. Zones 6, 7, 8, 9.
Form	Upright, semi-conical with vertical branching. Medium density. Foliage — alternate, simple, serrated, 2-3½ inches long. Flower — early April; 1 inch diameter in clusters. Fruit — May to June; ½ inch diameter.
Texture	Medium.
Color	Foliage — glossy green; fall, red. Flower — white. Fruit — orange-brown.
Culture	Sun or part shade. Soil — medium to good drainage; medium to low fertility. Moisture — medium. Pruning — lightly for strength and shape. Pest Problems — scale, fruit worms, cedar apple rust and scab. Growth rate — rapid.
Notes	Showy display of flowers in early spring; fruit adds interest without creating litter. Beautiful fall foliage color. Useful in formal design. Long lived.
Varieties	**Aristocrat** — branches more horizontal; vigorous growth. Yellow to red fall foliage. Susceptible to fire blight. **Bradford** — vigorous habit of growth; blossoms very cold hardy. Excellent as specimen, screen, or street tree. **Capitol** — upright habit of growth, forms tighter head than 'Bradford'. Susceptible to fire blight. Copper fall foliage. **Chanticleer** — narrow pyramidal habit of growth; red-purple fall foliage. **Redspire** — loose pyramidal form; yellow fall foliage. Susceptible to fire blight. **Whitehouse** — narrow pyramidal growth habit with strong central leader. Red to red-purple fall color.

Salix (say'licks)
 classical Latin
 for willow

caprea (kap'ree-a)
 pertaining to
 goat

GOAT WILLOW

Family Salicaceae

Size	Height 15-25 feet; spread 8-15 feet.	Zones 6, 7, 8.

Form
: Upright and shrubby with several trunks. Foliage — alternate, simple, toothed, 3-4 inches long. Flower — early spring; showy catkins about 1-1½ inches long. Fruit — capsule.

Texture
: Medium.

Color
: Foliage — gray-green. Flower — silvery-gray. Fruit — brown. Twigs — lustrous brown.

Culture
: Sun or part shade. Soil — medium drainage; medium to high fertility. Moisture — medium to high. Pruning — heavy thinning for renovation every 3-5 years. Pest Problems — leaf defoliators, scale, and rusts. Growth Rate — rapid.

Notes
: Used in landscaping as fast growing material. Interesting flowers and fruit for floral arrangements. Short lived.

Varieties
: **Pendula** — branches pendulous, shiny foliage. **Variegata** — leaves variegated with white.

Sassafras (sas'a-fras)
Spanish salsafras or
Saxifraga supposed to
have similar medicinal
properties

albidum (al'bee-dum)
white

COMMON SASSAFRAS

Family Lauraceae

Size	Height 25-40 feet; spread 20-25 feet.	Zones 6, 7, 8.

Form   Relatively small with numerous crooked branches forming horizontal branching outline. Foliage — late spring to early fall; alternate, simple, 3-5 inches long, 1-3 lobed or entire. Flower — spring; inconspicuous fragrant racemes. Fruit — late summer; drupes on female plants. Bark — aromatic, thick, rough, and fissured on old trunks, with firm, flat ridges.

Texture   Coarse in youth, medium with age.

Color   Foliage — bluish-green; fall, orange to red. Flower — light yellow. Fruit — dark blue with red stalks. Bark — red-brown.

Culture   Sun or part shade. Soil — very tolerant; good drainage; medium fertility in light soil. Moisture — medium. Pruning — remove dead wood and control suckers. Pest Problems — borers and Japanese beetles. Growth Rate — slow.

Notes   Valuable for gorgeous fall color and fragrant spring bloom. Useful for thickets, borders of woodland parks, and mass plantings. Excellent small tree for landscape use. Horizontal branching habit lends interest; excellent specimen. Difficult to transplant. May be trained to form multiple trunks.

Sorbus (sor'bus)
ancient Latin name

aucuparia (aw-kew-pay'ri-a)
specific name implying
bird-catching, from use
of fruits for this purpose

MOUNTAIN-ASH

Family Rosaceae

Size	Height 25-30 feet; spread 20-25 feet. Zones 6, 7.
Form	Slender trunk with spreading branches curving up, forming ovate head, fairly dense. Foliage — spring to early fall; alternate, pinnately compound, 9-15 leaflets, each 1-2 inches long. Flower — late spring, after leaves; flat-topped corymbs 4-6 inches wide. Fruit — late summer, persisting; showy clusters of ½ inch wide berries. Bark — smooth and lustrous, becoming rough at base on old trees.
Texture	Fine.
Color	Foliage — light green; fall, reddish. Flower — white. Fruit — orange to red. Bark — gray-green to red-brown.
Culture	Sun. Soil — very tolerant; medium drainage; medium fertility. Moisture — medium. Pruning — remove weak branches. Pest Problems — borers. Growth Rate — rapid.
Notes	Interesting specimen, showy with fruit, valuable for rocky hills, lawns, and parks. Good small tree for mountains. Easy to transplant. Somewhat short lived.
Varieties	**Apricot Lady** — apricot-yellow fruit; bright green foliage. **Beissneri** — orange-brown bark; large red berries persisting into winter. Graceful form. **Cardinal Royal** — very narrow habit of growth; red berries. **Edulis** — large edible fruit. **Fastigiata** — narrow upright habit of growth; dark green leaves and large red fruit. **Xanthocarpa** — orange-yellow fruit.

Ulmus (ul'mus)
   classical Latin name
   of elm

parvifolia (par-vi-fo'li-a)
   small-leaved

CHINESE ELM

Family Ulmaceae

Size	Height 30-40 feet; spread 25-30 feet. Zones 6, 7, 8, 9.
Form	Graceful and rounded with open or spreading crown. Foliage — alternate, simple, elliptic to obovate, 1-2½ inches long, ½-1½ inches wide. Flower — late summer or autumn; in axillary clusters, inconspicuous. Fruit — September; samara, decorative. Bark — mottled and exfoliating.
Texture	Medium to fine.
Color	Foliage — shiny deep green. Bark — shades of gray, green, and orange.
Culture	Sun or part shade. Soil — very tolerant; good drainage; medium fertility. Moisture — high to medium. Pruning — none. Pest Problems — usually resistant to Dutch elm disease. Growth Rate — moderate.
Notes	Superior tree for any situation; especially good in urban areas. Tough and durable, tolerates drought. Beautiful bark in all seasons; sometimes called Lacebark Elm.
Varieties	**Brea** — upright form; large leaves. **Drake** — sweeping, upright branches; foliage persists into winter. **Dynasty** — vase-shaped; smooth dark gray bark. **Prairie Shade** — excellent selection with small dark green leaves; extremely hardy. **Sempervirens (Pendens)** — attractive foliage persisting into winter; spreading branches. **True Green** — glossy leaves; graceful round head.

Viburnum (vy-bur'num)
classical Latin name
of wayfaring tree

prunifolium (pru-ni-fo'li-um)
with cherrylike leaves

BLACKHAW VIBURNUM

Family Caprifoliaceae

Size	Height 15-20 feet; spread 10-15 feet. Zones 6, 7, 8, 9.
Form	Broad, rounded head with low horizontal branching, usually multi-trunked. Foliage — opposite, broad-elliptic to ovate, 1½-3½ inches long and 1-2 inches wide. Flower — late spring; numerous flat-topped cymes 2-4 inches diameter. Fruit — September; drupe ½ inch long.
Texture	Medium.
Color	Foliage — dark green above, pale green beneath; fall, red to purple-bronze. Flower — white. Fruit — blue-black.
Culture	Sun or part shade. Soil — tolerant; medium drainage; medium fertility. Moisture — medium to low. Pruning — none. Pest Problems — none. Growth Rate — slow to moderate.
Notes	Attractive as multi-trunked specimen and in large shrub borders. May substitute for hawthorn and dogwood where these are not hardy. Graceful and adaptable tree which should be more widely used in residential landscaping and naturalized areas.

Viburnum (vy-bur'num)
    classical Latin name
    of wayfaring tree

rufidulum (ru-fid'u-lum)
    somewhat reddish

SOUTHERN BLACKHAW

Family Caprifoliaceae

Size	Height 20-25 feet; spread 15-20 feet. Zones 6, 7, 8, 9.
Form	Open, rounded or flat-topped; short trunk; stiff, stout branches. Foliage — opposite, simple, oval, 2-3 inches long, 1-1½ inches wide. Flower — May; conspicuous flat-topped clusters, 4-6 inches wide. Fruit — autumn; drupe ¼ inch diameter, in drooping clusters.
Texture	Medium.
Color	Foliage — shiny dark green above, rusty-tomentose beneath; fall, rich burgundy-red. Flower — white. Fruit — bright blue to blue-black.
Culture	Sun or shade. Soil — tolerant; medium drainage; medium fertility. Moisture — high to medium. Pruning — none. Pest Problems — none. Growth Rate — moderate.
Notes	Attractive as specimen and in shrub borders. Useful as substitute for dogwood; tolerates most soil conditions and transplants easily.

LARGE TREES — EVERGREEN

Abies (a'bi-ez)
  classical name for fir

firma (fir'ma)
  firm, strong

JAPANESE FIR

Family Pinaceae

Size	Height 50-70 feet; spread 40-60 feet.	Zones 6, 7.
Form	Symmetrically pyramidal; branched to base; opening up with age. Branchlets grooved. Foliage — 1½ inch long; apex rounded and notched; inconspicuous bands beneath. Fruit — 5 inch long cylindrical cones.	
Texture	Medium.	
Color	Foliage — green. Fruit — yellowish-green.	
Culture	Sun to part shade. Soil — acid, well-drained; medium to high fertility. Moisture — medium to high. Pruning — none. Pest Problems — spruce budworm, woolly aphid and cankers. Growth Rate — slow.	
Notes	Use as specimen and accent material. Good for screens and planted in groups. Does not tolerate air pollution, not suited for city planting. Pruning should be kept to minimum.	

Cedrus (see'drus)
old Greek name
for resinous tree

atlantica (at-lan'ti-ka)
of Atlas Mountains

ATLAS CEDAR

Family Pinaceae

Size	Height 40-50 feet; spread 35-45 feet. Zones 6, 7, 8, 9.
Form	Erect, pyramidal with stiff horizontal branches to ground in youth, flat-topped with spreading horizontal branches when mature. Foliage — stiff, needlelike, less than 1 inch long in clusters. Flower — inconspicuous. Fruit — barrel-shaped cone 1-3 inches long, upright on upperside of branches.
Texture	Medium.
Color	Foliage — blue-green to silver. Fruit — purple-green and light green becoming light brown. Bark — shiny gray.
Culture	Sun. Soil — good drainage; medium fertility. Moisture — medium. Pruning — none. Pest Problems — root rot, scale, tip blight, and deodar weevil. Growth Rate — slow when mature, rapid when young.
Notes	Picturesque specimen for large, open space. Resistant to drought and air pollution. Casts dense shade.
Varieties	**Argentea** — pale silver-gray foliage. **Fastigiata** — upright form; blue-green foliage. **Glauca** — bright blue-green foliage. Blue Atlas Cedar. **Glauca Pendula** — beautiful weeping form with blue-green foliage; stake to develop desired form.

Cedrus (see'drus)
old Greek name
for resinous tree

deodara (dee-o-dar'ra)
native name in India
for deodar

DEODAR CEDAR

Family Pinaceae

Size	Height 40-50 feet; spread 30-40 feet.	Zones 6, 7, 8.
Form	Pyramidal with pendulous branches. Foliage — needles 1-2 inches long borne in dense bunches. Fruit — 4 inch long upright cones, rarely produced.	
Texture	Fine.	
Color	Foliage — bluish-green. Fruit — green.	
Culture	Sun or part shade. Soil — medium drainage; medium fertility. Moisture — medium. Pruning — none. Pest Problems — borers may destroy central leader. Growth Rate — rapid.	
Notes	Seedlings vary considerably in foliage color. Should be planted where lower limbs may touch ground. Use as specimen or screen in large-scale areas.	
Varieties	**Compacta** — slow-growing; dense and rounded habit of growth. **Kashmir** — silvery blue-green leaves; very hardy. **Pendula** — long and drooping branches. **Shalimar** — blue-green leaves; very hardy. **Viridis** — dark green leaves.	

Cedrus (see'drus)
  old Greek name
  for resinous tree

libani (li'ba-nee)
  of Mount Lebanon

CEDAR OF LEBANON

Family Pinaceae

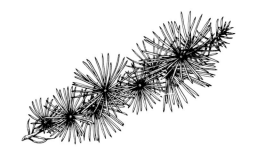

Size	Height 40-50 feet; spread 45-55 feet. Zones 6, 7, 8, 9.
Form	Pyramidal when young, thick trunk with wide spreading branches sweeping ground; picturesque flat top when mature. Foliage — stiff, dense and needlelike, 1 inch long, 30-40 per spur. Flower — inconspicuous. Fruit — barrel-shaped cones 3-4 inches long, rigidly upright.
Texture	Medium.
Color	Foliage — bright green or dark green. Fruit — purple-brown. Bark — gray-brown.
Culture	Sun. Soil — good drainage; medium fertility. Moisture — low. Pruning — none. Pest Problems — none. Growth Rate — slow when mature, rapid when young.
Notes	Distinctive in character; popular as park and garden specimen for open spaces. Somewhat stiff and rigid in appearance.
Varieties	**Argentea** — silver-blue foliage. **Sargentii** — dwarf and shrubby weeping form; slow-growing. **stenocoma** — dark green foliage; very hardy.

Cryptomeria (krip-to-me'ree-a)
   Greek referring to
   concealed parts of flower

japonica (ja-pon'i-ka)
   from Japan

JAPANESE CRYPTOMERIA

Family Taxodiaceae

Size	Height 60-80 feet; spread 25-35 feet.

Zones 6, 7, 8.

Form	Tall and narrowly conical with wide-spreading branches covered with sprays of foliage. Foliage — needles ¼ inch long, spirally arranged along drooping branchlets. Flower — inconspicuous catkins. Fruit — ¾ inch diameter globose cones.
Texture	Fine to medium.
Color	Foliage — dark green, bronze-green in winter. Bark — cinnamon-brown, shredding in long strips.
Culture	Sun or part shade. Soil — tolerant; medium drainage; medium fertility. Moisture — high to medium. Pruning — remove all dead branchlets. Pest Problems — none. Growth Rate — moderate to slow.
Notes	Needs fully exposed site in clean air for best growth. Handsome and graceful specimen for parks or for windscreen along country roads. Foliage and bark attractive in all seasons.
Varieties	**Cristata** — height 25-40 feet; conical and rather narrow. **Elegans** — height 12-16 feet; green feathery foliage, fall color soft red-bronze, unique texture. **Lobbii** — dense branching with shiny green needles all year. Grows well in southern climates. **Nana** — height and spread 3 feet; green foliage all winter.

x Cupressocyparis (kew-pres-o-si'pa-ris)
  intergeneric hybrid

leylandii (la-lan'de-i)
  after C.J. Leyland of
  Haggerston Hall

LEYLAND CYPRESS

Family Cupressaceae

Size	Height 60-70 feet; spread 12-17 feet.	Zones 6, 7, 8, 9.

Form
: Upright and graceful pyramid with dense pendulous branches.
Foliage — soft pointed leaves ¼ inch long on flattened branchlets.
Fruit — cones ¾ inch diameter with 8 scales.

Texture
: Fine.

Color
: Foliage — young leaves soft green, mature leaves dark blue-green.
Fruit — brown. Bark — red-brown, scaly.

Culture
: Sun. Soil — very tolerant; medium drainage; medium fertility.
Moisture — medium. Pruning — very tolerant. Pest Problems — bag-worms. Growth Rate — rapid.

Notes
: Looks best unpruned. Forms excellent upright hedge or dense wind-screen and background with judicious pruning. Good contrast with broadleaf evergreens.

Varieties
: **Castlewellan** — more compact form; gold-tipped leaves. Excellent for hedges in cool climates. **Leighton Green** — dense branching with dark green foliage; columnar form; hardy in zones 7, 8, 9. **Naylor's Blue** — blue-gray foliage; columnar form. **Silver Dust** — wide spreading form with blue-green foliage.

Juniperus (jew-nip'er-us)
   juniperlike

virginiana (vir-gin-i-a'na)
   from Virginia

EASTERN RED CEDAR

Family Cupressaceae

Size	Height 40-50 feet; spread 8-20 feet.	Zones 6, 7, 8, 9.

Form   Widely pyramidal with dense branching; grooved trunk. Foliage —
           minute and scale-like, clasping stem; opposite. Juvenile leaves awl-
           shaped. Fruit — 2-seeded berry-like cones ¼ inch diameter. Bark — thin
           and peeling in long strips.

Texture   Fine.

Color   Foliage — rich blue-green, rust-brown in winter. Fruit — pale blue-
           green to dark blue with silvery bloom. Bark — reddish-brown.

Culture   Sun or part shade. Soil — very tolerant; good drainage; medium fertility.
           Moisture — medium. Pruning — very tolerant. Pest Problems —
           bagworms; host for cedar apple rust, do not plant near apples or
           crabapples. Growth Rate — very slow.

Notes   Widely used for screening, windbreaks, and hedges; tolerant of salt
           spray.

Varieties **Burkii** — height 30 feet; narrowly pyramidal with dense growth; summer foliage
           color silver-green, winter color purple-green. **Columnaris** — dense columnar
           form; useful as screen. **Emerald Sentinel** — height 25 feet; upright conical form;
           emerald green foliage, darker in winter. **Gray Owl** — height 3 feet; feathery
           steel blue foliage; blue berries. **Pendula** — spreading branches and drooping
           branchlets; light green foliage. **Skyrocket** — very narrow columnar growth;
           foliage color blue-gray. Prefers full sun and dry soil. Grows well in containers.

Magnolia (mag-no'li-a)
named for Pierre Magnol

grandiflora (gran-di-flo'ra)
large or showy flowered

SOUTHERN MAGNOLIA

Family Magnoliaceae

Size	Height 40-60 feet; spread 25-30 feet. Zones 7,8,9.
Form	Conical and symmetrical; medium density. Foliage — alternate, 5-8 inches long. Flower — May to June; 4-6 inch diameter, fragrant. Fruit — late summer and fall; 3-4 inches long, conelike, splitting to disclose seeds.
Texture	Coarse.
Color	Foliage — lustrous dark green. Flower — white. Fruit — gray-brown with red seeds.
Culture	Sun or part shade. Soil — good drainage; medium fertility with high organic content. Moisture — high. Pruning — train young trees for shape. Pest Problems — occasional leaf spot and sun scald. Growth Rate — moderate to rapid.
Notes	Allow branches to touch ground to hide litter of leaves, flowers, and fruit. Needs ample space to develop well. Use as specimen or large screen. Seedlings vary in characteristics. Difficult to transplant when large.
Varieties	**Cairo** — glossy medium green leaves; early and long-flowering. **Charles Dickens** — leaves broad, nearly blunt; large flowers; large red fruit. **Goliath** — exceptionally large flowers to 12 inches in diameter; long flowering; bushy habit of growth. **Little Gem** — height 20-25 feet; small leaves and flowers; blooms when 3-4 feet high. Excellent as sheared evergreen hedge. **Majestic Beauty** — very large dark green leaves; profuse large flowers. **Praecox Fastigiata** — upright growth habit. **St. Mary** — dark green leaves; blooms when young. **Samuel Sommer** — rapid grower; flower 10-14 inch diameter. **Victoria** — leaves rust-red beneath; flowers small. Very hardy.

Picea (pi'se-a)
  Latin name for pitch-
  producing pine, spruce

abies (a'beez)
  Latin name for fir

NORWAY SPRUCE

Family Pinaceae

Size	Height 40-60 feet; spread 25-30 feet. Zones 6, 7.
Form	Conical with straight trunk; dense, regular tiers of branches becoming slightly pendulous with age. Foliage — sharp, stiff, square needles ¾ inch long. Fruit — terminal, pendant cones 5-7 inches long, slender; persisting through winter.
Texture	Medium.
Color	Foliage — bright green becoming dark green with age. Fruit — light brown. Bark — red-brown.
Culture	Sun or part shade. Soil — good drainage; medium fertility. Moisture — medium to high. Pruning — tolerant. Pest Problems — none. Growth Rate — rapid when young.
Notes	Use as temporary formal specimen or as screening and hedge in parks or large scale borders.
Varieties	**Arnold's Dwarf** — height 3-4 feet; spreading and bushy growth habit. **Argenteo-spica** — new shoots cream-white; foliage dark green. **Little Gem** — height 1 foot; dense rounded growth. **Microsperma** — dense pyramidal form; 10-15 feet height and spread. **Repens** — height 1-2 feet; wide-spreading with dense branches.

Picea (pi'se-a)
    Latin name for
    pitch-producing
    pine, spruce

orientalis (or-i-en-ta'lis)
    oriental, eastern

ORIENTAL SPRUCE

Family Pinaceae

Size	Height 50-70 feet; spread 30-40 feet. Zones 6, 7.
Form	Pyramidal, dense; branches stiffly horizontal or pendulous. Foliage — 4-sided, ¼-½ inch long. Flower — inconspicuous. Fruit — cylindrical cone 2-4 inches long and 1 inch wide. Bark — exfoliating.
Texture	Medium to fine.
Color	Foliage — lustrous dark green. Fruit — purple becoming cinnamon brown. Bark — brown.
Culture	Sun to part shade. Soil — tolerant; good drainage; medium fertility. Moisture — medium. Pruning — none. Pest Problems — spruce bud worm. Growth Rate — slow.
Notes	Handsome and graceful specimen in selected spaces. Does not tolerate southern heat and drought. Ornamental cones.
Varieties	**Aurea** — foliage gold tinged. **Gracilis** — height 18-20 feet; conical habit of growth with dense branching; bright green needles. Grows well in containers. **Skylands** — golden foliage. **Weeping Dwarf (Pendula)** — compact form with pendulous branchlets; slow-growing.

Picea (pi'se-a)
Latin name for
pitch-producing
pine, spruce

pungens (pun'jenz)
piercing, sharp
pointed

COLORADO SPRUCE

Family Pinaceae

Size	Height 70-90 feet; spread 30-40 feet.	Zones 6, 7.
Form	Broadly pyramidal with stiff horizontal branches, dense in appearance. Foliage — stiff, sharp, square needles 1-1¼ inches long. Fruit — oblong cones 2-4 inches long.	
Texture	Medium to coarse.	
Color	Foliage — gray-green to blue-green, blue in youth. Fruit — yellow-brown. Bark — gray-brown.	
Culture	Sun. Soil — good drainage; high fertility. Moisture — medium to high. Pruning — tolerant. Pest Problems — none. Growth Rate — slow.	
Notes	Best as specimen; does not combine well with other plants. Tolerant of dry climates.	
Varieties	**Foxtail** — heat resistant; excellent blue foliage, rapid growth. **Glauca Globosa** — height and spread 3 feet; compact flattened globe form with silver-blue needles. **Glauca Procumbens** — prostrate growth habit, forms weedproof mat. **Hoopsii** — dense pyramidal form with excellent waxy silver-blue foliage.	

Pinus (py'nus)
old Latin name for pine

bungeana (bun-je-ay'na)
named for Alexander von Bunge

LACEBARK PINE

Family Pinaceae

Size	Height 40-50 feet; spread 30-40 feet. Zones 6, 7, 8.
Form	Often multi-trunked, rounded to pyramidal with ascending branches. Foliage — 2-4 inches long, 3 needles in bundle, stiff and sharp to touch; needles held 3-5 years. Flower — monoecious, clustered. Fruit — cone 2-3 inches long, oval to pointed. Bark — exfoliating in irregular plates.
Texture	Fine.
Color	Foliage — bright green. Fruit — yellow-brown. Bark — cream, green, gray, brown.
Culture	Sun. Soil — well-drained; medium fertility; prefers acid soil. Moisture — medium. Pruning — none. Pest Problems — rusts, weevils, cankers, borers, bark beetles, and aphids. Growth Rate — slow.
Notes	Picturesque and exotic; extraordinarily beautiful as specimen. Branching form and bark interesting in all seasons; excellent contrast for broadleaf evergreens.

Pinus (py'nus)
old Latin name
for pine

palustris (pa-lus'tris)
marsh-loving

LONGLEAF PINE

Family Pinaceae

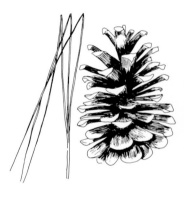

Size	Height 80-100 feet; spread 30-40 feet.	Zones 7, 8, 9.
Form	Ascending branches and open, rounded head. Foliage - 3 needles in bundle, 8-10 inches long. Fruit — cone 4-6 inches long, stemless.	
Texture	Fine.	
Color	Foliage — bright green. Fruit — reddish-brown. Buds — white.	
Culture	Sun to part shade. Soil — well-drained; medium fertility. Moisture — medium. Pruning — none. Pest Problems — rusts, bark beetles, sawflies, pine-shoot moth, and pine weevils. Growth Rate — rapid.	
Notes	Excellent in mass or as specimen for suburban areas, roadsides or lawns. Of limited use in upper Piedmont and mountains; needles accumulate heavy ice and snow. Difficult to transplant except when young.	

Pinus (py'nus)
old Latin
name for pine

strobus (stro'bus)
coned

WHITE PINE

Family Pinaceae

Size	Height 80-100 feet; spread 30-40 feet.　　　　Zones 6, 7.
Form	Symmetrical and pyramidal in youth, becoming irregular with age. Foliage — 3-4 inches long, 5 needles in bundle. Fruit — cone 5-6 inches long, slender and tapering, often curved.
Texture	Fine.
Color	Foliage — gray-green. Fruit — brown. Bark — gray; greenish-gray or tinged red when young.
Culture	Sun. Soil — well-drained; medium fertility. Moisture — medium to high. Pruning — none. Pest Problems — blister rust, weevils, borers, aphids, and woodrot. Growth Rate — rapid in youth.
Notes	Very handsome when used as ornamental specimen, mass or background; valuable for parks and estates. Good screen until lower branches fall. May be trained as tall hedge. Easy to transplant in large or small sizes. Limited to use in cooler parts of Piedmont and mountains.
Varieties	**Contorta** — branches twisted, bearing twisted needles. Height 20-30 feet. **Dawsoniana** — dwarf, spreading. **Fastigiata** — narrowly upright growth when young, wider with age. Excellent for narrow space. **glauca** — foliage light blue-green. **Hillside Winter Gold** — pale green and amber needles; excellent contrast for rhododendrons. **Nana (Densa)** — dwarf and bushy growth habit, becoming open with age. **Pendula** — pendulous branches; fine specimen. **Prostrata** — height 5-7 feet with trailing branches.

Pinus (py'nus)
old Latin name
for pine

sylvestris (sill-ves'triss)
growing in forests

SCOTCH PINE

Family Pinaceae

Size	Height 40-70 feet; spread 15-30 feet.	Zones 6, 7, 8.
Form	In youth symmetrical pyramid with short, spreading branches; with age very picturesque and open. Foliage — twisted needles 1-3 inches long, 2 in bundle. Fruit — cone 2-3 inches long. Bark — rough, scaling.	
Texture	Medium.	
Color	Foliage — dark green; winter, bluish-green. Fruit — brown. Bark — red-brown; upper bark bright orange if in favorable environment.	
Culture	Sun. Soil — well-drained; medium fertility. Moisture — medium. Pruning — none. Pest Problems — aphids, sawflies, rusts, borers, needle scales, and woodrot. Growth Rate — rapid.	
Notes	Valued for form and character; useful as specimen or in masses. Not suitable for base shrub planting. Easily transplanted.	
Varieties	**Aurea** — needles blue-green in spring, yellow and gold in summer and winter; height 16-18 feet. **Argentea** — silvery colored needles. **Compressa** — dwarf, conical in growth habit. **Fastigiata** — very narrow and columnar in growth habit, height to 30 feet. **Nana** — height 2 feet; bushy growth habit; gray-green needles. **Watereri** — dense slow-growing form with steel blue needles.	

Pinus (py'nus)
old Latin name
for pine

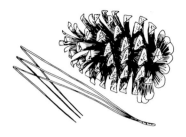

taeda (tae'da)
cone-bearing, torch-bearing

LOBLOLLY PINE

Family Pinaceae

Size	Height 70-90 feet; spread 30-40 feet. Zones 6, 7 ,8, 9.
Form	Horizontal or ascending branches and rounded head. Foliage — slender, stiff needles 5-10 inches long, 3 in bundle. Fruit — cone 2-5 inches long. Bark — scaly plates; branchlets often glaucous.
Texture	Fine.
Color	Foliage — bright green. Fruit — pale reddish-brown. Bark — red-brown to cinnamon.
Culture	Sun to part shade. Soil — well-drained; medium fertility. Moisture — medium. Pruning — none. Pest Problems — rusts, bark beetles, sawflies, pine-shoot moth, and pine weevils. Growth Rate — rapid.
Notes	Plant seedlings 12-18 inches in height. Useful in masses as tall windbreak or free-standing as specimen and shade tree. Provides protection for plants requiring light shade. Tolerates poor soil and severe exposures. Difficult to transplant successfully when 4 feet or more in height.
Variety	**Nana** — height 8-16 feet; dense and beautiful rounded growth habit. Slow-growing.

Pinus (py'nus)
old Latin name
for pine

thunbergiana (thun-ber-gee-a'na)
named for
C.P. Thunberg

JAPANESE BLACK PINE

Family Pinaceae

| Size | Height 50-70 feet; spread 25 feet. | Zones 6, 7, 8. |

Size   Height 50-70 feet; spread 25 feet.   Zones 6, 7, 8.

Form   Irregular with broad asymmetric head. Branches dense, wide spreading
            and pendulous. Terminal buds large. Foliage — needles in clusters of 2,
            3-5 inches long, stiff and sharply pointed. Fruit — cones 2-3 inches long.

Texture   Medium.

Color   Foliage — dark, bright green. Fruit — brown. Bud — whitish gray.

Culture   Sun. Soil — tolerant. Moisture — low. Pruning — shape. Pest Problems —
            tip moth and scale larvae of sawfly. Growth Rate — moderate to slow.

Notes   Best growth in seashore conditions. Useful in rows for bordering drives,
            property lines, and particularly as screening material spaced 4-6 feet
            apart. As specimen may be pruned and trained to desired form.

Pseudotsuga (su-doe-su'ga)
   from Greek false
   and *Tsuga*

menziesii (men-zeez'ee-i)
   after Archibald Menzies,
   naval surgeon and botanist

DOUGLAS FIR

Family Pinaceae

Size	Height 40-60 feet; spread 15-20 feet. Zones 6, 7.
Form	Open and pyramidal with straight, stiff, widespreading branches, lower branches drooping. Foliage — needlelike, straight and flat, 1-1½ inches long, thin and soft. Flower — inconspicuous. Fruit — pendulous cones 3-4 inches long and 1½-2 inches wide, prominent bracts with 3-lobed forklike projection. Bark — thick and ridged when old.
Texture	Medium.
Color	Foliage — shiny dark green. Fruit — light brown.
Culture	Sun. Soil — good drainage; medium fertility. Moisture — medium. Pruning — none. Pest Problems — borers, aphids, scale, and blight. Growth Rate — moderate.
Notes	Excellent as windbreak, background, and as specimen or in groups. Ornamental cones.
Varieties	**Compacta Viridis** — compact pyramidal form; dark green needles. **Fastigiata** — dense conical form; beautiful as specimen. **glauca** — dense, slow-growing form; blue-green needles. **Glauca Pendula** — weeping branches; blue-green foliage.

Quercus (kwer'kus)
    classical Latin name
    for oak

laurifolia (lor-ri-fo'li-a)
    with leaves like laurel

LAUREL OAK

Family Fagaceae

Size	Height 40-60 feet; spread 30-40 feet. Zones 7, 8, 9.
Form	Dense, upright with round top. Foliage — alternate, entire or slightly lobed, semi-evergreen, 2-5 inches long. Flower — spring; staminate in drooping catkins, pistillate in spikes. Fruit — acorn ⅝ inch long.
Texture	Medium to fine.
Color	Foliage — shining dark green above, light green beneath. Fruit — brown.
Culture	Sun or part shade. Soil — medium drainage; high fertility. Moisture — medium to high. Pruning — none. Pest Problems — none. Growth Rate — slow.
Notes	Frequently used as street tree. Excellent specimen. Not as strong or long lived as *Q. virginiana*.
Variety	**Darlington** — more compact than species, leaves more persistent.

Quercus (kwer'kus)
  classical Latin
  name for oak

virginiana (vir-gin-i-a'na)
  from Virginia

LIVE OAK

Family Fagaceae

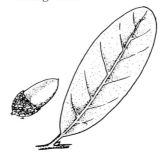

Size	Height 30-50 feet; spread 30-50 feet. Zones 7, 8, 9.
Form	Short trunk; very wide-spreading with horizontal branching. Foliage — alternate, 3-5 inches long, leathery, wavy margin. Flower — hanging catkins. Fruit — acorn 1 inch long.
Texture	Medium.
Color	Foliage — dark green; new growth, bright olive-green. Fruit — dark brown.
Culture	Sun or part shade. Soil — good drainage; medium fertility with high organic content. Moisture — medium. Pruning — none. Pest Problems — none. Growth Rate — slow.
Notes	May be trained to multiple trunk growth. Magnificent and long-lived specimen for spacious areas in Coastal Plain and Piedmont. Difficult to transplant in large sizes. Needs protection from salt spray. Naturally pruned to large shrub size by sea winds.

Tsuga (soo'ga)
Japanese name
for one of
Asiatic hemlocks

canadensis (kan-a-den'sis)
from Canada

CANADIAN HEMLOCK

Family Pinaceae

Size	Height 30-80 feet; spread 15-30 feet. Zones 6, 7.
Form	Slender horizontal branches forming graceful pyramid. Foliage — flat needles ½ inch long. Fruit — cone ½ inch long. Bark — scaly and deeply furrowed.
Texture	Fine.
Color	Foliage — dark green; spring, yellow-green. Fruit — brown. Bark — cinnamon-red to gray.
Culture	Shade or part shade. Soil — good drainage; medium fertility; prefers acid soil. Moisture — medium to high. Pruning — very tolerant. Pest Problems — heart-rot. Growth Rate — rapid.
Notes	Useful in cool shade and on north slopes in moist soil. Adaptable to formal shearing for high or low hedges or occasional pruning to reduce size. Excellent as screen, border, or large specimen.
Varieties	**Dawsoniana** — slow-growing and compact, to 6 feet in height. **Globosa** — dense and rounded form, to 6 feet in height. **Hussii** — dwarf; short twiggy branches. **Kingsville** — columnar growth habit. **Pendula** — Sargent Hemlock. Broad and moundlike with slightly pendulous branches. Height 6 feet; 10-12 feet wide. **Westonigra** — dark green needles.

Tsuga (soo'ga)
    Japanese name
    for one of
    Asiatic hemlocks

caroliniana (ka-ro-lin-i-a'na)
    from Carolinas

CAROLINA HEMLOCK

Family Pinaceae

Size	Height 30-70 feet; spread 20-25 feet. Zones 6, 7.
Form	Compact and pyramidal with rather pendulous branches. Foliage — needles ¾ inch long, encircling twig. Fruit — cone 1½ inches long. Bark — furrowed and scaly.
Texture	Fine.
Color	Foliage — lustrous dark green; new growth, yellow-green. Fruit — brown. Bark — reddish-brown, becoming dull-brown, tinged orange.
Culture	Part shade. Soil — good drainage; high fertility. Moisture — medium to high. Pruning — tolerant. Pest Problems — heart-rot. Growth Rate — rapid.
Notes	Adapts to city conditions; excellent in cool shaded areas as screen, hedge, and specimen. Limited to use in mountains and Piedmont areas.
Varieties	**Arnold Pyramid** — dense, pyramidal growth habit. **Compacta** — dwarf, with rounded top and dense needle growth.

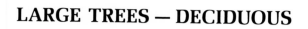

LARGE TREES — DECIDUOUS

Acer (a'sir)
  ancient Latin
  name of maple

platanoides (pla-ta-noy'deez)
  like plane tree

NORWAY MAPLE

Family Aceraceae

Size	Height 60-80 feet; spread 50-70 feet.	Zones 6, 7.

Form   Dense and very broad-spreading, regular in outline; in youth almost globose. Foliage — opposite, simple, lobed, 4-7 inches wide. Flower — late March before leaves appear; flat-topped clusters. Fruit — samara, paired.

Texture Coarse.

Color   Foliage — deep green; fall, yellow. Flower — greenish-yellow. Fruit — brown. Bark — brownish-black.

Culture Sun. Soil — good drainage; high fertility. Moisture — high. Pruning — none. Pest Problems — none. Growth Rate — moderate.

Notes   Low-branched, casts dense shade; effect heavier than native maples, stands city conditions better. Easily transplanted. Roots compete with other plantings.

Varieties **Almira** — height 18-20 feet; loose globe-shaped form. **Cleveland** — upright oval tree; leaves large and dark green, bright golden-yellow in autumn. **Drummondii** — leaves dark green edged with white; suitable for small gardens; less vigorous than species. Height 20-30 feet. **Emerald Queen** — glossy dark green foliage, fall color bright yellow; upright rapid grower. **Greenlace** — deeply cut leaves; ascending branches. Fast-growing. **Summer Shade** — leaves large, dark and leathery; heat resistant and fast-growing.

Acer (a'sir)
   ancient Latin
   name of maple

rubrum (roo'brum)
   red

RED MAPLE

Family Aceraceae

Size	Height 40-50 feet; spread 25-35 feet. Zones 6, 7, 8, 9.
Form	Spreading and symmetrical with ovate or narrow head and ascending branches. Head more irregular than *A. platanoides*. Foliage — opposite, simple, 3-5 lobed, irregularly toothed, 2-4 inches long. Flower — February and March; small but profuse. Fruit — samara, paired, ¾ inch long.
Texture	Medium.
Color	Foliage — medium green, pale green beneath with red petioles; fall, brilliant red or yellow. Flower — red. Fruit — red. Bark — light gray.
Culture	Sun or shade. Soil — medium drainage; medium fertility. Moisture — medium to high. Pruning — shape. Pest Problems — maple insects and diseases. Growth Rate — rapid but does not become brittle.
Notes	Valuable shade tree of excellent habit and beautiful color sequence; superior to other soft maples. Plant in groups for best effect. Easily transplanted. Long lived.
Varieties	**Autumn Flame** — small leaves with early scarlet fall color; dense, round form. **Bowhall** — red fall color; pyramidal upright growth habit. **Columnare** — densely upright growth habit. **October Glory** — heavy lustrous green leaves held later than most maples; fall color crimson. **Red Sunset** — pyramidal to rounded outline; orange to red fall color. Excellent cultivar and very hardy. **Scanlon** — leaves turning orange to red in fall; pyramidal, compact form. **Schlesingeri** — vigorous, upright and spreading form; leaves turning brilliant red-purple in early autumn.

Acer (a'sir)
   ancient Latin
   name of maple

saccharinum (sack-a-ry'num)
   sugary

SILVER MAPLE

Family Aceraceae

Size	Height 60-80 feet; spread 50-75 feet.	Zones 6, 7, 8, 9.

Form   Short trunk, upright, and fairly open. Foliage — opposite, simple, deeply 5-lobed, 3-6 inches wide. Flower — before leaves appear; inconspicuous. Fruit — samara, 2 inches wide.

Texture   Medium.

Color   Foliage — medium green, silvery beneath; fall, pale yellow. Flower — greenish-yellow. Fruit — greenish-yellow. Bark — silver and gray.

Culture   Sun. Soil — medium drainage; medium to high fertility. Moisture — medium to high. Pruning — during dormant season for growth correction, removal of dead or damaged wood and interfering branches. Pest Problems — leaf gall. Growth Rate — rapid.

Notes   Soft wood which breaks easily; roots compete with other plantings including lawns. For temporary use only in landscaping. Occasionally useful in parks or estates near water. Easily transplanted.

Varieties   **Blairii** — vigorous, well-shaped form with stronger branches. **Pyramidale** — broad columnar habit. **Silver Queen** — large, rapid grower; seedless. **Skinneri** — leaves dissected; pyramidal form with horizontal branches; fall color yellow.

Acer (a'sir)
ancient Latin name
of maple

saccharum (sack-kar'rum)
old Greek word for sugar

SUGAR MAPLE

Family Aceraceae

Size	Height 50-75 feet; spread 30-40 feet. Zones 6, 7, 8.
Form	Conical to round top; very dense. Foliage — opposite, simple, 5-lobed, 3-6 inches wide. Flower — inconspicuous. Fruit — samara, paired.
Texture	Medium to coarse.
Color	Foliage — dark green; fall, yellow to orange-red. Flower — yellow. Fruit — greenish-yellow. Bark — dark gray-brown.
Culture	Sun or part shade. Soil — good drainage; medium to high fertility. Moisture — medium. Pruning — none. Pest Problems — anthracnose, leaf spot, leaf blister, and scales. Growth Rate — slow.
Notes	Gorgeous fall coloring. Young trees susceptible to sun scald if not protected. Grows best in association with other trees and in clean atmosphere. Not suited to Coastal Plain.
Varieties	**Bonfire** — excellent red fall color. **Globosum** — dwarf, rounded shrub form; leaves yellow in fall. **Green Mountain** — dense dark green leaves turning orange to scarlet in fall; more heat and drought tolerance than species; upright oval form. **Sweet Shadow** — dark green foliage with deeply cut lobes, light in texture; bright yellow-orange leaves in autumn. **Temple's Upright** — columnar form.

Carpinus (kar-py'nus)
ancient name of
hornbeam

betulus (bet'you-lus)
classical name

EUROPEAN HORNBEAM

Family Betulaceae

Size	Height 40-50 feet; spread 30-40 feet. Zones 6, 7.
Form	Pyramidal, becoming round-headed with age; dense foliage. Foliage — alternate, oblong, doubly serrated with 7-14 pairs of straight veins, 1½-3½ inches long, 1-2 inches wide. Flower — early spring; catkins 1½-3 inches long. Fruit — September; nutlets ¼ inch long, hanging in decorative chains.
Texture	Medium.
Color	Foliage — dark green; fall, yellow. Fruit — light brown. Bark — smooth gray.
Culture	Sun to part shade. Soil — tolerant; low to medium drainage; medium to high fertility. Moisture — medium to high. Pruning — very tolerant. Pest Problems — none. Growth Rate — very slow.
Notes	Elegant small tree for any landscape use; grows well in planter boxes and in low shady spots. With pruning forms tall hedge of 8-10 feet. Slender branches especially attractive in winter.
Varieties	**Fastigiata** — erect vase-shaped growth habit, formal in appearance. Good windscreen if closely planted; faster growing than species. Excellent in containers. **Globosa** — rounded with no central trunk; very slow growing. Good windscreen. **Pendula** — pendulous branches.

Carya (ka'ri-a)
  Greek for walnut

illinoinensis (ill-i-no-i-en'sis)
  of Illinois

PECAN

Family Juglandaceae

Size	Height 60-100 feet; spread 30-40 feet.

Zones 6, 7, 8, 9.

Form — Irregular and open with medium density. Foliage — alternate, compound, 12-20 inches long with 11-17 leaflets. Flower — inconspicuous. Fruit — nut enclosed in 4-winged husk.

Texture — Medium.

Color — Foliage — medium green, lighter beneath. Fruit — dark brown.

Culture — Sun or part shade. Soil — medium to good drainage; medium to high fertility. Moisture — high. Pruning — train young trees for strength of branches. Pest Problems — pecan aphid, weevil, scab disease, and leaf defoliators. Growth Rate — moderate.

Notes — Unprotected young trees highly susceptible to sun scald. Used as shade tree in parks and estates. Not recommended for residential landscaping since green husks fall all summer, littering lawns and patios. Brittle. No fall color. Difficult to transplant large sizes.

Varieties — **Cheyenne** — semi-dwarf spreading form; medium to large fruit. **Chickasaw** — fine texture and spreading form; disease resistant; medium to large fruit. **Elliot** — upright habit of growth with fine texture; small fruit; disease resistant. **Owens** — compact growth habit; medium to large fruit. **Shoshonii** — upright growth habit and strong branches; large fruit; disease resistant. **Stuart** — vase-shaped form; large fruit.

Catalpa (ka-tal'pa)
    North American Indian
    name for these trees

bignonioides (big-known-i-oy'deez)
    resembling crossvine

SOUTHERN CATALPA

Family Bignoniaceae

Size	Height 30-50 feet; spread 20-30 feet. Zones 6, 7, 8, 9.
Form	Short, thick trunk and long crooked branches, coarse branchlets and twigs, forming loose, open, irregular head. Foliage — opposite or in 3's, heart-shaped, to 4 inches long. Flower — May; panicles 7 inches long. Fruit — summer; 15 inch pods with beanlike seeds.
Texture	Coarse.
Color	Foliage — dull green. Flower — white. Fruit — green turning brown. Bark — light brown.
Culture	Sun. Soil — good drainage; high fertility. Moisture — high. Pruning — tolerance limited; remove dead and broken branches and maintain shape. Pest Problems — sphinx moth and larvae. Growth Rate — rapid.
Notes	Loose, coarse, untidy tree with handsome flowers and interesting winter effect; useful in parks and large areas. Good as large specimen and for exotic effects. Transplants best when young. Strong, long lived.
Variety	**Aurea** — bright yellow leaves all summer.

Celtis (sel'tis)
  Greek name of tree

laevigata (lev-i-ga'ta)
  smooth

SUGAR HACKBERRY

Family Ulmaceae

Size	Height 60-80 feet; spread 50-70 feet. Zones 6, 7, 8, 9.
Form	Rounded open crown with slender, spreading branches. Foliage — alternate, simple, oblong-lanceolate, 2½-5 inches long. Flower — inconspicuous. Fruit — profuse; inconspicuous drupe. Twigs — slender, smooth, somewhat angled in growth.
Texture	Medium to coarse.
Color	Foliage — light green; fall, dull yellow. Bark — silver gray, slick.
Culture	Sun to part shade. Soil — very tolerant; medium drainage; medium fertility. Moisture — medium. Pruning — remove awkward branches. Pest Problems — none. Growth Rate — moderate.
Notes	Good shade and street tree even when young; tolerant of drought and pollution. Fruit attracts birds; bark attractive in winter.
Variety	**All Seasons** — rounded crown; bright yellow fall foliage; very hardy.

Celtis (sel'tis)
   Greek name of tree

occidentalis (ok-si-den-tay'lis)
   western, from
   American continent

COMMON HACKBERRY

Family Ulmaceae

Size	Height 40-55 feet; spread 35-50 feet. Zones 6, 7, 8, 9.
Form	Broad top with arching branches when mature, pyramidal when young. Foliage — alternate, ovate to oblong-ovate, serrated, 2-5 inches long. Flower — inconspicuous. Fruit — September, October; drupe 1/3 inch diameter.
Texture	Medium to coarse.
Color	Foliage — lustrous bright green above, pale green beneath. Fruit — orange-red to dark purple. Bark — gray.
Culture	Sun. Soil — very tolerant; medium drainage; medium to high fertility. Moisture — medium. Pruning — none. Pest Problems — powdery mildew, witches' broom, leaf spot, and scale. Growth Rate — moderate to rapid.
Notes	Grows well in adverse conditions; useful for rapid shade in parks and large open areas. Immune to Dutch elm disease.
Variety	**Prairie Pride** — uniform growth; glossy green foliage and less fruit. Resistant to witches' broom.

Cladrastis (kla-dras'tis)
    Greek meaning branch
    and fragile

lutea (loo'tee-a)
    yellow

YELLOWWOOD

Family Leguminosae

Size	Height 30-50 feet; spread 40-55 feet. Zones 6, 7, 8.
Form	Short trunk with wide, graceful, spreading crown. Foliage — alternate, 8-12 inches long and pinnately compound with 7-9 leaflets 3-4 inches long. Flower — June; drooping panicles 12-14 inches long; slightly fragrant. Fruit — thin pods 4 inches long. Bark — smooth with occasional ridges and wrinkles.
Texture	Medium.
Color	Foliage — bright green; fall, clear yellow. Flower — white. Fruit — brown. Bark — silver gray.
Culture	Sun to part shade. Soil — good drainage essential; medium fertility. Moisture — medium. Pruning — none. Pest Problems — none. Growth Rate — moderate.
Notes	Extremely handsome tree; withstands city conditions and drought. Deep roots permit planting beneath branches; usually flowers every other year. May be trained as multi-trunk specimen.
Variety	**Rosea** — pink flower panicles.

Diospyros (dy'os-py-ros)
  Greek grain of Jove,
  referring to edible fruit

virginiana (vir-gin-i-a'na)
  from Virginia

PERSIMMON

Family Ebenaceae

Size	Height 40-50 feet; spread 25-30 feet.	Zones 6, 7, 8, 9.

Form
: Slender, very open and irregular; more symmetrical in open than when mingled with other trees. Foliage — late spring to early fall; alternate, simple, entire, 4-6 inches long. Flower — late spring; small, bell-shaped, inconspicuous. Fruit — autumn; pulpy, round berry, 1½ inch diameter; very astringent until frost occurs, then sweet. Bark — deeply cut into rectangles.

Texture
: Coarse.

Color
: Foliage — deep green; fall, orange. Flower — yellow. Fruit — yellow to orange, marked with purple.

Culture
: Sun. Soil — good drainage; high fertility. Moisture — medium to high. Pruning — none. Pest Problems — none. Growth Rate — slow.

Notes
: Grown for fruit and interesting foliage; rather picturesque; landscape value limited. Withstands city conditions. Useful for natural areas, large parks and roadsides. Difficult to transplant. Fruit attracts wildlife.

Variety
: **Gehron** — seedless fruit.

Fagus (fay'gus)
    classical Latin
    for beech

grandifolia (gran-di-fo'lee-a)
    large-leaved

BEECH

Family Fagaceae

Size	Height 60-80 feet; spread 40-60 feet. Zones 6, 7, 8, 9.
Form	Dense and very low-branching with broad rounded crown. Foliage — late spring to very late fall; alternate, simple, sharply toothed, conspicuous parallel veins, 2-5 inches long. Flower — late spring after leaves appear; inconspicuous. Fruit — autumn; triangular nuts in prickly bur. Buds — ¾ inch long, very sharply pointed and slender with many scales.
Texture	Medium.
Color	Foliage — bright green; fall, golden-brown. Bark — light gray, smooth. Bud — brown.
Culture	Sun. Soil — medium drainage; high fertility. Moisture — high. Pruning — tolerant. Pest Problems — bark aphid. Growth Rate — slow.
Notes	Magnificent specimen casting dense shade which does not permit undergrowth. Shallow, exposed roots at trunk. Excellent for background and framing. Leaves frequently hang on all winter, giving added interest, particularly against dark background. Most suitable for parks and public areas where strong, long lived trees are needed. Difficult to transplant. Grows best in association with other trees.

Fagus (fay′gus)
     classical Latin for beech

sylvatica (sil-vat′i-ka)
     forest-loving

EUROPEAN BEECH

Family Fagaceae

Size	Height 50-60 feet; spread 35-45 feet. Zones 6, 7, 8.
Form	Oval and upright when young, more rounded with age, branching to ground. Foliage — alternate, 2-4 inches long, oval or oblong with 5-9 pairs of veins. Flower — April; inconspicuous. Fruit — autumn; nut enclosed in bur. Bark — thin and smooth, becoming crackled with age.
Texture	Medium.
Color	Foliage — dark green; fall, yellow to bronze. Bark — gray.
Culture	Sun. Soil — good drainage; medium fertility. Moisture — medium to high. Pruning — none. Pest Problems — chestnut borers. Growth Rate — moderate.
Notes	Ideal as free-standing specimen or shade tree; casts dense shade; shallow roots deter growth of groundcovers.
Varieties	**Asplenifolia** — lustrous green fern-like leaves; exceptionally beautiful slow-growing cultivar. Fall foliage golden brown. Structure interesting in winter. **Cuprea** — red-purple leaves in summer. Copper Beech. **Dawyckii** — narrow columnar form; slow-growing. **Dawyckii Gold** — golden yellow leaves in spring and fall; narrow columnar form; slow-growing. **Pendula** — graceful drooping branches; dark green foliage becomes bronze in fall. **Purpurea** — height 50 feet; dark purple folige all summer. **Riversii** — dark purple foliage all summer. River's Purple Beech. **Rotundifolia** — rounded leaves 1 inch wide; beautiful pyramidal form.

Fraxinus (frax'i-nus)
   classical Latin
   for ash

americana (a-me-ri-cay'na)
   from North or South
   America

WHITE ASH

Family Oleaceae

Size	Height 60-80 feet; spread 50-70 feet. Zones 6, 7, 8, 9.
Form	Broad, rounded head and stout, ascending branches, often broken and ragged from lightning. Foliage — late spring to early fall; opposite, 5-9 leaflets, pinnately compound, 8-12 inches long. Flower — midspring; inconspicuous. Fruit — late summer, often persistent; samara. Bud — broader than long, blunt.
Texture	Medium.
Color	Foliage — bright green; fall, yellow to purple. Bark — deep gray. Bud — brown.
Culture	Sun. Soil — medium drainage; medium to high fertility. Moisture — high. Pruning — tolerant. Pest Problems — scale and stem borer if transplanted from wild. Growth Rate — rapid while young, moderate later.
Notes	Resists heat and drought well. Good park tree for mass planting. May reseed sufficiently to become nuisance. Survives well in severe exposures. Easily transplanted.
Varieties	**Autumn Applause** — burgundy fall color; dense form; seedless. **Autumn Purple** — pyramidal form with deep green leaves turning mahogany-purple in fall; seedless. **Elk Grove** — shiny dark green foliage turning purple in fall. **Pendula** — weeping branches.

Ginkgo (gink'o)
Chinese name for
this tree

biloba (by-low'ba)
two-lobed

MAIDENHAIR TREE

Family Ginkgoaceae

Size	Height 40-70 feet; spread 20-40 feet.	Zones 6, 7, 8.

Form   In youth slender, pyramidal and rather spiky; with age broad and more regular in outline. Foliage — late spring to midfall; alternate, sometimes clustered, 2-lobed, margin wavy or entire, fan-shaped, 2-3½ inches wide. Flower — late spring with leaves; inconspicuous. Fruit — autumn; plumlike, 1 inch diameter. Bark — smooth.

Texture   Medium.

Color   Foliage — bright green; fall, bright yellow. Flower — yellow. Fruit — orange-yellow.

Culture   Sun. Soil — very tolerant; medium drainage; medium fertility. Moisture — medium. Pruning — none. Pest Problems — none. Growth Rate — slow.

Notes   Exceptional vitality and handsome foliage; excellent as street tree or specimen for large areas. Casts light shade; sheds leaves rapidly in fall. Avoid planting female tree which produces foul-smelling fruit. May require 20 years to attain mature form. Transplants easily.

Varieties   **Autumn Gold** — broad spreading form; male tree. **fastigiata** — columnar habit of growth. Excellent for street plantings. **Laciniata** — deeply divided leaves. **Macrophylla** — very large leaves. **Pendula** — slightly drooping branches. **Princeton Sentry** — superior cultivar; columnar form.

Gleditsia (gle-dit'si-a)
named for
Johann G. Gleditsch,
director of botanic
garden at Berlin

triacanthos (try-a-kan'thoss)
with 3 spines

inermis (in-er'mis)
thornless

THORNLESS HONEYLOCUST
Family Fabaceae

Size	Height 50-75 feet; spread 25-40 feet. Zones 6, 7, 8, 9.
Form	Upright, semi-conical, open with age; medium to open density. Foliage — alternate, may be clustered, singly or doubly pinnately compound, 7-12 inches long, leaflets ½-1½ inches long. Flower — inconspicuous. Fruit — fall, persistent; 12-18 inch long twisted pod. Twigs — typically branched.
Texture	Fine.
Color	Foliage — medium green; fall, yellow. Fruit — brown.
Culture	Sun. Soil — medium to good drainage; medium fertility. Moisture — medium to low. Pruning — train young trees for strength of branches; avoid large pruning wounds. Pest Problems — locust borer, canker, and webworms. Growth Rate — moderate.
Notes	Casts light shade and endures poor soils; withstands city conditions. Select fruitless varieties for landscape use.
Varieties	**Bujotii** — delicate pendulous form. Very slender branches and leaves. **Elegantissima** — dense and bushy form; height 8-12 feet. Excellent foliage. **Green Glory** — rapid growth rate, pyramidal when young. Dark green leaves, holds foliage longer than most varieties. Some resistance to webworm. **Imperial** — height 30-35 feet; graceful branches at right angles to straight trunk. **Majestic** — dark green leaves; branches spreading and slightly upright; compact growth. **Moraine** — fruitless. Outstanding for framing, background or specimen; excellent lawn tree. Some resistance to webworm. **Shademaster** — upright growth habit with dark green leaves; essentially fruitless. Excellent tree. **Skyline** — pyramidal in general habit with ascending branches and dark green leaves. Useful as street tree.

Gymnocladus (gim-no-kla'dus)
from Greek meaning
naked branch

dioicus (die-o'ee-kus)
dioecious

KENTUCKY COFFEE TREE

Family Leguminosae

Size	Height 60-75 feet; spread 40-50 feet.	Zones 6, 7, 8.
Form	Irregular and open with horizontal branching and globose crown. Foliage — alternate, bipinnately compound, 1-3 feet long with leaflets 2-4 inches long, oval to ovate. Flower — spring; dioecious, terminal panicles 1 foot long on female trees, 4 inches long on male trees. Fruit — thick pods 4-10 inches long. Bark — thick and ridged.	
Texture	Coarse.	
Color	Foliage — dark blue-green; fall, yellow. Flower — white, fragrant on female trees. Fruit — red-brown, persisting through winter. Bark — gray-brown tinged with red.	
Culture	Sun. Soil — tolerant; medium drainage; medium fertility. Moisture — medium. Pruning — remove broken branches in early spring. Pest Problems — none. Growth Rate — slow to moderate.	
Notes	Most useful for parks and large open areas; withstands city conditions. Bark and branching interesting in winter. Select male forms to avoid seed pods.	

Liquidambar (liquid-am'bar)
from Latin for liquid
and Arabic for amber, in
allusion to fragrant
resin of Asiatic species

styraciflua (sty-ra-see-flew'a)
sweet-gum-flowing

SWEET-GUM

Family Hamamelidaceae

Size	Height 60-100 feet; spread 50-75 feet.	Zones 6, 7, 8, 9.

Form   Upright and semi-conical. Foliage — alternate, simple, 5-7 lobed, star-shaped, 5-7 inches long. Flower — inconspicuous. Fruit — fall; 1 inch diameter, round and prickly. Twigs — frequently winged with cork.

Texture   Medium.

Color   Foliage — dark green; fall, brilliant scarlet and purple. Fruit — brown.

Culture   Sun or part shade. Soil — medium to good drainage; medium to high fertility. Moisture — medium to high. Pruning — train young trees to central trunk. Pest Problems — none. Growth Rate — slow to moderate.

Notes   Good specimen and attractive all year. Allow sufficient space to develop symmetrically. Most useful for shade, framing, or background in large open areas in parks and along highways. Fruit causes litter in fall and winter. Difficult to transplant in large sizes.

Varieties   **Burgundy** — deep wine-red fall foliage. **Festival** — more narrow and upright in form; fall foliage red in southeast, yellow in midwest. **Levis** — beautiful fall color. **Moraine** — uniform and rapid growth rate; beautiful shiny dark green leaves, brilliant red fall color. **Palo Alto** — uniform growth habit and beautiful orange-red fall color; pyramidal form. **Rotundiloba** — rounded lobes on leaves; fruitless. Fall color varies from yellow to dark burgundy.

Liriodendron (lir-i-o-den'dron)
　　Greek for lily and tree, in
　　allusion to shape of
　　flowers

tulipifera (too-lip-iff'er-a)
　　bearing tuliplike flowers

TULIP-TREE

Family Magnoliaceae

Size	Height 60-150 feet; spread 30-40 feet. Zones 6, 7, 8, 9.
Form	Very tall and erect with giant columnar trunk and cylindrical head; high branching and spreading with age. Foliage — mid-spring to mid-fall; alternate, simple, lobed, 3-5½ inches long. Flower — mid-April after leaves appear; tuliplike. Fruit — mid-summer; persisting; cone-shaped aggregate of samaras.
Texture	Coarse to medium.
Color	Foliage — light green; fall, bright yellow. Flower — greenish-yellow with orange centers. Fruit — tan.
Culture	Sun. Soil — good drainage; medium fertility. Moisture — medium. Pruning — not tolerant. Pest Problems — aphids. Growth Rate — moderate to rapid.
Notes	Handsome, stately tree valued for flowers and foliage; useful as specimen or for mass planting in very large areas. Good fall color. Partial leaf drop during dry periods. Difficult to transplant, should be moved when young and in active growth.
Varieties	**Aureo-marginatum** — leaves margined with yellow. **Compactum** — dwarf form with small leaves. **Fastigiatum** — upright pyramidal form.

Magnolia (mag-no'li-a)
name for Pierre Magnol

acuminata (a-ku-mi-na'ta)
tapering to point

CUCUMBER TREE

Family Magnoliaceae

Size	Height 50-70 feet; spread 40-60 feet. Zones 6, 7, 8.
Form	Pyramidal when young, spreading oval when mature. Foliage — alternate, broadly elliptical, 6-10 inches long, 3-5 inches wide. Flower — inconspicuous, 2-3 inches wide. Fruit — cucumber-like, 2-3 inches long. Bark — thin, rough and furrowed.
Texture	Coarse.
Color	Foliage — bright dark green above, pale green beneath. Flower — yellow-green. Fruit — red in fall. Bark — gray-brown.
Culture	Sun to part shade. Soil — very good drainage; medium fertility. Moisture — medium to high. Pruning — none. Pest Problems — none. Growth Rate — rapid.
Notes	Excellent for roadside and ornamental plantings in parks and natural areas. Casts dense shade; looks best unpruned.
Variety	**Elizabeth** — hybrid with *M. heptapeta*; flowers clear lemon yellow. Height 25-35 feet; spread 10-15 feet. Use as shade or specimen tree; flowers when young.

Metasequoia (met-a-se-quoi'a)
   from Greek meaning changed
   and Sequoia

glyptostroboides (glip-to-stro-boi'deez)

DAWN REDWOOD

Family Taxodiaceae

Size	Height 70-90 feet; spread 25-30 feet. Zones 6, 7, 8.
Form	Pyramidal when young, broadly rounded crown with age. Foliage — opposite, narrow needles ¾ inch long. Flower — inconspicuous. Fruit — oval cone ¾ inch long. Bark — fissured.
Texture	Fine.
Color	Foliage — bright green; fall, orange-brown. Fruit — dark brown. Bark — red-brown becoming gray with age.
Culture	Sun. Soil — tolerant; good drainage; medium fertility. Moisture — high. Pruning — none. Pest Problems — none. Growth Rate — rapid.
Notes	Needs large area for best growth; best suited to golf courses and parks. Attractive feathery foliage. Plant in groups for screen.
Variety	**National** — very narrow and pyramidal in habit of growth.

Nyssa (nis'sa)
    water nymph, referring
    to habitat of
    native species in
    swampy places

sylvatica (sil-vat'i-ka)
    forest-loving

BLACK TUPELO

Family Nyssaceae

Size	Height 40-60 feet; spread 20-30 feet. Zones 6, 7, 8, 9.
Form	Tall and narrow with picturesque crown when young; open and irregular in outline with branches spreading horizontally. Foliage — alternate, entire, 2-4 inches long. Flower — midspring; inconspicuous. Fruit — midsummer; berrylike, ½ inch long.
Texture	Medium.
Color	Foliage — lustrous green; fall, brilliant red. Flower — greenish. Fruit — dark blue.
Culture	Sun or shade. Soil — tolerant; medium drainage; medium fertility. Moisture — high. Pruning — tolerance limited. Pest Problems — none. Growth Rate — moderate.
Notes	Gorgeous fall color and distinctive winter habit; valued for foliage and form. Useful in mass or woodland; good specimen while young. Long lived. Difficult to transplant. May be trained to form multiple trunks.
Variety	**biflora** — smaller than species; for swamps and pond edges.

Paulownia (paul-o'ni-a)
  named for Princess
  Anna Pavlovna
  of Netherlands

tomentosa (toe-men-toe'sa)
  densely covered with
  matted, flat hairs

EMPRESS-TREE

Family Scrophulariaceae

Size	Height 30-50 feet; spread 20-30 feet.	Zones 6, 7, 8, 9.
Form	Low and spreading branches forming broadly oval and rather open crown. Foliage — opposite, simple, entire or shallowly lobed, to 2 feet wide, pubescent. Flower — midspring before leaves appear; conspicuous 1 foot clusters. Fruit — fall, persisting all winter; ovoid capsule 1½ inches long.	
Texture	Very coarse.	
Color	Foliage — dark green. Flower — lavender. Fruit — brown.	
Culture	Sun. Soil — tolerant; medium drainage; medium fertility. Moisture — medium. Pruning — remove dead wood. Pest Problems — none. Growth Rate — moderate to rapid.	
Notes	Strikingly handsome when in bloom; flower color unusual for trees. Brittle wood but useful as specimen for bold effects in lawns and parks. Transplants best while young.	
Variety	**Somaclonal Snowstorm** — leaves variegated with cream-white and yellow-green.	

Platanus (pla'ta-nus)
   classical Greek name
   for plane tree

x acerifolia (a-sir-ee-fo'lee-a)
   maple-leaved

LONDON PLANE-TREE

Family Platanaceae

Size	Height 70-100 feet; spread 50-70 feet.　　　　　　　　Zones 6, 7, 8.
Form	Medium or short trunk with crown of far-reaching branches; pendulous lower branches; rounded with age. Foliage — late spring to midfall; alternate, simple, lobes to 1/3 depth of blade, 5-10 inches wide. Flower — late spring with leaves; inconspicuous. Fruit — fall; globular heads 1½ inch diameter, usually in 2's. Bark — upper very smooth; lower flaking off in large patches.
Texture	Coarse.
Color	Foliage — yellow-green; fall, tan. Fruit — rusty brown. Bark — outer greenish-gray; inner, white.
Culture	Sun or part shade. Soil — medium drainage; high fertility. Moisture — high. Pruning — remove dead and broken wood. Pest Problems — fungi, borers, anthracnose, and lacebug. Growth Rate — rapid.
Notes	Very long lived; withstands worst city conditions. Valuable for streets and parks. Requires occasional cleanup of leaves, fruit, and bark. Easily transplanted. Hybrid of *P. occidentalis* x *P. orientalis*.
Varieties	**Bloodgood** — rapid growth rate; tolerates soil compaction, heat and drought. **Pyramidalis** — upright growth habit with lower branches not drooping.

Platanus (pla'ta-nus)
    classical Greek name
    for plane tree

occidentalis (ok-si-den-tay'lis)
    western, from
    American continent

SYCAMORE

Family Platanaceae

Size	Height 70-100 feet; spread 60-80 feet.	Zones 6, 7, 8, 9.
Form	Very tall and broad with open growth. Often forked into several large secondary trunks with massive, spreading limbs. Foliage — late spring to midfall; alternate, simple, 3-5 shallow lobes, 5-9 inches wide, downy beneath. Flower — inconspicuous. Fruit — fall; globular heads 1½ inch diameter, 1 or 2 together.	
Texture	Coarse.	
Color	Foliage — light green. Fruit — rusty brown. Bark — upper, green-gray; inner, white; lower, brown-gray.	
Culture	Sun or part shade. Soil — medium drainage; high fertility. Moisture — high. Pruning — remove dead and broken wood. Pest Problems — fungi, especially anthracnose, and twig blight. Growth Rate — very rapid.	
Notes	Withstands severe conditions and city atmosphere; useful as specimen or for mass planting; need ample space to develop. Bark peels to expose white beneath. Requires periodic cleanup of leaves, fruit, and bark. Easily transplanted.	

Prunus (proo'nus)
    classical Latin name
    of plum

sargentii (sar-jent'ee-eye)
    named for Charles Sprague
    Sargent, first director of
    Arnold Arboretum

SARGENT CHERRY

Family Rosaceae

Size	Height 40-60 feet; spread 30-40 feet. Zones 6, 7, 8.
Form	Upright, rounded and dense with wide-spreading branches. Foliage — alternate, 1-2 inches long. Flower — early spring; single, profuse, 1½ inches wide. Fruit — summer; ½ inch diameter, inconspicuous.
Texture	Medium.
Color	Foliage — medium green; new leaves red-bronze; fall, vivid orange-red. Flower — bright pink. Fruit — black. Bark — shiny black.
Culture	Sun. Soil — good drainage; medium fertility. Moisture — medium. Pruning — tolerant. Pest Problems — usually none; occasionally borers, scale, and aphids. Growth Rate — moderate.
Notes	Excellent flowering tree for large estates and parks. Casts dense shade; most effective as specimen. Bark effective in winter.
Varieties	**Columnaris** — columnar form. **Rancho** — upright form growing to 25 feet; for screening, accent, or street tree.

Quercus (kwer'kus)
   classical Latin
   name for oak

acutissima (a-ku-tis'i-ma)
   very acute

SAWTOOTH OAK

Family Fagaceae

Size	Height 35-45 feet; spread 35-50 feet. Zones 6, 7, 8, 9.
Form	Oval or broadly rounded with wide-spreading low branches when mature, pyramidal when young. Foliage — alternate, oblong and serrated with bristle-toothed margins, 3½-7 inches long and 1-2 inches wide. Flower — conspicuous catkins. Fruit — acorn 1 inch long. Bark — ridged and furrowed.
Texture	Medium.
Color	Foliage — lustrous dark green above, pale green beneath; new leaves light yellow. Flower — golden yellow. Fruit — brown. Bark — light gray.
Culture	Sun or part shade. Soil — tolerant; good drainage; medium fertility. Moisture — medium. Pruning — none. Pest Problems — none. Growth Rate — rapid to moderate.
Notes	Superior lawn tree which should be more widely used. Easily grown and thrives in variety of soils. Casts dense shade; grows rapidly in southern areas.

Quercus (kwer'kus)
    classical Latin name
    for oak

alba (al'ba)
    white

WHITE OAK

Family Fagaceae

Size	Height 60-100 feet; spread 50-90 feet. Zones 6, 7, 8, 9.
Form	Massive and spreading with thick trunk; upper branches ascending and twisting with age, forming broad head. Foliage — late spring to very late fall, often persisting through winter; alternate, simple, 5-9 rounded lobes, 5-8 inches long. Flower — hanging catkins. Fruit — acorn ¾ inch long.
Texture	Coarse to medium.
Color	Foliage — bluish-green; fall, dark red. Flower — pale yellow. Fruit — brown.
Culture	Sun or part shade. Soil — good drainage; medium fertility. Moisture — high. Pruning — none. Pest Problems — none. Growth Rate — slow.
Notes	Majestic specimen, splendid for any permanent planting in spacious areas. Slow growing but very long lived. Avoid planting near driveway or patio. Very difficult to transplant.

Quercus (kwer'kus)
classical Latin
name for oak

coccinea (kok-sin'ee-a)
scarlet

SCARLET OAK

Family Fagaceae

Size	Height 60-80 feet; spread 40-50 feet. Zones 6, 7, 8, 9.
Form	Symmetrical with rounded crown; branches gradually spreading and curving upward. Foliage — late spring to very late fall; alternate, simple, 5-9 toothed lobes, 4-6 inches long, glabrous and thin. Flower — hanging catkins. Fruit — ovoid acorn ¾ inch long.
Texture	Coarse to medium.
Color	Foliage — deep green; fall, red. Flower — pale yellow. Fruit — brown.
Culture	Sun. Soil — good drainage; medium fertility. Moisture — medium. Pruning — none. Pest Problems — none. Growth Rate — rapid.
Notes	Excellent foliage, pleasing fall color and rapid growth; excellent for framing, background, shade, and street plantings. Difficult to transplant successfully.
Variety	**Splendens** — foliage more glossy than species.

Quercus (kwer'kus)
   classical Latin name
   for oak

macrocarpa (ma-kro-car'pa)
   large carpel

BUR OAK

Family Fagaceae

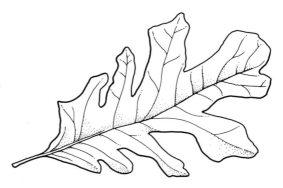

Size	Height 70-80 feet; spread 70-80 feet. Zones 6, 7, 8.
Form	Majestic broad head with spreading branches beginning high on trunk. Foliage — alternate, obovate, 8-10 inches long and 4-5 inches wide with 7-10 pairs of lobes; leaf shaped like bass fiddle. Flower — stalked catkins. Fruit — acorn 1-2 inches long with conspicuously fringed cup. Bark — thick and deeply furrowed.
Texture	Coarse.
Color	Foliage — lustrous deep green above, gray-white beneath. Fruit — brown. Bark — dark gray-brown.
Culture	Sun. Soil — very tolerant; medium drainage; medium fertility. Moisture — high. Pruning — none. Pest Problems — none. Growth Rate — slow.
Notes	Excellent focal point for large areas; withstands city conditions. Attractive branching pattern in winter. Difficult to transplant.

Quercus (kwer'kus)
classical Latin name
for oak

nigra (ny'gra)
black

WATER OAK

Family Fagaceae

Size	Height 50-75 feet; spread 30-40 feet.	Zones 6, 7, 8, 9.
Form	Semi-conical to round or irregular top; dense; lower branches pendulous. Foliage — alternate, semi-evergreen, leaves vary from rounded to 3-lobed, 1½-3 inches long. Flower — hanging catkins. Fruit — acorn ½ inch long.	
Texture	Medium.	
Color	Foliage — glossy dark green; fall, yellowish. Flower — yellow-green.	
Culture	Sun or part shade. Soil — medium to good drainage; medium to high fertility. Moisture — medium to high. Pruning — train young trees for central trunk. Pest Problems — gall insects and scale. Growth Rate — moderate to rapid.	
Notes	Frequently used as specimen, canopy, and background. Hybridizes easily, many leaf variations, drooping branches limit use as shade tree. Easily transplanted.	

Quercus (kwer'kus)
   classical Latin
   name for oak

palustris (pa-lus'tris)
   marsh-loving

PIN OAK

Family Fagaceae

Size	Height 60-80 feet; spread 40-50 feet. Zones 6, 7, 8, 9.
Form	Pyramidal with low branching; dense. Foliage — alternate, 5-9 lobed, 4-5 inches long. Flower — hanging catkins. Fruit — acorn ½ inch long.
Texture	Medium to slightly coarse.
Color	Foliage — medium green; fall, red. Flower — yellow green. Fruit — brown.
Culture	Sun or part shade. Soil — medium to good drainage; medium fertility with high clay content. Moisture — medium. Pruning — train young trees to central trunk; permit low branching to ground. Pest Problems — none. Growth Rate — rapid.
Notes	Excellent lawn tree for large open areas. Not recommended for street or roadway plantings because lower branches block visibility. Holds leaves through winter. Easily transplanted.
Variety	**Sovereign** — lower branches ascending slightly; may be used as canopy tree.

Quercus (kwer'kus)
    classical Latin
    name for oak

phellos (fell'os)
    willow

WILLOW OAK

Family Fagaceae

Size	Height 60-80 feet; spread 30-40 feet. Zones 6, 7, 8, 9.
Form	Graceful and conical in youth, round-topped with age. Foliage — late spring to late fall; alternate, entire, lance-shaped, 2½-5 inches long. Flower — hanging catkins. Fruit — round acorn ½ inch long.
Texture	Fine.
Color	Foliage — bright green; fall, light yellow. Flower — pale yellow. Fruit — brown.
Culture	Sun. Soil — good drainage; medium fertility. Moisture — high. Pruning — none. Pest Problems — none. Growth Rate — rapid to moderate.
Notes	Of finer texture than other oaks; useful as specimen, framing, background, and canopy. Allow low-branching where space permits. Excellent shade or street tree. Easily transplanted.

Quercus (kwer'kus)
   classical Latin name
   for oak

rubra (roo'brah)
   red

maxima (macks'i-ma)
   large or largest

EASTERN RED OAK

Family Fagaceae

Size	Height 50-70 feet; spread 40-60 feet. Zones 6, 7, 8.
Form	Erect and high-branching with several large, spreading branches and slender branchlets; crown pyramidal in youth, round-topped with age. Foliage — late spring to late fall; alternate, simple, 7-11 pointed lobes, 5-9 inches long. Flower — hanging catkins. Fruit — acorn 1 inch long.
Texture	Medium to coarse.
Color	Foliage — deep green; fall, red. Flower — yellow-green. Fruit — brown.
Culture	Sun to part shade. Soil — good drainage; medium fertility. Moisture — medium. Pruning — none. Pest Problems — borers when growth not vigorous. Growth Rate — rapid.
Notes	Withstands most city conditions. Valued for rapid growth; handsome shade tree for streets, lawns, and mass planting. Transplants more easily than most oaks.

Quercus (kwer'kus)
   classical Latin
   name for oak

velutina (vel-loo'ti-na)
   velvety

BLACK OAK

Family Fagaceae

Size	Height 60-80 feet; spread 30-60 feet.	Zones 6, 7, 8, 9.
Form	Wide, irregular, rounded crown; occasionally more narrow with slender branches; sometimes low-branching. Foliage — late spring to late fall, holding dead leaves to midwinter; alternate, usually 7-lobed, base wedge-shaped, to 8 inches long. Flower — hanging catkins. Fruit — acorn ¾ inch long.	
Texture	Medium to coarse.	
Color	Foliage — lustrous dark green; fall, dull red. Flower — pale yellow. Fruit — brown. Bark — black.	
Culture	Sun or part shade. Soil — medium drainage; medium fertility. Moisture — high. Pruning — none. Pest Problems — none. Growth Rate — moderate to slow.	
Notes	One of largest growing oaks; excellent shade tree for parks and woodlands. Tolerates poor soil. Not suitable for small residential lots. Difficult to transplant.	

Salix (say'licks)
   classical name
   for willow

babylonica (bab-i-lon'i-ka)
   from ancient Babylon

WEEPING WILLOW

Family Salicaceae

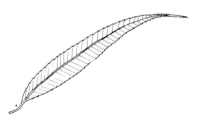

Size	Height 30-50 feet; spread 20-40 feet.　　　　　　　Zones 6, 7, 8.
Form	Slender pendulous branches; fairly compact growth habit. Foliage — alternate, simple, toothed, 5-6 inches long, less than ⅝ inch wide and glabrous. Flower — catkins. Fruit — capsule.
Texture	Fine.
Color	Foliage — medium green. Flower — greenish-yellow. Fruit — brown. Bark — dark brown-black.
Culture	Sun or part shade. Soil — medium drainage; medium to high fertility. Moisture — high. Pruning — head back when young for rigid trunk. Pest Problems — leaf defoliators and cankers. Growth Rate — rapid.
Notes	Somewhat untidy and aggressive but picturesque when located where billowing form shows to advantage. Use in groups in moist areas as accent or to emphasize rolling terrain. Attractive large screen for areas used in spring and summer; leaves appear in early spring. Should not be planted near underground pipes.

Sophora (soff'or-a)
   from Sophero, Arabic
   name for papilionaceous-
   flowered tree

japonica (ja-pon'i-ka)
   from Japan

JAPANESE PAGODA TREE

Family Fabaceae

Size	Height 50-70 feet; spread 50 feet.	Zones 6, 7.

Form   Wide branching with rounded head. Foliage — alternate, compound with leaflets 2 inches long. Flower — mid-July to September; 1/3 inch long in upright clusters 15 inches long. Fruit — winter; pods 3 inches long.

Texture   Fine.

Color   Foliage — bright green; fall, yellow-brown. Flower — yellowish-white. Fruit — yellow turning brown. Bark — black on trunk; dark green on smaller branches.

Culture   Sun or shade. Soil — very tolerant. Moisture — low. Pruning — tolerant. Pest Problems — none. Growth Rate — moderately rapid.

Notes   Excellent large street tree or specimen. Use as shade tree for parks and suburban gardens; light foliage permits adequate turf growth.

Varieties **fastigiata** — upright growth. **Pendula** — dense, globe-shaped head with pendulous branches. Rarely flowers. **Regent** — faster and straighter growth habit than species, large oval crown eventually becoming vase-shaped. Glossy deep green leaves; flowers in 6-8 years. **violacea** — leaflets pubescent; flowers with purplish coloration.

Taxodium (tacks-o'di-um)
  Greek meaning taxuslike

distichum (dis'ti-kum)
  two-ranked, with leaves
  or flowers in ranks on
  opposite sides of stem

BALD CYPRESS

Family Taxodiaceae

Size	Height 50-100 feet; spread 20-30 feet. Zones 6, 7, 8, 9.
Form	Pyramidal when young; rounded, spreading, and more open with age. Foliage — needles ½ inch long on lateral branchlets. Fruit — late fall; round cones 1 inch diameter, subdivided into sections.
Texture	Fine.
Color	Foliage — light green; fall, reddish-brown. Fruit — green turning brown.
Culture	Sun or part shade. Soil — tolerates poor drainage; medium fertility. Moisture — high to medium. Pruning — none. Pest Problems — none. Growth Rate — slow.
Notes	Often used as specimen for poorly drained sites but also grows well in average soil. Exotic in appearance.
Varieties	**Monarch of Illinois** — very wide-spreading form. **Shawnee Brave** — narrow pyramidal form; 15-20 feet wide.

Tilia (till'i-a)
old Latin name
of linden

americana (a-mer-i-cay'na)
from North or South
America

AMERICAN LINDEN

Family Tiliaceae

Size	Height 60-80 feet; spread 50-60 feet.	Zones 6, 7, 8.
Form	Tall and stately with rounded head and low wide-spreading branches. Foliage — alternate, simple, toothed, usually heart-shaped, 3-6 inches long. Flower — early summer; drooping cymes, fragrant. Fruit — early fall; nutlike with stalk attached to narrow leafy bract.	
Texture	Coarse.	
Color	Foliage — bright green; fall, yellow. Flower — ivory or creamy. Fruit — buff or mustard-color.	
Culture	Sun or part shade. Soil — good drainage; high fertility. Moisture — medium to high. Pruning — tolerant. Pest Problems — root rot. Growth Rate — rapid.	
Notes	Useful as shade or canopy for parks. Recommended for cooler areas. Easily transplanted while young.	
Varieties	**Fastigiata** — narrow pyramidal form. **Redmond** — pyramidal growth habit with large leaves; useful as street tree.	

Tilia (till'i-a)
   old Latin name
   of linden

cordata (kor-day'ta)
   heart-shaped

LITTLELEAF LINDEN

Family Tiliaceae

Size	Height 30-50 feet; spread 25-40 feet. Zones 6, 7, 8.
Form	Pyramidal and dense with ascending, spreading branches. Foliage — mid-spring to late fall; alternate, simple, toothed, usually broader than long, 1½-3 inches long. Flower — May; fragrant cymes. Fruit — fall, persisting; nutlike with stalk attached to narrow leafy bract.
Texture	Fine to medium.
Color	Foliage — dark green, bluish gray beneath. Flower — creamy yellow.
Culture	Sun or part shade. Soil — good drainage; medium fertility. Moisture — medium to high. Pruning — remove unduly heavy side limbs in youth. Pest Problems — Leopard Moth larvae. Growth Rate — moderate to slow.
Notes	Valuable for city conditions and poor soil. Useful as street tree and for areas requiring dense shade. More refined than *T. americana*. Useful as lawn tree but casts dense shade which limits turf growth. Easily transplanted.
Varieties	**Chancellor** — fastigiate, pyramidal with age; rapid growth. **Greenspire** — dark green foliage; straight single trunk; excellent shade tree. **Pyramidalis** — widely pyramidal habit. **Rancho** — upright growth habit with small glossy green leaves. **Swedish Upright** — narrow and upright with short side branches.

Ulmus (ul'mus)
   classical Latin
   name of elm

americana (a-me-ri-cay'na)
   from North or South
   America

AMERICAN ELM

Family Ulmaceae

Size	Height 75-125 feet; spread 60-120 feet.	Zones 6, 7, 8, 9.
Form	Irregular, widely arching branches forming vase shape; angles of branches acute. Foliage — alternate, simple, toothed, 4-6 inches long. Flower — inconspicuous. Fruit — samara ½ inch long.	
Texture	Medium to coarse.	
Color	Foliage — dark green; fall, yellow. Fruit — green. Bark — dark gray.	
Culture	Sun or part shade. Soil — medium drainage; medium fertility. Moisture — medium. Pruning — remove broken or dying branches. Pest Problems — insects, Dutch Elm disease, and mildew. Growth Rate — slow.	
Notes	Beautiful habit of growth; formerly widely planted on boulevards and parkways but susceptibility to Dutch Elm disease now limits landscape use.	
Varieties	**Augustine** — rapid growing columnar form; excellent yellow fall color. **Moline** — narrow tree with upright trunk; older branches become horizontal. **Princeton** — large thick leaves; vigorous growth. Resistant to elm leaf beetle.	

Zelkova (zel-ko'va)
    after vernacular name
    Zelkoua in Crete or
    Selkeva in Caucasus

serrata (ser-ra'ta)
    serrate

JAPANESE ZELKOVA

Family Ulmaceae

Size	Height 50-60 feet; spread 40-50 feet.	Zones 6, 7, 8.
Form	Short trunk with ascending branches and round head, graceful. Foliage — alternate, simple, toothed, 2-5 inches long. Flower — inconspicuous. Fruit — pea-size, hard, inconspicuous.	
Texture	Medium to fine.	
Color	Foliage — deep green; fall, yellow to reddish-brown.	
Culture	Sun or part shade. Soil — tolerant. Moisture — medium. Pruning — none. Pest Problems — none. Growth Rate — moderate to rapid.	
Notes	Excellent shade tree. Frequently used as street tree or lawn specimen. Substitute for elm; apparently resistant to Dutch Elm disease. Trunk subject to sun scald.	
Varieties	**Green Vase** — vigorous growth and handsome form; golden yellow to bronze-red fall foliage. **Green Veil** — beautiful pendulous branches. **Village Green** — excellent tree. Dark green foliage turning wine-red in fall. Smooth, straight trunk. Slightly arching branches, similar in form to American elm.	

BIBLIOGRAPHY

Bailey, L. H. 1949. *Manual of Cultivated Plants.* The Macmillan Company. New York, N. Y.

Bailey, L. H. and Ethel Bailey. 1976. *Hortus Third.* The Macmillan Company. New York, N. Y. and Collier Macmillan Publishers, London.

Coombes, Allen J. 1985. *Dictionary of Plant Names.* Timber Press. Portland, Oregon.

Dirr, Michael A. 1983. *Manual of Woody Landscape Plants.* Stipes Publishing Company. Champaign, Illinois.

Galle, Fred C. 1985. *Azaleas.* Timber Press. Portland, Oregon.

Graetz, Karl E. 1973. *Seacoast Plants of the Carolinas.* U. S. Department of Agriculture, Soil Conservation Service.

Hastings, Donald M., Jr. 1987. *Gardening in the South.* Taylor Publishing Company. Dallas, Texas.

Hightshoe, Gary L. 1978. *Native Trees for Urban and Rural America.* Iowa State University Research Foundation. Ames, Iowa.

Hobhouse, Penelope. 1985. *Color in your Garden.* Little, Brown and Company. Boston, Massachussets.

Hume, H. Harold. 1953. *Hollies.* The Macmillan Company. New York, N.Y.

Lee, Frederick P. 1965. *The Azalea Book.* D. Van Nostrand Company. Princeton, New Jersey.

Pirone, Pascal P. 1960. *Diseases and Pests of Ornamental Plants.* The Ronald Press Company. New York, N. Y.

Poor, Janet Meakin. 1984. *Plants That Merit Attention.* Timber Press. Portland, Oregon.

Raulston, J. C. 1987. *Friends of the NCSU Arboretum Newsletter.* Department of Horticultural Science, North Carolina State University. Raleigh, North Carolina.

Robinson, Florence Bell. 1960. *Useful Trees and Shrubs.* Garrard Publishing Company. Champaign, Illinois.

Schmieman, Susan and R. Gordon Halfacre. 1986. *Computer - Augmented Plant Selector for the Southeast.* Terisan. Astoria, Oregon.

Taylor, Norman. 1957. *Taylor's Encyclopedia of Gardening.* Houghton Mifflin Company. Boston, Massachusetts.

Taylor, Norman. 1965. *The Guide to Garden Shrubs and Trees.* Houghton Mifflin Company. Boston, Massachusetts.

Thode, Frederick W. 1974. *Woody Plant Material for Landscape Use*. Department of Horticulture, Clemson University, Clemson, South Carolina.

Van Veen, Ted. 1969. *Rhododendrons in America*. Sweeney, Krist and Dimm, Inc. Portland, Oregon.

Whitcomb, Carl E. 1976. *Know It and Grow It*. C. E. Whitcomb. Tulsa, Oklahoma.

Wigginton, Brooks, E. 1963. *Trees and Shrubs for the Southeast*. University of Georgia Press. Athens, Georgia.

Wyman, Donald. 1965. *Trees for American Gardens*. The Macmillan Company. New York, N. Y.

Wyman, Donald. 1969. *Shrubs and Vines for American Gardens*. The Macmillan Company. New York, N. Y.

Wyman, Donald. 1970. *Ground Cover Plants*. The Macmillan Company. New York, N. Y.

INDEX